Biography of World Greatest Political Thinkers

Biography of World Greatest Political Thinkers

Amir Ansari

CYBER TECH PUBLICATIONS
4264/3, Ansari Road, Daryaganj, New Delhi-110002 (India)
Ph.: 011-23244078, 011-43559448 Fax: 011-23280028
E-Mail: cyberpublicationsdelhi@yahoo.com
Website: www.cybertechpublications.com

BIOGRAPHY OF WORLD GREATEST POLITICAL THINKERS

Amir Ansari

First Edition 2010

Published by :

G.S. Rawat for **Cyber Tech Publications**
4264/3, Ansari Road, Daryaganj, New Delhi-110002 (India)
Ph.: 011-23244078, 011-43559448 Fax: 011-23280028
E-Mail: cyberpublicationsdelhi@yahoo.com
Website: www.cybertechpublications.com

Printed at: Asian Offset Printers, Delhi-53

Preface

That context assumes that politics is neither solely governed by economic interests, nor shaped entirely by historical causes beyond the control of participants in political life. The political ideas and opinions held by citizens actively shape a society's consciousness of what its economic interests are, and what forces may be beyond its control. Our ideas determine what we believe to be significant, possible, and right in politics. Students of political science properly hunger, therefore, for comprehensive approaches to political theory which place in theoretical perspective the major ideas which govern the world today.

Sixty years ago this desire was largely filled by the undergraduate liberal arts curriculum which gave to students a grounding in intellectual and cultural history. But today a college education no longer provides grounding in history or philosophy. The educational "reforms" that began in the 1960s have created an intellectual elite which is ignorant of most of what previously was the mark of an educated man. It is especially worrisome that at a time when politics has become more important in our daily lives, and the state more intrusive, we are less knowledgeable of the ideas which give it direction and shape. This work, written in response to what in effect is an intellectual vacuum, attempts to provide the essential background necessary for an intelligent view of contemporary intellectual culture. As such, however, we have felt it necessary to reject some assumptions traditionally held by authors of political theory texts.

Since the end of World War II, for example, several great scholars in Egyptology, Comparative Religions, and Old Testament studies have given political theorists an expanded and substantively improved understanding of the context within which political theory originated. Discoveries in neolithic Anatolia indicate that human communities thrived, and developed artifacts interpreting their order almost 40,000 years ago. A study of the development of political theory today, therefore, cannot simply begin with the Homer, the Presocratics, Socrates, Plato, and Aristotle. Political theory, Eric Voegelin and others have argued, emerged in reaction against a more ancient mythic perspective of order which was prevalent throughout the ancient world. The nature of that revolution in thought must be comprehended if political theory itself is to be understood. For that reason, Chapter One begins with analysis of ancient, mythic concepts of political order.

More importantly, most traditional political theory texts are afflicted by the "historicist" approach of their authors. "Historicism" assumes that political ideas have validity only for the historical moment in which those ideas were created and that political theory does not have universal value, only individual psychological value for the creators of those ideas and those persons and communities which accept or live by them. A view such as this, of course, negates the critique of moral relativism in which political theory originated as the science of valid knowledge of political order. Works on political theory as they are written traditionally, with the exception of Eric Voegelin and Leo Strauss and their students, do not philosophically distinguish between higher and lower modes of theoretical discourse. We believe, on the contrary, that the history of political theory reveals a hierarchy of concepts of political order, some higher, others lower.

—*Author*

CONTENTS

Biography of World Greatest Political Thinkers

ABDUS SALAM

Abdus Salam (January 29, 1926; Jhang Punjab – November 21, 1996; Oxford, England) was a Pakistani theoretical physicist and Nobel laureate in Physics for his work in Electro-Weak Theory. Salam, Sheldon Glashow and Steven Weinberg shared the prize for this discovery. Salam holds the distinction of being the first Pakistani Nobel Laureate, and was the first Muslim Nobel Laureate in science. The validity of the theory was ascertained through experiments carried out at the Super Proton Synchrotron facility at CERN in Geneva, particularly, through the discovery of the W and Z Bosons.

Biography

Salam's father was an official in the Department of Education in a poor farming district. His family has a long tradition of piety and learning.

At the age of just fourteen, Salam scored the highest marks ever recorded for the Matriculation Examination at the University of the Punjab. He won a scholarship to the Government College, University of the Punjab, in Lahore. As a fourth-year student there, he published his work on Srinivasa Ramanujan.. He took his master's degree at the Government College in 1946. That same year, he was awarded a scholarship to St. John's College, Cambridge University, where he took a BA degree with Double First-Class Honours in Mathematics and Physics in 1949. In 1950, he received the Smith's Prize from Cambridge University for the most outstanding predoctoral contribution to Physics. He obtained a PhD degree in Theoretical Physics at Cambridge. His doctoral thesis contained fundamental work in Quantum Electrodynamics. By the time it was published in 1951, it had already gained him an international reputation and the Adams Prize.

ARNO ALLAN PENZIAS

Arno Allan Penzias (born April 26, 1933) is an American physicist and Nobel laureate in physics.

Penzias was born in Munich, Germany. At age six he was among the Jewish children evacuated to Britain as part of the Kindertransport rescue operation. Six months later his parents also fled Nazi Germany for the U.S., and the family settled in the garment district of New York City in 1940. In 1946, Penzias became a naturalized citizen of the United States. He graduated Brooklyn Technical High School in 1951 and received a bachelor's degree from the City College of New York in 1954. From Columbia University, he received his Master's degree in 1958 and his Ph.D. in 1962.

He went on to work at Bell Labs in Holmdel, New Jersey where, with Robert Woodrow Wilson, he worked on ultra-sensitive cryogenic microwave receivers intended for radio astronomy observations. In 1964, on building their most sensitive antenna/ receiver system, the pair encountered radio noise which they could not explain. It was far less energetic than the radiation given off by the Milky Way, and it was isotropic, so they assumed their instrument was subject to interference by terrestrial sources. They tried, and then rejected, the hypothesis that the radio noise emanated from New York City. An examination of the microwave horn antenna showed it was full of pigeon droppings (which Penzias described as "white dielectric material"). After the pair removed the guano buildup, and the pigeons were shot (each physicist says the other ordered the deed), the noise remained. Having rejected all sources of interference, the pair published a paper announcing their findings. This was later identified as the cosmic microwave background radiation (CMB), the radio remnant of the Big Bang. This allowed astronomers to confirm the Big Bang, and to correct many of their previous assumptions about it.

Penzias and Wilson received the 1978 Nobel Prize, sharing it with Pyotr Leonidovich Kapitsa (Kapitsa's work was unrelated to Penzias and Wilson's). The two had received the Henry Draper Medal the previous year. Penzias is also the recipient of The International Centre in New York's Award of Excellence.

Penzias has been a resident of Highland Park, New Jersey. He currently serves as a venture partner at New Enterprise Associates.

ABRAHAM PAIS

Abraham (Bram) Pais (May 19, 1918, Amsterdam, The Netherlands — July 28, 2000, Copenhagen, Denmark) was a Dutch-born American physicist and science historian. Pais earned his Ph.D. from University of Utrecht just prior to a Nazi ban on Jewish participation in Dutch universities during World War II. When the Nazis began the forced relocation of Dutch Jews, he went into hiding, but was later arrested and saved only by the end of the war. He then served as an assistant to Niels Bohr in Denmark and was later a colleague of Albert Einstein at the Princeton Institute for Advanced Study. Pais wrote books documenting the lives of these two great physicists and the contributions they and others made to modern physics. He was a physics professor at Rockefeller University until his retirement.

Early Life

Pais was born in Amsterdam, the first child of middle-class Dutch Jewish parents. His father, Isaiah "Jacques" Pais, was the descendant of Sephardic Jews who migrated from Portugal to the Low Countries around the beginning of the 17th century. His mother, Kaatje "Cato" van Kleeff, was the daughter of an Ashkenazi diamond cutter. His parents met while studying to become elementary-school teachers. They both taught school until his mother quit when they married on December 2, 1916. His only sibling, Annie, was born on November 1, 1920. During Pais's childhood his father was an elementary schoolmaster, headmaster, and later the headmaster of the Sephardic Hebrew school.

Pais was a bright student and a voracious reader during his early education and said he had a happy childhood and felt integrated in Dutch society. At age twelve he passed examinations to enter a higher burgher school and attended a school in Amsterdam with a five-year curriculum of basic subjects. He passed his final examinations as number one in his class. He was graduated with a working knowledge of English, French, and German.

AMEDEE MOUCHEZ

Amedee Ernest Barthelemy Mouchez (August 24, 1821 – June 29, 1892) was a French naval officer who became director of the Paris Observatory and launched the ill-fated *Carte du Ciel* project in 1887.

Life

Born in Madrid, Spain, Mouchez embarked on a career in the French Navy as an ensign in 1843. This was a period of relative international maritime peace and much of the navy's activities were dedicated to exploration and discovery. Mouchez was initially occupied on hydrographic studies along the coasts of Korea, China and South America, penetrating 320 km up the Paraguay River and exploring the Abrolhos Islands. He improved the practice of surveying at sea, adapting terrestrial instruments for naval use, and was especially concerned with the problems of determining longitude. He developed the use of the theodolite and meridian telescope to improve the error in establishing longitude from around 303 to 3-43.

Attaining the rank of post captain in 1868, he embarked on a series of expeditions to chart the coast of Algeria. However, in 1870, during the Franco-Prussian War, he was called upon to make an heroic defence of the port of Le Havre.

Returning to his Algerian survey, he brought it to a conclusion in 1873, when he was elected to the Bureau des Longitudes and, in the following year, was sponsored by the *Academie des sciences* to observe the transit of Venus from St. Paul Island in the Indian Ocean. On December 9, he made a sequence of superb photographic plates of the event.

In 1875, the *Academie* elected him a member of the astronomy section and in 1878 he was promoted to rear admiral and awarded the role of director of the Paris Observatory. The observatory had fallen into disrepair and disrepute since the chaos of the 1870 war and the Paris Commune of 1871. Mouchez set about a programme of reconstruction but failed to persuade the government to fund a new observatory outside the centre of Paris.

In 1887, he collaborated with Sir David Gill to host an international astronomical conference in Paris. The principal outcome of the conference was a multi-national project to compile and index a photographic atlas of the heavens, the *Carte du Ciel.* The project consumed massive effort over several decades before it was rendered obsolete by modern astronomical methods.

Mouchez died in Wissous, Seine-et-Oise.

ALBERT ABRAHAM MICHELSON

Albert Abraham Michelson (December 19, 1852 – May 9, 1931) was a Prussian-born American physicist known for his work on the measurement of the speed of light and especially for the Michelson-Morley experiment. In 1907 he received the Nobel Prize in Physics. He became the first American to receive the Nobel Prize in sciences.

Biography

Michelson, the son of a Jewish merchant, was born to a Jewish family in what is today Strzelno, Poland (then Strelno, Provinz Posen in the Kingdom of Prussia). He moved to the United States with his parents in 1855, when he was two years old. He grew up in the rough mining towns of Murphy's Camp, California and Virginia City, Nevada, where his father was a merchant. He spent his high school years in San Francisco in the home of his aunt, Henriette Levy (nee Michelson), who was the mother of author Harriet Lane Levy.

President Ulysses S. Grant awarded Michelson a special appointment to the U.S. Naval Academy in 1869. During his four years as a midshipman at the Academy, Michelson excelled in optics, heat and climatology as well as drawing. After his graduation in 1873 and two years at sea, he returned to the Academy in 1875 to become an instructor in physics and chemistry until 1879. From 1880 to 1882, Michelson undertook postgraduate study at Berlin under Hermann Helmholtz and at Paris.

Michelson was fascinated with the sciences and the problem of measuring the speed of light in particular. While at Annapolis, he conducted his first experiments of the speed of light, as part of a class demonstration in 1877. After two years of studies in Europe, he resigned from the Navy in 1881. In 1883 he accepted a position as professor of physics at the Case School of Applied Science in Cleveland, Ohio and concentrated on developing an improved interferometer. In 1887 he and Edward Morley carried out the famous Michelson-Morley experiment which seemed to rule out the existence of the aether. He later moved on to use astronomical interferometers in the measurement of stellar diameters and in measuring the separations of binary stars.

In 1889 Michelson became a professor at Clark University at Worcester, Massachusetts and in 1892 was appointed professor and the first head of the department of physics at the newly organized University of Chicago. In 1899, he married Edna Stanton and they raised one son and three daughters.

In 1907, Michelson had the honour of being the first American to receive a Nobel Prize in Physics "for his optical precision instruments and the spectroscopic and metrological investigations carried out with their aid". He also won the Copley Medal in 1907, the Henry Draper Medal in 1916 and the Gold Medal of the Royal Astronomical Society in 1923. A crater on the Moon is named after him.

Michelson died in Pasadena, California at the age of 78. The University of Chicago Residence Halls remembered Michelson and his achievements by dedicating Michelson House in his honour. Case Western Reserve has also dedicated a Michelson House to him, and an academic building at the United States Naval Academy also bears his name. Michelson Laboratory at Naval Air Weapons Station China Lake in Ridgecrest, California is named after him. There is an interesting display in the publicly accessible area of the Lab of Michelson's Nobel Prize medal, the actual prize document, and examples of his diffraction gratings.

ALEKSANDR LYAPUNOV

Aleksandr Mikhailovich Lyapunov (June 6, 1857 – November 3, 1918, all new style) was a Russian mathematician, mechanician and physicist. Sometimes his name is also written as Ljapunov, Liapunov or Ljapunow, and often improperly pronounced 'la-yapunov'.

Biography

Lyapunov was born in Yaroslavl, Imperial Russia. His father Mikhail Vasilyevich Lyapunov (1820-1868) was a well known astronomer and a head of the Demidovski lyceum. Because of the reaction of the university administration, after the departure of Lobachevsky, he gave up his work entirely in 1864 at the observatory of the University of Kazan. He moved with his family on his wife's estate in Simbirsk province (now Ulyanovsk Oblast), where he devoted his time to the education of his oldest sons, Aleksandr and Sergei (1859-1924). During long winter nights he stayed with his sons and he taught them assiduously with the aid of games on maps of the world. He possessed a lot of books in Russian, German and French on subjects as varied as mathematics, astronomy, philosophy, history, ethnography, political economy and literature. After the sudden death of his father Aleksandr was educated by his uncle R. M. Sechenov, brother of the famous physiologist Ivan Mikhailovich Sechenov. At his uncle's Lyapunov learned with his cousin, his intended Nataliya Rafailovna. In 1870 his mother moved with her sons to Nizhny Novgorod, where he started to attend the third class of the gymnasium. He passed gymnasium in 1876 with distinction.

Education

He studied at the Physico-Mathematical department of the University of Saint Petersburg, where he was a schoolfellow of Markov. In the beginning he listened to Mendeleyev's lectures on chemistry. After a month he transferred to the mathematics department of the university, but he continued attending the chemistry lectures. Mathematics was taught at that time by Chebyshev and his students Aleksandr Nikolaevich Korkin and Yegor Ivanovich Zolotarev. Lyapunov wrote his first independent scientific works under the guidance of professor of mechanics, D. K. Bobylev. In his fourth year he received the gold medal for a work on hydrostatics, which had been suggested by the faculty. This was the basis for his first published scientific work *About the equilibrium of solid bodies in vessels with arbitrary forms, filled with dense fluids* and *About the potential of hydrostatic pressure.* In both works he used many new approaches and developed new rigorous proofs of a few earlier incomplete theorems from hydrostatics. With the first work he gained the title of candidate in mathematical sciences. Now he was able to leave the university to prepare for a professorial calling.

He graduated in 1880. He received a Master's degree in applied mathematics in 1884 with the thesis *About the stability of elliptic forms in the equilibrium of turbulent fluid.* This work treated an important and difficult task about understanding the shapes of celestial bodies. This task was offered by Chebyshev to Zolotarev and to Sofia Vasilyevna Kovalevskaya and Chebyshev was aware of the difficulty. As was said by Vladimir Andreevich Steklov, "Chebyshev saw in the young man such an immense research power, that he had dared to lay on him such a toilsome task". Lyapunov had already begun to study this stability in his previous two-years attempts at solving the task. After the public announcement his work instantly attracted the attention of mathematicians, mechanicians, physicists and astronomers all over the world.

ARCHIBALD LOW

Professor *Archibald Montgomery Low* (1888-September 1956) was an English Astronautics engineer, research physicist and inventor, and author of more than 40 books.

Low has been called the ***"father of radio guidance systems"*** due to his pioneering work on guided rockets, planes and torpedoes. He was a pioneer in many fields though, often leading the way for others, but his lack of discipline meant he hardly ever saw a project through, being easily distracted by new ideas. If it weren't for this inability to see things to a conclusion, Low could well have been remembered as one of the great men of science. Many of his scientific contemporaries disliked him, due in part to his using the title *Professor*, which technically he wasn't entitled to do as he didn't occupy an academic chair. His love of the limelight and publicity probably also added to the dislike.

Later Life

Low died in 1956 from a malignant tumour on his lung. He is buried in Brompton Cemetery, London.

In 1976 Low was inducted into the International Space Hall of Fame

ALFRED LEE LOOMIS

Alfred Lee Loomis (November 4, 1887-August 11, 1975) was an American attorney, investment banker, physicist, philanthropist, and patron of scientific research. He established the Loomis Laboratory in Tuxedo Park, New York, and his role in the development of radar is considered instrumental in the Allied victory in World War II. In 2002 the book displayed to the right was published about him and his secret research in his private laboratory. He is the inventor of the *Aberdeen Chronograph*, the LORAN navigational system, and the electroencephalograph; participated in the development of a ground controlled approach technology for aircraft, the centrifuge microscope, and the preliminary meetings of the Manhattan Project.

He married Elizabeth Ellen Farnsworth of Dedham, Massachusetts, a member of a prominent Boston society family, on June 22, 1912 and they had three sons, Albert Lee Jr., William Farnsworth, and Henry. In 1945 he married Manette Seeldrayers Hobart. The theme of the comic books and movie, *Batman*, is based on the life of Alfred Loomis and he is considered the model for Bruce Wayne.

Early Years

Born in Manhattan, Loomis was the son of Julia Stimson and Henry Patterson Loomis. There were distinguished members on both sides of his family, primarily physicians, and they held high positions in society. Loomis' mother and father separated when he was very young and his father died when Alfred was in college. His first cousin was Henry Stimson, secretary of war and secretary of state in the Taft administration. Stimson became a great influence upon him from an early age.

He completed his undergraduate work at Yale University in mathematics and science, and was graduated, *cum laude*, from Harvard Law School in 1912. Immediately following his graduation, Loomis married and began the practice of corporate law in the law firm of Winthrop and Stimson and achieved great success.

In 1917 he and his brother-in-law, Landon K. Thorne, the wealthy husband of his sister Julia, purchased 17,000 acres of Hilton Head Island and established the property as a private preserve for riding, boating, fishing, and hunting. His hobbies included automobiles and yachting—racing America's Cup yachts against the Vanderbilts and the Astors—and the pursuit of many sciences.

ADOLF KRATZER

B. Adolf Kratzer (October 16, 1893 in Gunzburg, Germany –) was a German theoretical physicist who made contributions to atomic physics and molecular physics, and was an authority on molecular band spectroscopy.

From 1912 to 1914, Kratzer studied physics at the Technische Hochschule Munchen (today, Technische Universitat Munchen), and then he spent two years in the army, after which he began studies at the University of Munich under Arnold Sommerfeld. He was granted his doctor of philosophy in 1920; his thesis was on the band spectra of molecules. While at Munich, he was Sommerfeld's assistant; he had been trained by Sommerfeld's assistant and student Wilhelm Lenz to fill this role. While at Munich, Kratzer extended the theory of diatomic molecular spectroscopy by including anharmonic forces between the nuclei, which changed the oscillation frequencies.

It was Sommerfeld's practice to send some of his assistants to be personal assistants for physics to the mathematician David Hilbert, at the University of Gottingen. Kratzer was sent to Gottingen during the period 1920 to 1921. Upon his return to Munich, he became a Privatdozent, and it was during this time that he became acquainted with Werner Heisenberg, also a student of Sommerfeld.

Based on his work at Munich, it was in 1922 that Krazter's detailed analysis on the cyanide spectroscopic bands was published. His analysis resulted in the introduction of half-integral quantum numbers to account for molecular rotation. During 1922, he was also called as an ordinarius professor of theoretical physics to the University of Munster. Here, Kratzer made contributions to quantum mechanics and became a leading authority in the field of molecular band spectroscopy.

At this time, there were three centres of development for quantum mechanics and the interpretation of atomic and molecular structure, based on atomic and molecular spectroscopy, especially the Sommerfeld-Bohr model: the Theoretical Physics Institute at the University of Munich, under Arnold Sommerfeld, the Institute of Theoretical Physics at the University of Gottingen, under Max Born, and the Institute of Theoretical Physics, under Niels Bohr. These three institutes effectively formed a consortium for the exchange of assistants and researchers. Furthermore, with Sommerfeld educating such capable physicists as Kratzer, and others, when they were called to other facilities, they effectively became extensions of Sommerfeld's Institute of Theoretical Physics. This was the case with Kratzer when he went to Munster, as was the case of Sommerfeld's former student Paul Peter Ewald when he went to the Stuttgart Technische Hochschule.

Kratzer published a number of physics books, based on his lectures on electrodynamics, mechanics, optics, relativity, thermodynamics, and quantum mechanics (wave mechanics). A book on transcendental functions was written with Walter Franz, also a student of Sommerfeld.

The Kratzer potential, a central force in molecular physics, is named in his honour.

A. Q. KHAN

Abdul Qadeer Khan (born April 1, 1936) in Bhopal, undivided British India, is a Pakistani scientist and metallurgical engineer, widely regarded as the founder of Pakistan's nuclear programme. His middle name is occasionally rendered as Quadeer, Qadir or Gadeer, and his given names are usually abbreviated to A.Q.

In January 2004, Khan confessed to having been involved in a clandestine international network of nuclear weapons technology proliferation from Pakistan to Libya, Iran and North Korea. On February 5, 2004, the President of Pakistan, General Pervez Musharraf, announced that he had pardoned Khan, who is widely seen as a national hero. Recently Dr. Qadeer cleared the issue of confession which he said was handed to him by authorities.

In an August 23, 2005 interview with Kyodo News General Pervez Musharraf confirmed that Khan had supplied gas centrifuges and gas centrifuge parts to North Korea and, possibly, an amount of uranium hexafluoride.

On May 30th, 2008, ABC News reported that Khan, who previously confessed to his involvement with Iran and North Korea, now denies involvement with the spread of nuclear arms to those countries. He explained in an interview with ABC News that the Pakistani government and President Pervez Musharraf forced him to be a "scapegoat" for the "national interest." He denies ever travelling to Iran or Libya and claims that North Korea's nuclear programme was well advanced before his visit.

Early Life

Khan was born (Bhopal) into a middle-class Muslim-Muhajir family, which migrated from India to Pakistan in 1952. He obtained a B.Sc. degree in 1960 from the University of Karachi, majoring in physical metallurgy. He then obtained an engineer's degree in 1967 from Delft University of Technology, the Netherlands, and a Ph.D. degree in metallurgical engineering from the Catholic University of Leuven in Belgium in 1972..

ANDREW D. HUXLEY

Andrew D. Huxley (born 1966) is the chair of the physics department of Edinburgh University. Of no relation to Sir Andrew F. Huxley (the English physiologist and biophysicist), Prof. Andrew D. Huxley is of renown in the field of condensed matter physics. While at the CEA laboratory in Grenoble, Huxley and colleagues were involved in the revolutionary discovery of superconductivity in the ferromagnet UGe_2 under applied pressure. This was followed up by a series of breakthroughs in another ferromagnetic material, URhGe [3-5], which was found to turn superconducting under the application of an external magnetic field. This emergence of an unconventional superconducting state by the application of an external tuning parameter such as magnetic field or pressure is hypothesised to be closely related to a 'Quantum critical point' (QCP)-a special phase transition that occurs at temperatures approaching zero kelvins. Quantum fluctuations are enhanced at the QCP, destabilising the conventional phase that dominates under ambient conditions, making conditions propitious for the emergence of a novel unconventional phase such as superconductivity, or possibly even more exotic states.

Huxley earned a BA from Churchill College, Cambridge University, an MS from the University of Pennsylvania, and a PhD from Cambridge University. He was subsequently a postdoctorate fellow and then a scientist at CEA, Grenoble before joining Edinburgh University as a Professor of Physics in 2006.

Huxley is yet another of the prestigious alumnae of the Quantum Matter (formerly the Low Temperature Physics) group in the Cavendish Laboratory, Cambridge University that have gone on to become leading physicists. The current leader of the group, Prof. Gilbert (Gil) Lonzarich, is considered by many to be the visionary behind the burgeoning field within experimental condensed matter research that involves the discovery of novel phases in the vicinity of quantum critical points.

ANTONY HEWISH

Antony Hewish (born Fowey, Cornwall, May 11, 1924) is a British radio astronomer who won the Nobel Prize for Physics in 1974 (together with fellow radio-astronomer Martin Ryle) for his work on the development of radio aperture synthesis and its role in the discovery of pulsars. (Jocelyn Bell Burnell, Hewish's graduate student, was not recognized, although she was the first to notice the stellar radio source that was later recognised as a pulsar.) He was also awarded the Eddington Medal of the Royal Astronomical Society in 1969. His undergraduate degree at Gonville and Caius College, Cambridge was interrupted by war service at the Royal Aircraft Establishment, and at the Telecommunications Research Establishment where he worked with Martin Ryle. Returning to Cambridge in 1946, Hewish completed his degree and immediately joined Ryle's research team at the Cavendish Laboratory, obtaining his Ph.D. in 1952. Hewish made both practical and theoretical advances in the observation and exploitation of the apparent scintillations of radio sources due to their radiation impinging upon plasma.

This led him to propose, and secure funding for, the construction of the Interplanetary Scintillation Array, a large array radio telescope at the Mullard Radio Astronomy Observatory (MRAO), Cambridge in order to conduct a high time-resolution radio survey of interstellar scintillation. In the course of this project, one of his graduate students, Jocelyn Bell, first noticed the radio source which was ultimately recognised as the first pulsar.

The paper announcing the discovery had five authors, Hewish's name being listed first, Bell's second. The Nobel award to Ryle and Hewish without the inclusion of Bell as a co-recipient was controversial, and was roundly condemned by Hewish's fellow astronomer Fred Hoyle. Others however have noted that the prize was given to Ryle and Hewish for their work across the field of radio-astronomy as a whole, with particular mention of Ryle's work on aperture-synthesis, and Hewish's on pulsars.

Hewish was professor of radio astronomy at the Cavendish Laboratory from 1971 to 1989, and head of the MRAO from 1982 to 1988. He was made a Fellow of the Royal Society in 1968, and he and Martin Ryle were awarded the Nobel Prize in Physics in 1974.

Hewish is a fellow of Churchill College, Cambridge.

ALAN GUTH

Alan Harvey Guth (born February 27, 1947) is a theoretical physicist and cosmologist. Guth has researched elementary particle theory (and how particle theory is applicable to the early universe).

He graduated from the Massachusetts Institute of Technology in 1968 in physics and stayed to receive a master's and a doctorate, also in physics.

As a junior particle physicist, Guth first developed the idea of cosmic inflation in 1979 at Cornell after attending a Big Bang lecture by Robert Dicke, and gave his first seminar on the subject in January 1980. Moving on to Stanford University Guth formally proposed the idea of cosmic inflation in 1981, the idea that the nascent universe passed through a phase of exponential expansion that was driven by a positive vacuum energy density (negative vacuum pressure). The results of the WMAP mission in 2006 made the case for cosmic inflation very compelling.

Early Life

Alan Guth was born on February 27, 1947 in New Brunswick, New Jersey, USA to the middle-class couple Hyman and Elaine Guth, owners of a small grocery store and a dry-cleaning establishment.

Unlike their son, they were not highly educated: Hyman had only graduated from junior college, while his wife never went to college. Guth was the middle child between two sisters. He has stated that in his mostly uneventful childhood, he developed a great fondness for mathematics.

After attending several public schools, he skipped his senior year to start at the Massachusetts Institute of Technology. After his junior year, he enrolled a five-year programme where he could get his bachelor's and master's after two more years. MIT was easier for him than high school because all his courses were science and math. One reason he did this was because he was worried about the draft. He certainly was not a big fan of the Vietnam War, because in 1970 he participated in some speeches at political activities. Guth managed to obtain both a bachelor's and master's degree in 1969 and a doctorate in 1972. In 1971, he married Susan Tisch, his high school sweetheart, and they had two children: Lawrence (born 1977) and Jennifer (born 1983). However, Guth found a hard time finding a permanent job before he found his true calling in investigating the origins of the universe. Part of the problem was that the assistant professorships at the universities were filled, largely because of the baby boom.

At the very beginning, Guth did not have much interest in cosmology and tended to focus on particle physics. After he graduated in 1971, he spent nine years travelling across the country pursuing temporary postdoc jobs related to physics hoping to get a permanent job at a university somewhere, but did not meet much luck. He was at Princeton 1971 to 1974, Columbia 1974 to 1977, Cornell 1977 to 1979, and the Stanford Linear Accelerator Centre (SLAC) 1979 to 1980.

AUGUSTIN-JEAN FRESNEL

Augustin-Jean Fresnel (May 10, 1788 – July 14, 1827), was a French physicist who contributed significantly to the establishment of the theory of wave optics. Fresnel studied the behaviour of light both theoretically and experimentally.

Biography

Fresnel was the son of an architect, born at Broglie (Eure). His early progress in learning was slow, and he still could not read when he was eight years old. At thirteen he entered the Ecole Centrale in Caen, and at sixteen and a half the Ecole Polytechnique, where he acquitted himself with distinction. From there he went to the Ecole des Ponts et Chaussees. He served as an engineer successively in the departments of Vendee, Drome and Ille-et-Vilaine; but having supported the Bourbons in 1814 he lost his appointment on Napoleon's return to power.

On the second restoration of the monarchy, he obtained a post as engineer in Paris, where much of his life from that time was spent. His researches in optics, continued until his death, appear to have begun about the year 1814, when he prepared a paper on the aberration of light, which, however, was not published. In 1818 he wrote a memoir on diffraction for which in the ensuing year he received the prize of the Academie des Sciences at Paris. He was in 1823 unanimously elected a member of the academy, and in 1825 he became a member of the Royal Society of London, which in 1827, at the time of his last illness, awarded him the Rumford Medal. In 1819 he was nominated a commissioner of lighthouses, for which he was the first to construct a special type of lens, now called a Fresnel lens, as substitutes for mirrors. He died of tuberculosis at Ville-d'Avray, near Paris.

His labours in the cause of optical science received during his lifetime only scant public recognition, and some of his papers were not printed by the Academie des Sciences till many years after his death. But as he wrote to Young in 1824: in himself "that sensibility, or that vanity, which people call love of glory" had been blunted.

"All the compliments," he says, "that I have received from Arago, Laplace and Biot never gave me so much pleasure as the discovery of a theoretic truth, or the confirmation of a calculation by experiment."

ALEXANDER FRIEDMAN

Alexander Alexandrovich Friedman or Friedmann (June 16, 1888, Saint Petersburg, Imperial Russia – September 16, 1925, Leningrad, USSR) was a Russian and Soviet cosmologist and mathematician.

Life and Work

Alexander Friedman lived much of his life in Leningrad. He fought in World War I (on behalf of Imperial Russia) as a bomber and later lived through the Russian Revolution of 1917.

He discovered the expanding-universe solution to general relativity field equations in 1922, which was corroborated by Edwin Hubble's observations in 1929 (Ferguson, 1991: 67). Friedman's 1924 papers, including "Uber die Moglichkeit einer Welt mit konstanter negativer Krummung des Raumes" (On the possibility of a world with constant negative curvature of space) published by the German physics journal *Zeitschrift fur Physik* (Vol. 21, pp. 326-332), demonstrated that he had command of all three Friedman models describing positive, zero and negative curvature respectively, a decade before Robertson and Walker published their analysis.

This dynamical cosmological model of general relativity would come to form the standard for the Big Bang and steady state theories. Friedman's work supports both theories equally, so it was not until the detection of the cosmic microwave background radiation that the steady state theory was abandoned in favour of the current favourite Big Bang paradigm.

The classic solution of the Einstein field equations that describes a homogeneous and isotropic universe is called the "Friedmann-Lemaitre-Robertson-Walker metric", or "FLRW", after Friedman, and Robertson, Walker and Georges Lemaitre who worked on the problem in 1920's and 80's independently of Friedman.

In addition to general relativity, Friedman's interests included hydrodynamics and meteorology. In June 1925 he was given the job of the director of Main Geophysical Observatory in Leningrad. In July 1925 he participated in a record-setting balloon flight, reaching the elevation of 7400 m.

Friedman died on September 16, 1925, at the age of 37, from typhoid fever that he contracted during a vacation in Crimea.

Another famous physicist, George Gamow, was a student of Friedman.

ARPAD ELO

Arpad Emrick Elo (August 25, 1903 in Egyhazaskeszo, Hungary – November 5, 1992 in Brookfield, Wisconsin) is the creator of the Elo rating system for two-player games such as chess. Born in Hungary, he moved to the United States with his parents as a child in 1913.

Elo was a professor of physics at Marquette University in Milwaukee, Wisconsin. He was also a chess master. By the 1930s he was the strongest chess player in Milwaukee, one of the nation's leading chess cities. He won the Wisconsin State Championship eight times.

Elo died in Brookfield, Wisconsin in 1992.

The Elo Rating System

Elo is best known for his system of rating chess players. The original chess rating system was developed in 1950 by Kenneth Harkness, the Business Manager of the United States Chess Federation. By 1960, using the data developed through the Harkness Rating System, Elo developed his own formula which had a sound statistical basis and constituted an improvement on the Harkness System. The new rating system was approved and passed at a meeting of the United States Chess Federation in St. Louis in 1960.

In 1970, FIDE, the World Chess Federation, agreed to adopt the Elo Rating System. From then on until the mid-1980s, Elo himself made the rating calculations. At the time, the computational task was relatively easy because fewer than 2000 players were rated by FIDE.

FIDE reassigned the task of managing and computing the ratings to others, excluding Elo. FIDE also added new "Qualification for Rating" rules to its handbook awarding arbitrary ratings (typically in the 2200 range, which is the low end for a chess master) for players who scored at least 50 percent in the games he played at selected events, such as named Chess Olympiads. Elo and others objected to these new rules as arbitrary and politically-driven.

ARTHUR STANLEY EDDINGTON

Sir Arthur Stanley Eddington, OM (28 December 1882 – 22 November 1944) was an English astrophysicist of the early 20th century. The Eddington limit, the natural limit to the luminosity of stars, or the radiation generated by accretion onto a compact object, is named in his honour.

He is famous for his work regarding the Theory of Relativity. Eddington wrote a number of articles which announced and explained Einstein's theory of general relativity to the English-speaking world. World War I severed many lines of scientific communication and new developments in German science were not well known in England. He also conducted an eclipse expedition in 1919 that provided one of the earliest confirmations of relativity, and became known for his popular expositions and interpretations of the theory.

Biography

Eddington was born in Kendal, England, son of Quaker parents, Arthur Henry Eddington and Sarah Ann Shout. His father taught at a Quaker training college in Lancashire before moving to Kendal to become headmaster of Stramongate School. He died in the typhoid epidemic which swept England in 1884. When his father died, his mother was left to bring up her two children with relatively little income. The family moved to Weston-super-Mare where at first Stanley (as his mother and sister always called him) was educated at home before spending three years at a preparatory school.

In 1893 Stanley entered Brynmelyn School. He proved to be a brilliant scholar and excelled in mathematics and English literature. His records won him a 60 pounds scholarship in 1898, and he was able to attend Owens College in Manchester once he turned 16 later that year. He spent the first year in a general course, but turned to physics for the next three years. Eddington was greatly influenced by his physics and mathematics teachers, Arthur Schuster and Horace Lamb. At Manchester, Eddington lived at Dalton Hall, where he came under the lasting influence of the Quaker mathematician J.W. Graham. His progress continued to be rapid, winning him several additional scholarships and allowing him to graduate with a B.Sc. in physics with First Class Honours in 1902.

Based on his performance at Owens, he was awarded a 75 pound scholarship at Trinity College, Cambridge, which he entered in 1902. He was coached by the famous mathematician R.A. Herman, and in 1904 became the first second-year student to place as Senior Wrangler. After receiving his B.A. in 1905, he began research on thermionic emission in the Cavendish Laboratory. This did not go well, and meanwhile he spent time teaching mathematics to first year engineering students, without much satisfaction. But fortunately this hiatus was brief.

ARTHUR COMPTON

Arthur Holly Compton (September 10, 1892 – March 15, 1962) was an American physicist and Nobel laureate in physics for his discovery of the Compton effect. He served as Chancellor of Washington University in St. Louis from 1945 to 1953.

Biography

Arthur Holly Compton was born in Wooster, Ohio in 1892 to Elias and Otelia Compton. They were an academic family; his father Elias Compton was dean of The University of Wooster (later The

College of Wooster), which Arthur attended. His eldest brother Karl Taylor Compton also attended The University of Wooster, became a physicist, and was later president of MIT; his second brother Wilson M. Compton became a diplomat and president of the State College of Washington, later Washington State University. Around 1913, Compton devised a demonstration method for the Earth's rotation.

In 1918, Compton began studying X-ray scattering. In 1922, Compton found that X-rays wavelength increases due to scattering of the radiant energy by "*free electrons*". Scattered quanta have less energy than the quanta of the original ray. This discovery, known as the "Compton effect," or "Compton scattering" demonstrates the "*particle*" concept of electromagnetic radiation and earned Compton the Nobel Prize in physics in 1927. Compton developed the method for observing at the same instant individual scattered X-ray photons and the recoil electrons (developed with Alfred W. Simon). In Germany, Walther Bothe and Hans Geiger independently developed a similar method.

ARCHIMEDES

Archimedes of Syracuse (*c.* 287 BC – *c.* 212 BC) was a Greek mathematician, physicist, engineer, inventor, and astronomer. Although few details of his life are known, he is regarded as one of the leading scientists in classical antiquity. Among his advances in physics are the foundations of hydrostatics, statics and the explanation of the principle of the lever. He is credited with designing innovative machines, including siege engines and the screw pump that bears his name. Modern experiments have tested claims that Archimedes designed machines capable of lifting attacking ships out of the water, and setting ships on fire using an array of mirrors.

Archimedes is generally considered to be the greatest mathematician of antiquity and one of the greatest of all time. He used the method of exhaustion to calculate the area under the arc of a parabola with the summation of an infinite series, and gave a remarkably accurate approximation of Pi. He also defined the spiral bearing his name, formulas for the volumes of surfaces of revolution and an ingenious system for expressing very large numbers.

Archimedes died during the Siege of Syracuse when he was killed by a Roman soldier despite orders that he should not be harmed. Cicero describes visiting the tomb of Archimedes, which was surmounted by a sphere inscribed within a cylinder. Archimedes had proved that the sphere has two thirds of the volume and surface area of the cylinder (including the bases of the latter), and regarded this as the greatest of his mathematical achievements.

Unlike his inventions, the mathematical writings of Archimedes were little known in antiquity. Mathematicians from Alexandria read and quoted him, but the first comprehensive compilation was made only by Isidore of Miletus (*c.* 530 AD), while commentaries on the works of Archimedes written by Eutocius in the sixth century AD opened them to wider readership for the first time. The relatively few copies of Archimedes' written work that survived through the Middle Ages were an influential source of ideas for scientists during the Renaissance, while the discovery in 1906 of previously unknown works by Archimedes in the Archimedes Palimpsest has provided new insights into how he obtained mathematical results.

Biography

Archimedes was born *c.* 287 BC in the seaport city of Syracuse, Sicily, at that time a colony of Magna Graecia. The date of birth is based on a statement by the Byzantine Greek historian John Tzetzes that Archimedes lived for 75 years. In *The Sand Reckoner*, Archimedes gives his father's name as Phidias, an astronomer about whom nothing is known. Plutarch wrote in his *Parallel Lives* that Archimedes was related to King Hiero II, the ruler of Syracuse. A biography of Archimedes was written by his friend Heracleides but this work has been lost, leaving the details of his life obscure. It is unknown, for instance, whether he ever married or had children. During his youth Archimedes may have studied in Alexandria, Egypt, where Conon of Samos and Eratosthenes of Cyrene were contemporaries. He referred to Conon of Samos as his friend, while two of his works (*The Method of Mechanical Theorems* and the *Cattle Problem*) have introductions addressed to Eratosthenes.

Archimedes died *c.* 212 BC during the Second Punic War, when Roman forces under General Marcus Claudius Marcellus captured the city of Syracuse after a two-year-long siege. According to the popular account given by Plutarch, Archimedes was contemplating a mathematical diagram when the city was captured. A Roman soldier commanded him to come and meet General Marcellus but he declined, saying that he had to finish working on the problem.

The soldier was enraged by this, and killed Archimedes with his sword. Plutarch also gives a lesser-known account of the death of Archimedes which suggests that he may have been killed while attempting to surrender to a Roman soldier. According to this story, Archimedes was carrying mathematical instruments, and was killed because the soldier thought that they were valuable items. General Marcellus was reportedly angered by the death of Archimedes, as he considered him a valuable scientific asset and had ordered that he not be harmed.

The last words attributed to Archimedes are "Do not disturb my circles", a reference to the circles in the mathematical drawing that he was supposedly studying when disturbed by the Roman soldier. This quote is often given in Latin as "Noli turbare circulos meos", but there is no reliable evidence that Archimedes uttered these words and they do not appear in the account given by Plutarch.

The tomb of Archimedes carried a sculpture illustrating his favourite mathematical proof, consisting of a sphere and a cylinder of the same height and diameter. Archimedes had proved that the volume and surface area of the sphere are two thirds that of the cylinder including its bases. In 75 BC, 137 years after his death, the Roman orator Cicero was serving as quaestor in Sicily. He had heard stories about the tomb of Archimedes, but none of the locals was able to give him the location. Eventually he found the tomb near the Agrigentine gate in Syracuse, in a neglected condition and overgrown with bushes. Cicero had the tomb cleaned up, and was able to see the carving and read some of the verses that had been added as an inscription.

The standard versions of the life of Archimedes were written long after his death by the historians of Ancient Rome. The account of the siege of Syracuse given by Polybius in his *Universal History* was written around seventy years after Archimedes' death, and was used subsequently as a source by Plutarch and Livy. It sheds little light on Archimedes as a person, and focuses on the war machines that he is said to have built in order to defend the city.

ANDRE-MARIE AMPERE

Andre-Marie Ampere (January 20, 1775 – June 10, 1836), was a French physicist and mathematician who is generally credited as one of the main discoverers of electromagnetism. The SI unit of measurement of electric current, the ampere, is named after him.

Early Days

Ampere was born on January 20, 1775 in Lyon, France, and lived from 1775 to 1796 in the nearby burg of Poleymieux-au-Mont-d'Or. His father began to teach him Latin, but ceased on discovering the boy's greater inclination and aptitude for mathematical studies. The young Ampere, however, soon resumed his Latin lessons, to enable him to master the works of Euler and Bernoulli.

In later life he was accustomed to say that he knew as much about mathematics and science when he was eighteen as ever he knew; but, a polymath, his reading embraced nearly the whole round of knowledge—history, travels, poetry, philosophy and the natural sciences.

During the revolution his father stayed at Lyons expecting to be safer in the city. Nevertheless, after the revolutionaries had taken the city he fell a victim and was executed. This death was a great shock to Ampere.

In 1796 he met Julie Carron, the daughter of a blacksmith living near Lyon, and an attachment sprang up between them. In 1799 they were married. From about 1796 Ampere gave private lessons at Lyon in mathematics, chemistry and languages; and in 1801 he removed to Bourg, as professor of physics and chemistry, leaving his ailing wife and infant son (Jean Jacques Ampere) at Lyon. Her death, in July 1803, troubled Ampere for the rest of his life. Also in 1804, Ampere was appointed professor of mathematics at the *lycee* of Lyon.

Ampere used to say that "at eighteen years he found three culminating points in his life, his First Communion, the reading of Thomas's "Eulogy of Descartes", and the Taking of the Bastille... On the day of his wife's death he wrote two verses from the Psalms, and the prayer, 'O Lord, God of Mercy, unite me in Heaven with those whom you have permitted me to love on earth.' Serious doubts harassed him at times, and made him very unhappy. Then he would take refuge in the reading of the Bible and the Fathers of the Church."

ANDERS JONAS ANGSTROM

Anders Jonas Angstrom (August 13, 1814 – June 21, 1874) was a physicist in Sweden, one of the founders of the science of spectroscopy.

Born in Medelpad, he moved to and was educated at Uppsala University, where in 1839 he became docent in physics. In 1842 he went to the Stockholm Observatory in order to gain experience in practical astronomical work, and in the following year he was appointed keeper of the Uppsala Astronomical Observatory.

Becoming interested in terrestrial magnetism he made many observations of magnetic intensity and declination in various parts of Sweden, and was charged by the Stockholm Academy of Sciences with the task, not completed till shortly before his death, of working out the magnetic data obtained by the Swedish frigate "Eugenie" on her voyage round the world in 1851-1853.

In 1858 he succeeded Adolph Ferdinand Svanberg in the chair of physics at Uppsala. His most important work was concerned with the conduction of heat and with spectroscopy. In his optical researches, *Optiska Undersokningar*, presented to the Royal Swedish Academy of Sciences in 1853, he not only pointed out that the electric spark yields two superposed spectra, one from the metal of the electrode and the other from the gas in which it passes, but deduced from Leonhard Euler's theory of resonance that an incandescent gas emits luminous rays of the same refrangibility as those which it can absorb. This statement, as Sir Edward Sabine remarked when awarding him the Rumford medal of the Royal Society in 1872, contains a fundamental principle of spectrum analysis, and though overlooked for a number of years it entitles him to rank as one of the founders of spectroscopy.

From 1861 onwards he paid special attention to the solar spectrum. His combination of the spectroscope with photography for the study of the solar system resulted in proving that the sun's atmosphere contains hydrogen, among other elements (1862), and in 1868 he published his great map of the normal solar spectrum in *Recherches sur le spectre solaire*, including detailed measurements of more than 1000 spectral lines, which long remained authoritative in questions of wave-length, although his measurements were inexact to the extent of one part in 7000 or 8000 owing to the metre which he used as his standard having been slightly too short.

He was the first, in 1867, to examine the spectrum of the aurora borealis, and detected and measured the characteristic bright line in its yellow green region; but he was mistaken in supposing that this same line, which is often called by his name, is also to be seen in the zodiacal light.

He died at Uppsala on June 21, 1874.

The angstrom units with which the wavelength of light is measured are named for him. The units are used in crystallography as well as spectroscopy.

The Angstrom crater on the Moon was named in his honour.

His son Knut Angstrom was known for his research at Uppsala University on solar radiation, the radiation of heat from the sun and its absorption by the earth's atmosphere. For his research, he devised various delicate methods and instruments, including his electric compensation pyrheliometer, invented in 1893, and apparatus for obtaining a photographic representation of the infrared spectrum in 1895.

ALEXEI ALEXEYEVICH ABRIKOSOV

Alexei Alexeyevich Abrikosov (born June 25, 1928) is a Russian theoretical physicist whose main contributions are in the field of condensed matter physics. He was awarded the Nobel Prize in Physics in 2003.

Biography

Abrikosov was born in Moscow, Russian SFSR, USSR, on June 25, 1928. He graduated from Moscow State University in 1948. From 1948 to 1965, he worked at the Institute for Physical Problems of the USSR Academy of Sciences, where he received his Ph.D. in 1951 for the theory of thermal diffusion in plasmas, and then his Doctor of Physical and Mathematical Sciences degree in 1955 for a thesis on quantum electrodynamics at high energies. From 1965 to 1988, he worked at the Landau Institute for Theoretical Physics (USSR Academy of Sciences). He has been a professor at Moscow State University since 1965, and served as an acedemician at the USSR Academy of Sciences from 1987 to 1991. In 1991, he became an academician at the Russian Academy of Sciences.

In 1952, Abrikosov discovered the way in which magnetic flux can penetrate a superconductor. The phenomenon is known as type-II superconductivity, and the accompanying arrangement of magnetic flux lines is called the Abrikosov vortex lattice.

Since 1991, he has been working in the Materials Science Division at Argonne National Laboratory in Illinois on a contract basis. Abrikosov is an Argonne Distinguished Scientist at the Condensed Matter Theory Group in Argonne's Materials Science Division. His recent research at Argonne National Laboratory has focused on the origins of magnetoresistance, a property of some materials that change their resistance to electrical flow under the influence of a magnetic field.

He is a citizen of both Russia and the United States.

ALFRED WEGENER

Alfred Lothar Wegener (Berlin, November 1, 1880 – Greenland, November 2 or 3, 1930) was a German scientist and meteorologist. He is most notable for his theory of continental drift (*Kontinentalverschiebung*), proposed in 1912, which hypothesized that the continents were slowly drifting around the Earth. However, at the time he was unable to demonstrate a mechanism for this movement; this combined with a lack of solid evidence meant that his hypothesis was not accepted until the 1950s, when numerous discoveries provided evidence of continental drift.

Career

Wegener had early training in astronomy (Ph.D., University of Berlin, 1904). He became very interested in the new discipline of meteorology (he married the daughter of famous meteorologist and climatologist Wladimir Koppen) and as a record-holding balloonist himself, pioneered the use of weather balloons to track air masses. His lectures became a standard textbook in meteorology, *The Thermodynamics of the Atmosphere*. Wegener was part of several expeditions to Greenland to study polar air circulation, when the existence of a jet stream itself was highly controversial. On his last expedition, Alfred Wegener and his companion Rasmus Villumsen went missing in November 1930. Wegener's body was found on May 12, 1931. His suspected cause of death was heart failure through overexertion.

Continental Drift

Browsing the library at the University of Marburg, where he was teaching in 1911, Wegener was struck by the occurrence of identical fossils in geological strata that are now separated by oceans. The accepted explanations or theories at the time posited land bridges to explain the fossil anomalies; animals and plants could have migrated between fixed separate continents by crossing the land bridges.

But Wegener was increasingly convinced that the continents themselves had shifted away from a primal single massive supercontinent, which drifted apart about 180 million years ago, to judge from the fossil evidence. Wegener used land features, fossils, and climate as evidence to support his hypothesis of continental drift. Examples of land features such as mountain ranges in Africa and South America lined up; also coal fields on Europe matched up with coal fields in North America. Wegener noticed that fossils from reptiles such as Mesosaurus and Lystrosaurus were found in places that are now separated by oceans. Since neither reptile could have swum great distances, Wegener inferred that these reptiles had once lived on a single landmass that split apart.

From 1912 he publicly advocated the theory of "continental drift", arguing that all the continents were once joined together in a single landmass and have drifted apart.

In 1915, in *The Origin of Continents and Oceans* (*Die Entstehung der Kontinente und Ozeane*), Wegener published the theory that there had once been a giant supercontinent, which, in later editions, he named "Pangaea" (meaning "All-Lands" or "All-Earth") and drew together evidence from various fields. Expanded editions during the 1920s presented the accumulating evidence. The last edition, just before his untimely death, revealed the significant observation that shallower oceans were geologically younger.

Theory of Centrifugal Force

Alfred Wegener also came up with a theory to explain continental drift, although it was in error. His theory of continental drift proposed that centrifugal force moved the heavy continents toward the equator as the Earth spun. He thought that inertia, from centrifugal movement combined with tidal drag on the continents (caused by the gravitational pull of the sun and moon) would account for continental drift.

ABRAHAM GOTTLOB WERNER

Abraham Gottlob Werner (September 25, 1749 – June 30, 1817), was a German geologist who set out a now obsolete theory about the stratification of the Earth's crust and coined the now obsolete word Neptunism.

Life

Werner was born in Wehrau, a city in Prussian Silesia, southeastern Germany. His family had been involved in the mining industry for many years. His father, Abraham David Werner, was a foreman at a foundry in Wehrau. Werner was educated at Freiberg and Leipzig, where he studied law and mining, and was then appointed as Inspector and Teacher of Mining and Mineralogy at the small, but influential, Freiberg Mining Academy in 1775. While in Leipzig, Werner became interested in the systematic identification and classification of minerals. Within a year he published the first modern textbook on descriptive mineralogy, *Vonden ausserlichen Kennzeichen der Fossilien* (On the External Characters of Fossils, or of Minerals) (1774).

During his career, Werner published very little, but his fame as a teacher spread throughout Europe, attracting students, who became virtual disciples, and spread his interpretations throughout their homelands, *e.g.* Robert Jameson who became professor at Edinburgh and Andres Manuel del Rio who discovered vanadium. Socratic in his lecturing style, Werner developed an appreciation for the broader implications and interrelations of geology within his students, who provided an enthusiastic and attentive audience.

Unfortunately, Werner was plagued,widespread disease, by frail health his entire life, and passed a quiet existence in the immediate environs of Freiberg. An avid mineral collector in his youth, he abandoned field work altogether in his later life. There is no evidence that he had ever travelled beyond Saxony in his entire adult life. He died at Dresden from internal complications said to have been caused by his consternation over the misfortunes that had befallen Saxony during the Napoleonic Wars.

Legacy

Werner was certainly the most influential geologist of the early portion of the Industrial Revolution. His extraordinary abilities as a lecturer attracted students from all over Europe, who then returned to their native countries and applied his teachings and concepts. Those applications immediately fomented debate, particularly over the origin of basalt, and are commonly referred to as the Neptunist-Plutonist controversy. That controversy was the focus of much geological activity through the end of the 18th century, and well into the 19th century.

The variety of scapolite known as wernerite is named in his honour. He is credited with coining the term geognosy, for the geological study of the Earth's structure, specifically its exterior and interior construction.

ADAM SEDGWICK

Adam Sedgwick (22 March 1785–27 January 1873) was one of the founders of modern geology. He proposed the Devonian period of the geological timescale and later the Cambrian period. The latter proposal was based on work which he did on Welsh rock strata.

Sedgwick was born in Dent, Yorkshire, the third child of an Anglican vicar. He was educated at Sedbergh School and Trinity College, Cambridge.

He obtained his BA (5th Wrangler) from the University of Cambridge in 1808 and his MA in 1811. His academic mentors at Cambridge were Thomas Jones and John Dawson.

Sedgwick studied the geology of the British Isles and Europe. He founded the system for the classification of Cambrian rocks and with Roderick Murchison worked out the order of the carboniferous and underlying Devonian strata. He investigated the phenomena of metamorphism and concretion, and was the first to distinguish clearly between stratification, jointing, and slaty cleavage. He was elected to Fellow of the Royal Society on 1 February 1821.

Opposition to Evolution

While by no means a fundamentalist or evangelical by today's standards, Sedgwick always maintained a fine line between his science and his faith. His geological position was catastrophist, and he believed in a succession of Divine creative acts throughout the long expanse of history. Any form of development that denied a direct creative action smacked as materialistic and amoral. For Sedgwick, moral truths (the obtainment of which separates man from beast) were to be distinguished from physical truths, and to combine these or blur them together could only lead to disastrous consequences. In fact, one's own hope for immortality may ultimately rest on it.

So, when Robert Chambers anonymously published his own theory of evolution, or development, in the book *Vestiges of the Natural History of Creation* (1844), Sedgwick jumped at the chance to attack the book in the July, 1845 edition of the *Edinburgh Review*. *Vestiges* "comes before [its readers] with a bright, polished, and many-coloured surface, and the serpent coils a false philosophy, and asks them to stretch out their hands and pluck the forbidden fruit," he wrote in his review. Accepting the arguments in Vestiges was akin to falling from grace and away from God's favour.

He lashed out at the book in a letter to Charles Lyell, bemoaning the consequences of it conclusions. "...If the book be true, the labours of sober induction are in vain; religion is a lie; human law is a mass of folly, and a base injustice; morality is moonshine; our labours for the black people of Africa were works of madmen; and man and woman are only better beasts!" Later, Sedgwick would add a long preface to the 5th edition of his *Discourse on the Studies of the University of Cambridge* (1850), including a lengthy attack on *Vestiges* and theories of development in general.

Charles Darwin was one of his geological students and the two kept up a correspondence while Darwin was aboard the *HMS Beagle*. However, Sedgwick never accepted the case for evolution made in the *Origin of Species* any more than he did in the *Vestiges*. In response to receiving and reading Darwin's book, he wrote to Darwin saying:

"If I did not think you a good tempered and truth-loving man I should not tell you that... I have read your book with more pain than pleasure. Parts of it I admired greatly; parts I laughed at till my sides were almost sore; other parts I read with absolute sorrow; because I think them utterly false and grievously mischievous. You have deserted-after a start in that tram-road of all solid physical truth-the true method of induction..."

In the same letter, once again, Sedgwick emphasized his distinction between the moral and physical aspects of life, "There is a moral or metaphysical part of nature as well as a physical. A man who denies this is deep in the mire of folly." To break this distinction would be to degrade and brutalize humanity. In a letter to another correspondent, Sedgwick was even harsher on Darwin's book, calling it "*utterly false*" and writing that "It repudiates all reasoning from final causes; and seems to shut the door on any view (however feeble) of the God of Nature as manifested in His works. From first to last it is a dish of rank materialism cleverly cooked and served up."

Despite this difference of opinion, the two men remained friendly until Sedgwick's death.

ANTHONY J. NALDRETT

Anthony James "Tony" Naldrett, (born 1933) is an award-winning Canadian scientist. He is an authority on the geology and origin of nickel-copper-platinum group element deposits, the tectonic setting in which they occur, the petrology of associated rocks, and controls on their composition. He is considered an expert on the reaction between sulfide and silicate melts, fractional crystallization of sulfide melts, and the role of hydrothermal fluids.

Early Life

Naldrett was born in England. Between 1951-1953, he was a pilot officer in the Royal Air Force.

In 1957, he obtained a degree in geology from the University of Cambridge. Later that year he moved to Canada, where he worked in Sudbury as a geologist for Falconbridge Nickel Mines. In 1959 he moved to Kingston, Ontario to attend Queen's University. He received an MSc (1961) and a PhD (1964) for his research on nickel deposits.

Career

Naldrett took a position working in the Geophysical Laboratory of the Carnegie Institution of Washington. In 1967, he returned to Canada as an Assistant Professor at the University of Toronto. In 1972, he was appointed a full Professor, and University Professor in 1984. He worked there until his retirement in 1998. The university made him an Emeritus Professor.

Naldrett has authored, or co-authored 240 refereed publications, plus the writing or editing of 8 books covering his research in geology, mineralogy and chemistry of magmatic sulfide deposits and related rocks.

His research has covered most of the world's magmatic sulfide ores, including those at Sudbury, the Abitibi Belt, Voisey's Bay, the West Australian Widgiemooltha Komatiite deposits, the Zimbabwe Nickel deposits, deposits of the Raglan and Thompson Nickel belts, Norilsk, Pechenga, Jinchuan, the Duluth Complex, the Bushveld and Stillwater complexes, Zimbabwe's Great Dyke, and at Lac des Iles.

In addition to his research, he has consulted for over 30 companies including Chevron Corporation, Falconbridge Ltd., Western Mining Corporation, BHP Billiton, Rio Tinto Group, Cominco-American, and Kennecott.

ANDRIJA MOHOROVIEIAE

Andrija Mohorovieiae (January 23, 1857 – December 18, 1936) was a notable Croatian meteorologist and seismologist. He is best known as the eponym for the Mohorovieiae discontinuity.

Early Years

Mohorovieiae was born in Volosko near Opatija, where his father, also named Andrija, was a blacksmith making anchors. The younger Andrija himself loved the sea and he married a captain's daughter, Silvija Verni. Together, they had four sons.

Andrija Jr. obtained his elementary education in his home town, continued his study in the gymnasium of a neighbouring town, Rijeka, and received his higher education in mathematics and physics at the Faculty of Philosophy in Prague in 1875. There, one of his professors was the famous physicist Ernst Mach. At the age of 15 the junior Mohorovieiae knew Italian, English and French and later he learned German, Latin and Ancient Greek.

Education Career

His career began with a teaching post in the Zagreb gymnasium (1879-1880) and then secondary school in Osijek. In 1882, he began to teach at the Royal Nautical School in Bakar, near Rijeka, where he remained for nine years. Works initiated or done there were crucial for the beginning of Mohorovieiae's scientific work. From 1893, when he became a corresponding member, to 1917-18 he taught subjects in the fields of geophysics and astronomy at the Faculty of Philosophy, University of Zagreb. In 1898 he became a full member of what was then the Croatian Academy of Sciences and Arts in Zagreb where he was private docent, and in 1910 he became titular associate university professor.

ANDREW LAWSON

Andrew Cowper Lawson (1861-1952) was a professor of geology at the University of California, Berkeley. He was the editor and co-author of the 1908 report on the 1906 San Francisco Earthquake which became known as the "Lawson Report". He was also the first person to identify and name the San Andreas Fault in 1895, and after the 1906 quake, the first to delineate the entire length of the San Andreas Fault which previously had been noted only in the San Francisco Bay Area. He also named the Franciscan Complex.

Lawson was born on July 25, 1861 in Anstruther, Scotland. He moved to Hamilton, Canada with his parents at age six. In 1883, he received his B.A. degree in natural science from the University of Toronto. He worked for the Geological Survey of Canada while pursuing his graduate degrees. He received his M.A. from the University of Toronto in 1885, and his Ph.D. from Johns Hopkins University in 1888.

In 1890, he left the Geological Survey of Canada to work as a consulting geologist in Vancouver. In October of the same year, he accepted a position as Assistant Professor of Mineralogy and Geology at the University of California in Berkeley. He became a full professor in 1892, and a Professor Emeritus from 1928 to his death on June 16, 1952.

Professor Lawson was a consulting geologist for the construction of the Golden Gate Bridge in the 1930s.

His home in the La Loma Park area of the Berkeley Hills in Berkeley, California, now called the "Lawson House", was especially designed for him by noted architect Bernard Maybeck to withstand earthquakes. The house is an officially designated local landmark.

The mineral Lawsonite is named for him.

ARTHUR HOLMES

Arthur Holmes (January 14, 1890 – September 20, 1965) was a British geologist. As a child he lived in Low Fell, Gateshead.

He performed the first uranium-lead radiometric dating specifically designed to measure the age of a rock during his undergraduate studies. His result was 370 mya for a Devonian rock from Norway.

He graduated in 1910, and the result was published 1911, after he had already travelled to Mozambique for six months to prospect for minerals. He contracted blackwater fever and malaria so severe that an obituary was telegraphed back to Britain. However, he immediately left for home and recovered, and, because of this managed to avoid military service during World War I.

He joined the staff at Imperial College, where he pursued doctoral studies, obtaining a PhD in 1917.

He then took a job with an oil company in Burma, but the company went bankrupt and he had to return to England penniless in 1924. To make matters worse, his son had died of dysentery in Burma. He then became Professor of geology at the University of Durham, but moved on to the University of Edinburgh later in his career (1943), retiring in 1956.

He greatly furthered the newly created discipline of geochronology and published the world renowned book *The Age of the Earth* in 1913 in which he estimated the Earth's age to be 1.6 billion years. He championed the theory of continental drift, even when he was in a small minority. He proposed that Earth's mantle contained convection cells that dissipated radioactive heat and moved the crust at the surface.

His second famous book *Principles of Physical Geology* was published in 1944, which concludes with a chapter about continental drift. His later measurements of the age of the Earth (4,500 +/- 100 Ma) were based on measurements of the relative abundance of uranium isotopes by Alfred O. C. Nier.

He won the Wollaston Medal in 1956 and the Penrose Medal in the same year. The Arthur Holmes Medal of the European Geosciences Union is named after him.

A crater on Mars was named in his honour.

The Durham University Department of Earth Sciences' Arthur Holmes Isotope Geology Laboratory is named after him, as is the students' Geology society.

ALEXANDER HENRY GREEN

Alexander Henry Green (October 10, 1832 – August 19, 1896) was an English geologist.

Born at Maidstone, he was the son of the Rev. Thomas Sheldon Green, master of the Ashby Grammar School. He was educated partly at his father's school, Ashby-de-la-Zouch, and afterwards at Gonville and Caius College, Cambridge, where he graduated as sixth wrangler in 1855 and was elected a fellow of his college. In 1861 he joined the Geological Survey of Great Britain, and surveyed large areas of the midland counties, Derbyshire and Yorkshire.

He wrote (wholly or in part) memoirs on the *Geology of Banbury* (1864), of *Stockport* (1866), of *North Derbyshire* (1869, 2nd ed. 1887), and of the *Yorkshire Coal-field* (1878). In 1874 he retired from the Geological Survey, having been appointed professor of geology in the Yorkshire College at Leeds; in 1885 he became also professor of mathematics, while for many years he held the lectureship on geology at the school of military engineering at Chatham.

He was elected fellow of the Royal Society in 1886, and two years later was chosen professor of geology in the University of Oxford. In 1892 he was awarded the Murchison Medal of the Geological Society of London.

His wrote a manual of *Physical Geology* (1876, 3rd ed. 1882).

He died at Boars Hill, Oxford, on 19 August 1896.

A portrait of him, with brief memoir, was published in *Proc. Yorksh. Geol. and Polytechnic Soc.* xiii. 232.

AUSTRALIAN MUSEUM

The Australian Museum is the oldest museum in Australia, with an international reputation in the fields of natural history and anthropology. It features collections of vertebrate and invertebrate zoology, as well as mineralogy, palaeontology, and anthropology. Apart from exhibitions, the museum is also involved in indigenous studies research and community programmes.

It is located in College Street, Sydney and was originally known as the **Colonial Museum** or **Sydney Museum**. The museum was renamed in June 1836 by a Sub-Committee meeting, when it was resolved during an argument that it should be renamed the Australian Museum.

History

The museum was founded on March 30, 1827, by Earl Bathurst, then the Secretary of State for the Colonies, who wrote to the

Governor of New South Wales of his intent to found a public museum, and provisions to provide £200 yearly towards its upkeep.

The establishment of a museum had been planned in 1821 by the Philosophical Society of Australasia, and although specimens were collected, the Society folded in 1822. In 1826, however, upon the arrival of entomologist and Fellow of the Linnean Society of London Alexander Macleay, who, after being appointed New South Wales Colonial Secretary, began lobbying for a museum.

The first location of the museum was likely a room in the offices of the Colonial Secretary, although for the next 30 years it moved to several other locations in Sydney, until moving into its current location in 1849. This handsome sandstone building on the corner of College and Park Streets, opposite Hyde Park, was first opened to the public in May 1857. It was designed by the New South Wales Colonial Architect James Barnet. The first chairman of the museum was William Holmes, who was appointed on June 16, 1829. He was accidentally shot while at Moreton Bay on assignment, in August 1831.

The Museum was administered directly by the colonial government until June 1836, until the establishment of a Committee of Superintendence of the Australian Museum and Botanical Garden. Sub-committees were established for each institution. Members of these committees were generally the ruling members of the political and scientific elite of Sydney; and scions of the Macleay served until 1853, at which point the Committee was abolished. In that year, the government drafted the Australian Museum Act, thereby incorporating it and establishing a Board of Trustees consisting of 24 members. William Sharp Macleay, the former Committee chairman, continued to serve as the Chairman of this committee.

The first curator of the Australian Museum was well-known naturalist George Bennett, appointed in 1835, who was the first to catalogue the Museum's collections. After his 1841 resignation, he was succeeded by Rev. W.B. Clarke until 1843, and then by William Sheridan Wall, a longtime collector with the Museum. In these early years, collecting was the main priority of the Museum. Specimens were commonly traded with English and European institutions.

The scientific stature of the Museum was established under the curatorship of Gerard Krefft, who served until 1874, himself a well-published scientist. His successor, Edward Pierson Ramsay, who served until 1894, greatly increased the recruitment of scientific staff within the institution. The museum catalogues, first documented by Bennett, were the first scientific publications by the Museum, but with the addition of science staff, and thereby, research output, in 1890 Ramsay started the *Records of the Australian Museum* a publication which continues to this day.

In 1918, the position of *Curator* was renamed *Director and Curator*, and from 1921, *Director*. In 1948, the *Scientific Assistants* (the scientific staff) were redesignated *Curators* and *Assistant Curators*. In 1983, during a period of reorganisation, the position of *Curator* was changed, becoming *Collection Manager*.

During the 19th century, galleries mainly included large display cases overly filled with specimins and artifacts. Displays grew to include dioramas showing habitat groups beginning in the 1920s, but otherwise, the Museum was largely unchanged during the timespan beginning with the curatorship of Robert Etheridge Jr (1895-1919), until 1954, with the appointment of John Evans. Under his direction, additional buildings were built, several galleries were entirely overhauled, and a new Exhibitions department was created. The size of the education staff was also radically increased. By the end of the 1950s, all of the galleries had been completely overhauled.

The Museum's growth in the field of scientific research continued with Frank Talbot, who succeeded Evans in 1966, and a new department of Environmental Studies was created in 1968. The museum support society TAMS (*The Australian Museum Society*) was formed in 1972, and in 1973 the Lizard Island Research Station (LIMS), was established near Cairns.

Director Des Griffin, the successor to Talbot, oversaw extensions to the original Musum building, which were completed in 1988. His direction saw increased cooperation with Aborigines, leading to new exhibitions and policies, as well as repatriations of artefacts.

In 1991, the museum established Australian Museum Business Services (AMBS), a commercial consulting and project management consulting group. AMBS initially undertook ecological, Australian Aboriginal archaeological and exhibitions management consulting projects for a range of clients, and since 2007 has included historic heritage and archaeology in its range of expertise.

In 1995, the museum established new research centres in Conservation, Biodiversity, Evolutionary Research, Geodiversity, and People and Places. In 1998, the djamu gallery opened at Customs House, Circular Quay, the first major new venue for the Museum beyond College Street site. A series of exhibitions on Indigenous culture were displayed until the gallery closed at the end of 2000.

The current director is Frank Howarth.

ALEKSIS DREIMANIS

Aleksis Dreimanis (b. August 13, 1914 in Riga) is an award winning Quaternary geologist.

Dreimanis was born in Latvia. He first studied geology at the Institute of Palaeontology at the University of Latvia in Riga. In 1939, he worked as a lecturer at the University. As World War II was being fought, he also took on the responsibility of consulting in Quaternary mapping in the Latvian Institute of Mineral Resources. He volunteered for the Latvian Legion. After the war Dreimanis was appointed Associate Professor in the Baltic University in the Displaced Persons camps at Hamburg and Pinneberg in Germany.

In 1948, Dreimanis immigrated to Canada to assume a lecturer position at the University of Western Ontario in London, Ontario. Several Canadian institutions called on him for his Quaternary expertise, including the Geological Survey of Canada, the Ontario Department of Mines, and the Ontario Department of Planning and Development for the St. Lawrence Seaway Authority, the Thames

River Conservation Authority and various private companies. The university promoted him to Associate Professor in 1956, then to Professor in 1964. In 1980 the university gave made him an Emeritus Professor. In the over 40 years with the university, he has produced over 200 papers, notes and abstracts in the field of Quaternary research.

Between 1974 and 1982, Dreimanis acted as an international advisor for several groups including; the Polish Academy of Sciences, the Geological Survey of Finland, and the Ministry of Education in Finland.

Dreimanis maintained his link with Latvia. He made numerous visits as an invited lecturer to Riga, and to Tallinn in Estonia. He was a correspondent with the Dictionary of Latvian Technical Terminology from 1970 to 1986. He has been an associate editor of the Technical Review Journal (for Geology) from 1979. He served as s Chairman of the Commission on Technical and Natural Sciences at the Latvian Cultural Foundation from 1973 to 1976.

ALEXANDRE-EMILE BEGUYER DE CHANCOURTOIS

Alexandre-Emile Beguyer de Chancourtois (January 20, 1820 – November 14, 1886) was a French geologist and mineralogist who was the first to arrange the chemical elements in order of atomic weights, doing so in 1862. De Chancourtois only published his paper, but did not publish his actual graph with the proposed arrangement.

Although his publication was significant, it was ignored by chemists as it was written in terms of geology. It was Dmitri Mendeleyev's table published in 1869 that became most recognized. De Chancourtois was also a professor of mine surveying, and later geology at the Ecole Nationale Superieure des Mines de Paris. He also was the Inspector of Mines in Paris, and was widely responsible for implementing many mine safety regulations and laws during the time.

Life

De Chancourtois was born in Paris. At age eighteen, he entered the renowned Ecole Polytechnique, one of the best known French grandes ecoles of engineering and management. While he was there, de Chancourtois was a pupil of three famous French scientists, Jean-Baptiste Elie de Beaumont, Pierre Guillaume Frederic le Play, and Ours-Pierre-Armand Petit-Dufrenoy. After completing his studies at Ecole Polytechnique, de Chancourtois went on a geological expedition into Hungary, Armenia and Turkey. In 1848, de Chancourtois went back to Paris and joined the teaching faculty as professor of mine surveying at the Ecole Nationale Superieure des Mines de Paris. He worked with Pierre Guillaume Frederic le Play to organize a collection of minerals for the French government. In 1852, De Chancourtois was named the professor of geology at Ecole Nationale Superieure des Mines de Paris. In 1867, de Chancourtois was awarded the Legion d'honneur by Napoleon III of France. De Chancourtois led several overseas expeditions during the course of his life and served as the Inspector of Mines in Paris from 1875 until his death. As a mine inspector, he introduced safety laws to prevent methane gas explosions, which were frequent occurrences at the time.

ANTHONY R. BARRINGER

Anthony R. "Tony" Barringer (b. October 20, 1925) is a Canadian/American geophysicist. He has made numerous contributions to mineral exploration technology. His most famous work was the development of the INPUT airborne electromagnetic system, which has been credited in the discovery of tens of billions of dollars worth of ore deposits.

Before beginning his university studies, Barringer served with the British Army in World War II. In 1948, he began attending the University of London. In 1951, he obtained a B.Sc. in economic geology from the university's Imperial College of Science and Technology. He obtained a PhD degree in 1954, from the same institution.

Career

Barringer left the United Kingdom to accept a post in Toronto, Canada with Selco Exploration as an exploration geologist. Eventually he was promoted to Manager of its Airborne and Technical Services division. At this time, he invented the INPUT (Induced Pulse Transient) airborne electromagnetic system and the equipment for a portable ground electromagnetic system. This technology allows explorers to get a better understanding of the minerals in a rock formation, without extracting the rocks. The Society of Exploration Geophysicists said INPUT was "a meritorious technical achievement which has been instrumental in the discovery of many base metal deposits in a number of countries around the world." In 1961, he formed a private company, Barringer Research Ltd. He was the President and major shareholder. Barringer continued to develop the airborne system and licenses its use to exploration companies. Major oil and mining companies depended on this remote-sensing technology for their exploration. It has been credited in the discovery of over 25 commercial ore deposits, representing tens of billions of dollars. Barringer Research went public in 1967. Ten years later, Barringer moved to Denver, Colorado and brought the company's headquarters with him. He later became a citizen of the United States.

Barringer made numerous technical contributions to the mining industry, including a laser-induced fluorescence-based system used primarily in oil and gas exploration (FLUOROSCAN), correlation spectrometer used to measure atmospheric dispersions of various gases (COSPEC), an infrared remote sensor for atmospheric gases which has been used by NASA to measure the worldwide atmospheric distribution of carbon dioxide (GASPEC), two airborne conductivity mapping systems using very low frequency fields (E-phase and radiophase) and several particulate analyzers (COTRAN, SURTRACE, LASERTRACE and AIRTRACE). He has presented more than 80 technical papers and has been awarded more than 70 patents in Canada, the U.S., and other countries.

In 1989, Barringer officially retired.

ANDREW GEDDES BAIN

Andrew Geddes Bain (baptised 11 June 1797 Thurso, Scotland-20 October 1864 Cape Town), South African geologist, road engineer, palaeontologist and explorer.

Life History

The only child of Alexander Bain and Jean Geddes, both of whom died when Bain was still a young boy. He was raised by an aunt who lived near Edinburgh. Here he received a classical education, but no vocational training. In 1816 he emigrated to Cape Town accompanied by his uncle Lieutenant Colonel William Geddes of the 83rd Regiment, who was stationed in the Cape. He married Maria Elizabeth von Backstrom on 16 November 1818 and had 3 sons and 7 daughters. In 1822 he bought property in Graaff Reinet and carried on for some years the business of a saddler. In 1825 he accompanied John Burner Biddulph on a trading expedition to Kuruman, the mission outpost on the edge of the Kalahari and home of Dr. Robert Moffat (father-in-law of David Livingstone). They explored further north and reached Dithubaruba in Bechuanaland, becoming the first recorded Europeans to return safely from so far north. In 1829 they trekked to the vicinity of present-day Kokstad. They were forced to return by hordes of Bantu fleeing Dingaan.

During these journeys he discovered his talent for drawing and writing and became a regular correspondent for John Fairbairn's *South African Commercial Advertiser.* Outspoken, he was sued for libel a number of times by Gerrit Maritz, one of the eventual Voortrekker leaders. He was awarded a special medal in 1832 for 'gratuitously superintending the construction of Van Ryneveld's Pass, Graaff-Reinet'.

In 1834 he made another trip to Bechuanaland where he lost his wagons and collection of zoological specimens during an attack by the Matabele, caused by his Griqua guides' stealing some of the King's cattle. During the Cape Frontier Wars in 1833-1834 he served as captain of the Beaufort Levies raised for the defence of the frontier. He tried his hand at farming in the newly-annexed Queen Adelaide Province, but lost the farm when the land was returned to the Xhosa in 1836. Later he was engaged to construct a military road through the Ecca Pass, and displayed engineering talents which led to his being permanently employed as surveyor of military roads under the corps of Royal Engineers in 1836. During this period he had a part in building the Fish River bridge, then the largest bridge in the country.

He constructed the Queen's Road from Grahamstown to Fort Beaufort. He was appointed inspector by the Cape Roads Board in 1845 and built Michell's Pass near Ceres in 1848 and Bain's Kloof Pass near Wellington in 1853. He was presented with table silver and a candelabrum by grateful colonists. Returning to the Eastern Cape in 1854, he built numerous roads and passes including the Katberg Pass near Fort Beaufort. This occupation created an interest in geology, inspired in 1837 by a copy of Lyell's *Elements of Geology*.

He was friendly with William Guybon Atherstone, who was also a keen geologist and fossil collector and who was present at the discovery of *Paranthodon africanus* Broom at the farm Dassieklip on the Bushmans River, about half-way between Grahamstown and Port Elizabeth. Bain discovered many fossil remains, including the herbivorous mammal-like reptile dicynodon *Oudenodon bainii* Owen, which was excavated from the Karoo Beds on the farm Mildenhall south of Fort Beaufort and described by Sir Richard Owen. He was awarded £200 by the British government in 1845 for his researches.

Devoting his spare time to geological studies, Bain prepared in 1852 the first comprehensive geological map of South Africa, a work of great merit, which was published by the Geological Society of London in 1856. Sir Roderick Murchison and Sir Henry de la Beche, prominent geologists of the time, both recommended Bain's appointment as Cape Geological Surveyor in 1852, but since no funds were available, nothing came of it. Bain went to Namaqualand in 1854 and reported to the Government on the copper mines there.

ADOLPHE D'ARCHIAC

Etienne Jules Adolphe Desmier de Saint-Simon, Vicomte d'Archiac (September 24, 1802-December 24, 1868), was a French geologist and paleontologist.

Early Life

He was born at Reims and educated in the Military School of St. Cyr, and served for nine years as a cavalry officer until 1830, when he retired from the service. Prior to this he had published an historical romance; but now geology came to occupy his chief attention. In his earlier scientific works, which date from 1835, he described the Tertiary and Cretaceous formations of France, Belgium and England, and dealt especially with the distribution of fossils geographically and in sequence. Later on he investigated the Carboniferous, Devonian and Silurian formations.

Magnum Opus

His great work was *Histoire des Progres de la Geologie de 1834 a 1859*, published in eight volumes (1847-1860). In 1853 the Wollaston Medal of the Geological Society of London was awarded to him. In the same year, with Jules Haime (1824-1856), he published a monograph on the Nummulitic formation of India. In 1857 he was elected a member of the French Academy of Sciences, and in 1861 he was appointed professor of palaeontology in the Museum National d'Histoire Naturelle in Paris. Of later works his *Paleontologie Stratigraphique*, in three vols. (1864-1865); his *Geologie et paleontologie* (1866); and his paleontological contributions to de Tchihatcheff's *Asie mineure* (1866), may be specially mentioned.

Death

While suffering from severe depression he committed suicide by throwing himself into the River Seine on Christmas Eve, 1868.

ALLAN WILSON

Allan Charles Wilson (18 October 1934 – 21 July 1991) was a pioneer in the use of molecular approaches to understand evolutionary change and reconstruct phylogenies. One of the great innovators of science, he revolutionised the study of human evolution. He was one of the most controversial figures in post-war biology; his work attracted a great deal of attention both from within and outside the academic world. He is the only New Zealander to win the prestigious MacArthur Fellowship and was short listed for the Nobel Prize when he died at the age of 56. Allan Wilson's scientific achievements were nothing short of profoundly significant.

Alian Wilson was born in Ngaruawahia, New Zealand, and raised on a farm at Helvetia, Pukekohe. He attended King's College in Auckland and excelled in maths and chemistry. After school he gained a BSc from the University of Otago. It was here as a Masters student that Wilson met Professor C.P. 'Mac' McMeekan, a New Zealand pioneer in animal science. He suggested that Wilson further his study in biochemistry instead of genetics.

In 1955 Wilson was invited to do his PhD at the University of California, Berkeley. At the time the family thought Allan would only be gone two years; instead he stayed at Berkeley for 35 years, gaining his PhD in 1961 under the direction of Arthur Pardee, and setting up one of the world's most creative biochemistry labs and turning ideas of evolution on their ear.

Allan Wilson first came to world attention when he published a paper titled *Immunological Time-Scale For Human Evolution* in Science magazine in December 1967. Together with doctoral student Vincent Sarich, Wilson argued that the origins of the human species could be seen through, what he termed, a "molecular clock". This was a way of dating, not from fossils, but from the genetic mutations that had accumulated since they parted from a common ancestor. The molecular clock estimated the length of time from divergence, given a certain rate of change.

When Wilson, with his then-student Mary-Claire King, and Sarich analysed and compared genetic material of humans and chimpanzees, they found the material to be 99 percent identical. From King's work, using the 'molecular clock' reasoning (bigger differences equate to greater time since their last common ancestor) Wilson deduced that the earliest proto-hominids evolved only five million years ago. Most contemporary anthropologists, who favoured a date of around 25 million years, dismissed his work as absurd.

In the early 1980s, as his findings for the age of the proto-humans were starting to be more widely accepted, Wilson again dropped a bombshell on traditional anthropological thinking with his best known work with Rebecca Cann and Mark Stoneking on the so-called "Mitochondrial Eve" hypothesis. In his efforts to identify informative genetic markers for tracking human evolutionary history, he started to focus on mitochondrial DNA (mtDNA)—genes that sit in the cell, but not in the nucleus, and are passed from mother to child. This DNA material is important because it mutates quickly, thus making it easy to plot changes over relatively short time spans. By comparing differences in the mtDNA Wilson believed it was possible to estimate the time, and the place, modern humans first evolved. With his discovery that human mtDNA is genetically much less diverse than chimpanzee mtDNA, he concluded that modern human races had diverged recently from a single population while older human species such as Neandertal, Java erectus and Pekin erectus had become extinct. He and his team compared mtDNA in people of different racial backgrounds and concluded that all modern humans evolved from one 'lucky mother' in Africa about 150,000 years ago.

This finding was as, if not more, controversial than his 1967 findings. Accepted thinking had various human groups evolving from different ancestors, over a million years in separate geographic regions, but at basically the same rate around the world. In Europe with Homo sapiens Neanderthals, in Indonesia with Java Man, in China with Peking Man. Again, as in the 1960s, many palaeontologists rejected Wilson's conclusions; fossil scientists were unfamiliar with biochemistry and trusted their own data more than molecular data. It took 20 years to convince palaeontologists of the value of Wilson's theory, but when they did, it married their science with that of genetics.

ALFRED STURTEVANT

Alfred Henry Sturtevant (November 21, 1891 – April 5, 1970) was an American geneticist. Sturtevant constructed the first genetic map of a chromosome in 1913. Throughout his career he worked on the organism *Drosophila melanogaster* with Thomas Hunt Morgan. By watching the development of flies in which the earliest cell division produced two different genomes, he measured the embryonic distance between organs in a unit which is called the sturt in his honour. In 1967, Sturtevant received the National Medal of Science.

Biography

Alfred Henry Sturtevant was born in Jacksonville, Illinois, United States on November 21, 1891, the youngest of Alfred Henry and Harriet Sturtevant's six children. His grandfather Julian M. Sturtevant, a Yale University graduate, founded Illinois College where his father taught mathematics.

When Sturtevant was seven years old, his father quit his teaching job and moved the family to Alabama to pursue farming. Sturtevant attended a one room schoolhouse until entering high school in Mobile. In 1908, he enrolled at Columbia University. During this time, he lived with his older brother Edgar who taught nearby. Edgar taught Alfred about scholarship and research.

As a child, Sturtevant had created pedigrees of his father's horses. While in college, he read about Mendelism, which piqued Sturtevant's interest because it could explain the traits expressed in the horse pedigrees. He further pursued his interest in genetics under Thomas Hunt Morgan, who encouraged him to publish a paper of his pedigrees shown through Mendelian genetics. In 1914, Sturtevent completed his doctoral work under Morgan as well.

After earning his doctorate, Sturtevant stayed at Columbia as a research investigator for the Carnegie Institution of Washington. He joined Morgan's research team in the "fly room", in which huge advances were being made in the study of genetics through studies of the fruit fly *Drosophila*. In 1922, he married Phoebe Curtis Reed, and the couple subsequently had three children, the eldest of whom was William C. Sturtevant.

In 1928, the Sturtevant moved to Pasadena to work at the California Institute of Technology, where he became a Professor of Genetics and remained for the rest of his career, except for one year when he was invited to teach in Europe. He taught an undergraduate course in genetics at Caltech and wrote a textbook with George Beadle. He became the leader of a new genetics research group at Caltech, whose members included George W. Beadle, Theodosius Dobzhansky, Sterling Emerson, and Jack Schultz. In 1967, he received the National Medal of Science for his longtime work on the genetics of *Drosophila* and other organisms.

Sturtevant was interested in taxonomy as well as genetics. He loved solving all kinds of puzzles and saw genetics as a puzzle for him to decipher. He was widely read, interested in politics, newspapers, scientific journals across many subjects and crossword puzzles. He had an impressive memory and composed and edited papers in his head before writing them down from memory. He enjoyed a long and prosperous career in genetics until his death on April 5, 1970. He died in Pasadena, California at the age of 79.

ALFRED PLOETZ

Alfred Ploetz (August 22, 1860 – March 20, 1940) was a German physician, biologist, eugenicist known for introducing together with Wilhelm Schallmayer the concept of racial hygiene (*Rassenhygiene*) in Germany. "Rassenhygiene" ist another name for eugenics.

Life

Alfred Ploetz was born in Swinemunde, Germany (now Œwinoujœcie, Poland) grew up and attended school in Breslau (now Wroc³aw). Already then he began his friendship with Carl Hauptmann, brother of the famous author Gerhart Hauptmann. In 1879 he founded a secret schoolboy society for the improvement of the race. In Gerhart Hauptmanns Drama "Vor Sonnenaufgang" (before sunrise) which was first performed on October 20, 1889 in Berlin, the key figure of the journalist Loth bears the features of Ploetz. After his school time Ploetz at first studied political economy in Breslau. There he joined the "Freie wissenschaftliche Vereinigung" (free scientific union). Among his friends were-besides his brother-among others: his former school friend Ferdinand Simon (later son-in-law of August Bebel), the brothers Carl and Gerhart Hauptmann, Heinrich Laux, and Charles Proteus Steinmetz.

This circle enthusastically read the works of Ernst Haeckel and Charles Darwin. Carl Hauptmann was a student of Ernst Haeckel, and Gerhart Hauptmann and Ploetz attended some of his lectures. This circle extended itself, developed a plan of founding a colony in one of the pacific states and established itself as the association "Pacific". They planned a "community on friendly, socialist and maybe also pan-Germanic basis".

In consequence of the prosecution of socialistic minded persons in application of Bismarck's "socialist laws" (187-1890), in 1883 Ploetz flew to Zurich, where he continued to study political economy with Julius Platter (1844-1923). In his memoirs Ploetz states as an important reason for his choice of Zurich that in his studies in Breslau socialist theories were only incidentally mentioned. In Zurich he could occupy himself more intensively with them and make acquaintance with some socialist and social democrats. In the 1880s the free Switzerland, with its liberal asylum laws, was the destination of various persons who suffered political persecution.

For more of the association "Pacific" see the German article. After half a year in the USA Ploetz returned to Zurich and began to study medicine. In 1890 he became medical doctor and married Ernst Rudin's sister Pauline. The next four years both lived in the USA. The marriage remained childless. In 1898 they were divorced. Later Ploetz married Anita Nordenholz. This marriage led to three children Ulrich (called Uli), Cordelia (called Deda) and Wilfrid (called Fridl, born 1912, in 2007 still alive).

In 1904 Ploetz founded the periodical "Archiv fur Rassen-und Gesellschaftsbiologie" with Fritz Lenz as chief editor, and in 1905 the "Deutsche Gesellschaft fur Rassenhygiene" (German association of eugenics). He remained the Great Old Man of the German eugenics until his death in 1940. In 1930 he became honourary doctor of the university of Munich.

Ploetz first proposed the theory of racial hygiene (eugenics) in his "Racial Hygiene Basics" (*Grundlinien einer Rassenhygiene*) in 1895.

He died at the age of 79 and is buried at his home in Herrsching on the Ammersee in Bavaria.

ARTHUR PARDEE

Arthur Pardee (born July 13, 1921) is an American biochemist. One biographical portrait begins "Among the titans of science, Arthur Pardee is especially intriguing." There is hardly a field of molecular biology that is not affected by his work, which has advanced our understanding through theoretical predictions followed by insightful experiments. He is perhaps most famous for his part in the 'PaJoMo experiment' of the late 1950s, which greatly helped in the discovery of messenger RNA. He is also well known as the discoverer of the restriction point, in which a cell commits itself to certain cell cycle events during the G1 cycle. He has done a great deal of work on tumour growth and regulation, with a particular focus on the role of estrogen in hormone-responsive tumors. And he is also well known for the development of various biochemical research techniques, most notably the differential display methodology, which is used in examining the activation of genes in cells. More recently he has championed the acceptance and adoption of the conceptual review as a valuable approach to unearthing new knowledge from the enormous stores of information in the scientific literature.

Career

Pardee received his Bachelor of Science degree from the University of California, Berkeley in 1942 while his Masters (1943) and PhD (1947) degrees were earned at the California Institute of Technology under the mentorship of Linus Pauling, who he considered to be the greatest chemist of the 20th century. Pardee did postdoctoral work at the University of Wisconsin-Madison before returning to Berkeley as an instructor in biochemistry in 1949. In the 1950s, he was on a sabbatical with Jacob Francis and Jacques Monod in Paris. In 1961 Pardee became Professor in Biochemical Sciences at Princeton University while in 1975 he moved to Boston to become Professor of Biological Chemistry and Molecular Pharmacology at the Dana-Farber Cancer Institute and Harvard Medical School as well as Chief for the Division of Cell Growth and Regulation at the Dana-Farber Cancer Institute. Pardee became an emeritus professor at Dana-Farber in 1992. He has been a member of the National Academy of Sciences in 1968.

ARTHUR MOURANT

Arthur Ernest Mourant (April 11, 1904 – August 29, 1994) was a British chemist, hematologist and geneticist who pioneered research into biological anthropology and its distribution, genetics, clinical and laboratory medicine, and geology.

Mourant graduated from Oxford University with honours in chemistry and a Doctor of Philosophy in geology in 1931. He was an early advocate of the then discredited Wegener theory of continental drift, which subsequently gained acceptabtability as plate tectonics. When he left Oxford he failed to find a position in his chosen discipline and returned to his childhood home of Jersey, where he set up a pathology laboratory.

He later studied medicine and surgery at St Bartholomew's Medical College, London, joining the Galton Laboratory Serum Unit in 1946 and then founding the Blood Group Reference Laboratory in London, where he was director for 20 years.

He pioneered a study of hematology of the worldwide distribution of blood groups. This work help build the genetic map of the world by studying and classifying blood groups across many populations and ethnic groups. His book, *The Distribution of the Human Blood Groups*, definitively drew together current knowledge on blood groups and their distribution. It launched anthropology on a new scientific basis as it described the genetic evidence for biological relationships, and allowed theories of population genetics to be developed and examined. This had far-reaching effects on medicine, research into genetic diseases, blood transfusion, and public health.

Mourant also studied the new blood group antigens of the Lewis, Henshaw, Kell, and Rhesus systems, biological polymorphisms, and animal serological characteristics for fish stocks and cattle breeds.

Amongst his many honours and recognitions, he gained a Fellowship of the Royal Society, the Huxley Memorial Medal of the Royal Anthropological Institute, Landsteiner Memorial Award of the American Association of Blood Banks and honourary member of the Human Biology Council.

ALFRED MIRSKY

Alfred Ezra Mirsky (October 17, 1900–June 19, 1974) was an American pioneer in molecular biology.

Mirsky graduated from Harvard College in 1922, after which he studied for two years at the College of Physicians and Surgeons of Columbia University until 1924 when he moved to the University of Cambridge on a US National Research Council fellowship. He received his PhD from Cambridge in 1926, with a dissertation on the Haemoglobin molecule.

On May 25, 1926 Mirsky married Reba Paeff, who went on to become a renowned children's author; they had a daughter and a son.

In 1927 Mirsky was appointed Lab Assistant to Alfred E. Cohn at the then Rockefeller Institute for Medical Research, beginning his association with Rockefeller University. During a sabbatical year at the California Institute of Technology, Mirsky published a paper with Linus Pauling on the general theory of protein structure, suggesting that the structure of proteins are coiled in a specific configuration that accounts for the function in the body, and that the protein is denatured when that configuration is lost by breaking the hydrogen bonds that stabilize the structure. Mirsky became an official Member of the Rockefeller Institute in 1948, and in 1950 was internationally congratulated for the "grand discovery" of DNA constancy, which proved the concept of DNA as the hereditary material.

Mirsky was made Professor in 1954 when the Institute became Rockefeller University. He was also elected to the United States National Academy of Sciences in the same year. Mirsky was highly involved in university affairs, and in 1959 he initiated a series of lectures for high school students, now named the Alfred E. Mirsky Holiday Lecture on Science in his honour.

In 1962 Mirsky chose a new lab assistant from a pool of candidates, in choosing a woman, Ellie Donoghue, he set a precedent by making her the first female lab assistant in the Institute's history, the very same position which he first held upon his initial association with Rockefeller Institute. Mirsky proceeded to entrust Ms. Donoghue with assistance in his research and the running of his laboratory, setting an early precedent for the advancement of women in the labs at Rockefeller University.

Following retirement from his laboratory in an official capacity in 1964, he served as librarian of the Rockefeller University from 1965 until 1972, all the while being allowed to maintain his laboratory at the university for his personal research, He continued to make groundbreaking contributions to the study of cell nuclei in rodents and bovines in direct parallels to the structure of cell nuclei in humans.

After his wife, Reba Paeff Mirsky, died in 1966 he donated her valuable jewelry collection, save for a few pieces distributed to family and close friends, to the university's collection. This collection of jewelry, acquired during their many trips around the world, is a part of the university's holdings to this day. He went on to marry fellow Rockefeller employee Sonia Wohl in 1967. Mirsky became professor emeritus in 1971, after forty-four years at the Rockefeller Institute and University.

Mirsky travelled widely and was quite knowledgeable in archaeology and art history; his priceless collection of art and historical objects was willed to the Rockefeller University upon his death in 1974 and remains in their permanent collection.

BERNARD KETTLEWELL

Henry Bernard Davis Kettlewell (24 February 1907-1979) was a British geneticist, lepidopterist and medical doctor, who carried out important research into the influence of industrial melanism on natural selection in moths, showing why moths are darker in polluted areas.

Early Life

Kettlewell was born in Howden, Yorkshire, was educated at Charterhouse School, and from 1926 studied medicine with zoology at Gonville and Caius College, Cambridge. In 1929 he began clinical training at St Bartholomew's Hospital, London, then in 1935 joined a general medical practice in Cranleigh, Surrey. He also worked as an anesthetist at St. Luke's Hospital, Guildford. During World War II, from 1939 to 1945, he worked for the Emergency Medical Service at Woking War Hospital. He emigrated to South Africa in 1949, and from then until 1954 was a researcher at the International Locust Control Centre at Cape Town University, investigating methods of locust control and going on expeditions to the Kalahari, the Knysna Forest, the Belgian Congo and Mozambique. In 1952 he was appointed to a Nuffield Research Fellowship in the Department of Genetics of the Department of Zoology at Oxford University. Until 1954 he divided his time between South Africa and Oxford, then he gained the position of Senior Research Officer in the Department of Genetics and spent the rest of his career in Oxford as a genetics researcher. His supervisor was E. B. Ford.

Peppered Moth Investigation and Experiments

His grant was to study industrial melanism in general, and in particular the peppered moth *Biston betularia* which had been studied by William Bateson in the 1890s. Kettlewell's research from three surveys between 1952 and 1972 appeared to show a static pattern with a high frequency of the dark-coloured *carbonaria* phenotype in industrial regions, and the light coloured *typica* moths becoming the most common in more rural areas. In the first of Kettlewell's experiments moths were released into an aviary to observe how insectivorous birds reacted.

He showed that the birds ate the moths, and found that where the camouflage of the moths made them difficult for him to see against a matching background, the birds too had difficulty in finding the moths. Most famously he then carried out experiments involving releasing then recapturing marked moths in polluted woodlands in Birmingham, and in unpolluted rural woods at Deanend Wood, Dorset, England. He demonstrated experimentally the efficiency of natural selection as an evolutionary force: light-coloured moths are more conspicuous than dark-coloured ones in industrial areas, where the vegetation is darkened by pollution, and are therefore easier prey for birds, but are less conspicuous in unpolluted rural areas, where the vegetation is lighter in colour, and therefore survive predation better. His experiment led to better understanding of industrial melanism and its effects on the evolution of species.

In 1979 Kettlewell died from an accidental drug overdose.

BORIS EPHRUSSI

Boris Ephrussi (May 9, 1901–May 2, 1979) was a French geneticist of Russian origin. He was one of the many famous Jewish life scientists. He had published two papers in November 1966 which represented a key step in a decade of research in his laboratory. This research helped transform mammalian, and especially human, genetics.

Boris started his scientific training as a Russian emigre in 1920. He studied the initiation and regulation of embryological processes by intracellular and extracellular factors. A major strand of his early research concerned the effect of temperature on the development of fertilized sea urchin eggs. In this work he used a micromanipulator, which was developed by Robert Chambers, an American biologist.

During Ephrussi's time, writing a second dissertation was standard practice in France. Ephrussi's involved culturing tissues. Ephrussi ran into difficulties typically associated with early tissue culture techniques, but despite these obstacles Ephrussi managed to conclude from studies of brachyury in mice that intrinsic factors (i.e genes) play a key role in development.

As the next phase of his career, Ephrussi coupled his embryological concerns with a firm conviction that one must understand the role of genes in order to decipher embryological processes. He moved to Caltech in 1934 and stayed until 1935 to learn genetics within the intellectual empire of T.H. Morgan. This move was supported by the Rockefeller Foundation Fellowship. During this period he conducted important work with George Beadle, who joined him in Paris in the autumn of 1935. There they produced results from experiments with Drosophila eye transplants which became integral to the work of Beadle and Tatum, who were working with Neurospora, and from this research developed the 'one gene, one enzyme' hypothesis.

During World War II, Ephrussi spent most of his time as a refugee at Johns Hopkins University. Following this he began work in France on yeast and cytoplasmic genetics. He began working at the Institut de Biologie Physicochimique (the Rothschild Institute) in Paris, and later worked at the CNRS at Gif-sur-Yvette, where he studied the contribution of cytoplasm to the cell phenotype and pursued the interactions between nuclear and cytoplasmic genetic endowments necessary to the yielding of an intact, functioning (albeit single-celled) organism.

BARUJ BENACERRAF

Baruj Benacerraf (born 29 October 1920) is a US immunologist born in Venezuela, son of a Jewish family originating from North Africa, who shared the 1980 Nobel Prize in Physiology or Medicine for the "discovery of the Major histocompatibility complex genes which encode cell surface molecules important for the immune system's distinction between self and non-self". His brother is well-known philosopher Paul Benacerraf.

Born in Caracas, his parents were Sephardic Jews: his father was born in the Spanish Morocco and his mother in Algeria. Dr. Benacerraf moved to Paris from Venezuela with his family in 1925. After having come back to Venezuela, in 1940 he emigrated to the USA and in 1943, he became a naturalized citizen. He earned his B.S. at Columbia University School of General Studies. He then went on to attain the degree of Doctor of Medicine from the Medical College of Virginia, the only school to which he was accepted.

After his medical internship and US Army service (1945–48), and working at he military hospital of Nancy, he became a researcher at Columbia University College of Physicians and Surgeons (1948–50). He performed research in Paris (1950–6), relocated to New York University (1956–68), moved to the National Institutes of Health (1968–70), then joined Harvard University (1970–91), concurrently serving the Dana-Farber Cancer Institute, Boston (1980). He began studies of allergies in 1948, and discovered the Ir (immune response) genes that govern transplant rejection (1960s).

In 1990, Benacerraf also received National Medal of Science for his contributions to the world of medicine.

BARRY WAKEMAN

Barry Noble Wakeman (1939-September 21, 2004) was an American naturalist and educator.

Born in Glenridge, New Jersey, he became interested in nature as a child, having explored the woods near his home. He received a B.S. in biology from Colgate University and a M.S. in botany from Indiana University. He served in the Peace Corps in Uganda.

After working as a curator at the Oklahoma City Zoo he came to the Cincinnati Zoo in 1968. That year he was part of an expedition to Antarctica, where he visited the South Pole and brought penguins to Cincinnati. At the Cincinnati Zoo he worked to teach children about nature, establishing the Junior Zoologist Club for twelve-to-sixteen year olds in 1968. This became a model for other zoos. He became the Cincinnati Zoo's director of education in 1974 and retired in 1995. But after leaving the zoo he was still busy, serving as director of the Nature Academy, another programme for young people, and at the (Highlands Nature Santuary) in Bainbridge, Ohio.

Barry also taught (ILR) classes at the University of Cincinnati during his retirement, and shared his insights, writing and reading list with a circle of friends and students who met with him weekly at St. John's Unitarian Universalist Church, in Clifton, Cincinnati, Ohio. Barry continued teaching in that weekly meeting until just a few weeks before his passing.

Barry has four children;Barry, Amy Hunter and Brooke. He has three grandchildren;Gabriel, Morgan, and Orion. He died at his home in Pierce Township, Clermont County, Ohio.

BERNHARD RENSCH

Bernhard Rensch (21 January 1900–4 April 1990) was a German evolutionary biologist, and ornithologist who did field work in Indonesia and India. He is probably best known as one of the architects of the modern evolutionary synthesis, which he popularised in Germany. Besides his work on how environmental factors influenced the evolution of geographically isolated populations and on evolution above the species level, which contributed to the modern synthesis, he also worked extensively in the area animal behavior (ethology). His education and scientific work was interrupted by service in the German military during both World War I and World War II.

Biography

Rensch was born in Thale. He served in the German army from 1917-1920, and then continued his education. He received his PH.D from the university of Halle in 1922. He joined the zoological museum of the University of Berlin as an assistant in 1925. In 1927 he participated in a zoological expedition to the Sunda islands. He studied the geographical distribution of subspecies of polytypic species and of complexes of closely related species with attention to how local environmental factors influenced their evolution. In 1929 he published the book *Das Prinzip Geographischer Rassenkreise und das Problem der Artbildung* that discussed the relationship between geography and speciation. His work in this area would influence Ernst Mayr, who was also an assistant at the Berlin museum from 1927-1930, and contribute to the development of the modern evolutionary synthesis.

In 1937 he was forced to leave the Berlin museum because he refused to join the Nazy party and he took a position at a zoological garden in Munster. In 1940 he was recalled for military service, but was discharged for medical reasons in 1942. In 1947 he published a book that would later be translated into English under the title *Evolution Above the Species Level.* The book discussed how the evolutionary mechanisms that drove speciation could also explain the differences between higher taxa and it was considered a major document in the modern synthesis. That same year he became chairman of the zoology department and director of the zoological institute at the University of Munster. In 1953 he would take part in zoological expedition to India. Later in his career he would work extensively in the areas of animal behavior (ethology), learning, and memory. He published an autobiography in 1979 and remained scientifically active until his death in 1990..

BARRY MARSHALL

Barry James Marshall, (born 30 September 1951) is an Australian physician, Nobel Prize laureate in Physiology or Medicine, and Professor of Clinical Microbiology at the University of Western Australia. Marshall is well-known for proving that bacteria *Helicobacter pylori* are the cause of most stomach ulcers, reversing decades of medical doctrine which held that ulcers were caused by stress, spicy foods, and too much acid. He has recently accepted a part-time appointment at the Pennsylvania State University.

Early Years

Marshall was born in Kalgoorlie, Western Australia and lived in Kalgoorlie and Carnarvon until moving to Perth at seven. He attended High School at Newman College and the University of Western Australia, where he received a Bachelor of Medicine, Bachelor of Surgery in 1975. He married his wife Adrienne in 1972.

Life and Research

In 1979 Marshall was appointed as a Registrar in Medicine at the Royal Perth Hospital. He met Robin Warren, a pathologist interested in gastritis, during internal medicine fellowship training at Royal Perth Hospital in 1981. Together, the pair studied the presence of spiral bacteria in association with gastritis. The following year (1982), they performed the initial culture of *H. pylori* and developed their hypothesis related to the bacterial cause of peptic ulcer and gastric cancer. It has been claimed that the *H. pylori* theory was ridiculed by the establishment scientists and doctors, who did not believe that any bacteria could live in the acidic stomach. Marshall has been quoted as saying in 1998 that "Everyone was against me, but I knew I was right". On the other hand, it has also been argued that medical researchers showed a proper degree of skepticism until the *H. pylori* hypothesis could be proved.

After failed attempts to infect piglets in 1984, Marshall drank a petri-dish of the bacteria and soon developed gastritis with achlorhydria. Symptoms included vague stomach discomfort, nausea, vomiting and halitosis. On the 14th day of the infection, biopsies of Marshall's stomach did not reveal any bacteria-so spontaneous eradication may have occurred. However, on the insistence of his wife, he did take antibiotics immediately after that endoscopy so there was no way of double-checking the negative result. Interestingly, he did not develop antibodies to H.pylori, suggesting that innate immunity can sometimes eradicate acute H.pylori infection. His illness and recovery, based on a culture of organisms extracted from a patient, fulfilled Koch's postulates for *H. pylori* and gastritis, but not for peptic ulcer. This experiment was published in 1985 in the

Medical Journal of Australia and is among the most cited articles from the journal.

After this work at Fremantle Hospital, Marshall did research at Royal Perth Hospital (1985-86) and at the University of Virginia, USA (1986-1996), before returning to Australia. He held a Burnet Fellowship at the University of Western Australia from 1998-2003 and continues research related to *H. pylori* and runs the H.pylori Research Laboratory at UWA.

BERNARD GERMAIN DE LACEPEDE

Bernard-Germain-Etienne de La Ville-sur-Illon, comte de Lacepede or La Cepede (December 26, 1756 – October 6, 1825) was a French naturalist.

Biography

He was born at Agen in Guienne. His education was carefully conducted by his father, and the early perusal of Buffon's Natural History (*Histoire naturelle, generale et particuliere*) awakened his interest in that branch of study, which absorbed his chief attention. His leisure he devoted to music, in which, besides becoming a good performer on the piano and organ, he acquired considerable mastery of composition, two of his operas (which were never published) meeting with the high approval of Gluck; in 1781–1785 he also brought out in two volumes his *Poetique de la musique*. Meantime he wrote two treatises, *Essai sur l'electricite* (1781) and *Physique generale et particulaire* (1782–1784), which gained him the friendship of Buffon, who in 1785 appointed him subdemonstrator in the Jardin du Roi, and proposed that he continue Buffon's *Histoire naturelle*. This continuation was published under the titles *Histoire des quadrupedes, ovipares et des serpents* (2 vols., 1788–1789) and *Histoire naturelle des reptiles* (1789).

After the French Revolution Lacepede became a member of the Legislative Assembly, but during the Reign of Terror he left Paris, his life having become endangered by his disapproval of the massacres. When the Jardin du Roi was reorganized as the Jardin des Plantes, Lacepede was appointed to the chair allocated to the study of reptiles and fishes. In 1798 he published the first volume of *Histoire naturelle des poissons*, the fifth volume appearing in 1803, and in 1804 appeared his *Histoire des cetaces.* From this period until his death the part he took in politics prevented him making any further contribution of importance to science. In 1799 he became a senator, in 1801 president of the senate (a role he also fulfilled in 1807-08 and 1811-13), in 1803 grand chancellor of the Legion of Honour, in 1804 minister of state, and at the Bourbon Restoration in 1819 he was created a peer of France. He died at Epinay-sur-Seine. During the latter part of his life he wrote *Histoire generale physique et civile de l'Europe*, published posthumously in 18 volumes, 1826.

BERNARD DE JUSSIEU

Bernard de Jussieu (August 17, 1699-November 6, 1777) was a French naturalist, younger brother of Antoine de Jussieu.

Bernard de Jussieu was born in Lyon. He took a medical degree at Montpellier and began practice in 1720, but finding the work uncongenial he gladly accepted his brother's invitation to Paris in 1722, when he succeeded Sebastien Vaillant (1669-1722) as sub-demonstrator of plants in the Jardin des Plantes. In 1725 he brought out a new edition of Joseph Pitton de Tournefort's *Histoire des plantes qui naissent aux environs de Paris*, 2 vols., which was afterwards translated into English by John Martyn, the original work being incomplete. In the same year he was admitted into the French Academy of Sciences, and communicated several papers to that body.

Long before Abraham Trembley (1700-1784) published his *Histoire des polypes d'eau douce*, Jussieu maintained the doctrine that these organisms were animals, and not the flowers of marine plants, then the current notion; and to confirm his views he made three journeys to the coast of Normandy. Singularly modest and retiring, he published very little, but in 1759 he arranged the plants in the royal garden of the Trianon at Versailles, according to his own scheme of classification. This arrangement is printed in his nephew

Antoine Laurent de Jussieu's *Genera plantarum*, and formed the basis of that work. He cared little for the credit of enunciating new discoveries, so long as the facts were made public. On the death of his brother Antoine, he could not be induced to succeed him as professor of botany at the Jardin des Plantes, but prevailed upon L. G. Lemonnier to assume the higher position.

The standard botanical author abbreviation **B.Juss.** is applied to plants described by de Jussieu.

BERNARDO HOUSSAY

Bernardo Alberto Houssay (April 10, 1887 – September 21, 1971) was an Argentine physiologist who in 1947 with Carl Ferdinand Cori and Gerty Cori received Nobel Prize for Physiology or Medicine for their discovery of the role played by pituitary hormones in regulating the amount of blood sugar (glucose) in animals. He is the first Argentine and Latin American Nobel laureate in the Sciences.

Biography

Bernardo Alberto Houssay was born in Buenos Aires, to emigrees from France, Albert and Clara Houssay. A precocious youngster, he was admitted to the Pharmacy School at the University of Buenos Aires at 14 years of age and subsequently to the Medical School of the same University from 1904 to 1910, beginning when he was only 17 years old. While a third year medical student, Houssay took up a post as a research and teaching assistant in the Chair of Physiology.

Career

After graduating, he quickly developed and presented his M.D. thesis on the physiological activities of pituitary extracts, published in 1911, a theme he would pursue for the rest of his scientific career. Since 1908 he was already an assistant lecturer in the same department, and immediately after his doctorate he took up the post of Professor of Physiology in the University's School of Veterinary Medicine. Simultaneously, he started a private practice and as assistant physician at the municipal hospital of Buenos Aires. In 1913 he became Chief Physician at the Alvear Hospital, and, in 1915, Chief of the Section of Experimental Pathology at the National Public Health Laboratories in Buenos Aires.

In 1919 Houssay was appointed to the chair of physiology at the University of Buenos Aires Medicine School, and, until 1943, he transformed and directed it into a highly respected research department in experimental physiology and medicine of international class. In that year, however, the military dictatorship deprived him of his university posts, due to his liberal political ideas and Houssay was forced to re-establish his research lines and staff at a privately funded Instituto de Biologia—Medicina Experimental.

This situation, reinforced by a second dismissal by the Peronista government in 1945, was prolonged until 1955, when Peron was ousted from power and Houssay was reinstated in the University of Buenos Aires, where he remained till he died. His retirement. After this he was also director of the National Scientific and Technical Research Council, from 1957 on.

Houssay's worked in many fields of physiology, such as the nervous, digestive, respiratory and circulatory systems, but his main contribution, which was recognized by the Nobel Prize in Physiology or Medicine of 1947, was on the experimental investigation of the role of the anterior hypophysis gland in the metabolism of carbohydrates, particularly in diabetes mellitus. Houssay demonstrated in the 1930s the diabetogenic effect anterior hypophysis extracts and the decrease in diabetes severity with anterior hypophysectomy. These discoveries stimulated the study of hormonal feedback control mechanisms which are central to all aspects of modern endocrinology.

Houssay's many disciples along his years of activity became also influential by themselves as they spread around the world; such as Eduardo Braun-Menendez, and Miguel Rolando Covian (who went to become the "father" of Brazilian neurophysiology, as chairman of the Department of Physiology of the Medical Faculty of Ribeirao Preto of the University of Sao Paulo).

Houssay wrote with them the most influential textbook of Human Physiology in Latin America, in Spanish and Portuguese (the latter was translated by Covian and collaborators), which, since 1950 has been published in successive editions and used in almost all medical schools of the continent. Houssay published more than 600 scientific papers and several specialized books. Besides the Nobel, Houssay won many distinctions and awards from the Universities of Harvard, Cambridge, Oxford and Paris and 15 other universities, as well as the Dale Medal of the London Society for Endocrinology in 1960. Houssay was also very active as a scientific leader and promoter of the advancement of scientific research and medical education, in Argentina as well as in Latin America.

Personal Life

Houssay died in Buenos Aires at age 84. He is buried in the La Chacarita Cemetery.

BIRUTE GALDIKAS

Birute Marija Filomena Galdikas, OC Ph.D. (born May 10, 1946 (1946-05-10) (age 62), Wiesbaden, Germany), is a primatologist, conservationist, ethologist, and author of several books relating to the endangered species orangutan. Well known in the field of modern primatology, Galdikas is recognized as an authority on orangutans.

Early Life and Education

Galdikas was born in Germany to Lithuanian parents. She later became a naturalized Canadian and grew up in Toronto, Canada.

In college she studied psychology and biology. In 1966, Galdikas earned her bachelor's degrees in psychology and zoology from the University of British Columbia and the University of California, Los Angeles, her master's degree in anthropology from UCLA in 1969 and her doctorate in anthropology, also from UCLA, in 1978. It was there, as a graduate student, she first met famed Kenyan paleontologist Louis Leakey and expressed her desire to study orangutans in their natural habitats.

Leakey's Angels

Determined to study and understand the world of the elusive 'red ape', Galdikas convinced Leakey to help orchestrate her endeavour, despite his initial reservations. Orangutans comprise an exceedingly intelligent great ape genus native to Malaysia and Indonesia, who have long arms and reddish, sometimes brown, hair.

In 1971, Galdikas and her then husband, photographer Rod Brindamour, arrived in one of the world's few remaining wild places, Tanjung Puting Reserve, in Indonesian Borneo. Galdikas thus become the third of a trio of women hand-picked by Leakey to study mankind's nearest relatives, the other great apes, in their natural habitat. Known as 'Leakey's Angels', the other two were Jane Goodall, who studied chimpanzees, and Dian Fossey, who became a martyr in her quest to study and protect mountain gorillas.

Leakey and the National Geographic Society helped Galdikas initially set up her research camp to conduct field study on orangutans in Borneo. Before Leakey's fortuitous decision to anoint Galdikas as the third of his 'Angels', the orangutan was much less well understood than the African great apes. Galdikas went on to further burnish Leakey's legacy by greatly expanding scientific knowledge of orangutan behavior, habitat and diet.

Research and Advocacy

At 25, Galdikas arrived in Borneo to begin her field studies of orangutans in a jungle environment extremely inhospitable to most Westerners. Galdikas proceeded to make many invaluable contributions to the scientific understanding of Indonesia's biodiversity and the rainforest as a whole, while also bringing the orangutan to the attention of the rest of the world.

When she arrived in Borneo, Galdikas settled into a primitive bark and thatch hut, at a site she dubbed 'Camp Leakey', near the edge of the Java Sea. Once there, she encountered numerous poachers, legions of leeches, and swarms of carnivorous insects. Yet she persevered through many travails, remaining there for over 30 years while becoming an outspoken advocate for orangutans and the preservation of their rainforest habitat, which is rapidly being devastated by loggers, gold miners, and unnatural conflagrations. Galdikas' conservation efforts have extended well beyond advocacy, largely focusing on rehabilitation of the many orphaned orangutans turned over to her for care. Many of these orphans were once pets, before becoming too smart and difficult for their owners to handle. Galdikas' rehabilitation efforts have become the centre of several controversies for Galdikas and the Orangutan Foundation. The effectiveness of her rehabilitation efforts spawned widespread debate in the late 1990s, due in part to articles and books about Galdikas by Canadian Linda Spalding. It was suggested that wild orangutan populations might be harmed as a result of the manner in which rehabilitation was being conducted at the Camp Leakey field station.

BARRY FELL

Barry Fell (born Howard Barraclough Fell on June 6, 1917 in Lewes, Sussex, England; died on April 21, 1994, of heart failure in San Diego, California) was a professor of invertebrate zoology at the Harvard Museum of Comparative Zoology. His primary research was on starfish and sea urchins; however, Fell is also widely known for his controversial work in New World epigraphy.

Biography

Fell moved to New Zealand with his mother in the early 1920s, after his father, who was a merchant seaman, died in a shipboard fire. He received his Ph.D. at the University of Edinburgh in 1941, after which he served in the British Army during World War II. In 1946 he returned to New Zealand where he resumed his academic career. In 1964 he joined the Museum of Comparative Zoology at Harvard, where he stayed until retirement in 1979.

Epigraphy

Though Fell was an accomplished marine biologist at Harvard University, he is best known for his work on epigraphy. This interest began early in his career with a study of Polynesian petroglyphs published in 1940. His most famous work came much later, starting in 1976 with the publication of the book *America BC*, in which he proposed translations of alleged inscriptions found on rock surfaces and artifacts in North and South America that he believed to be written in Old World scripts and languages. He followed up this work in 1980 with *Saga America* and in 1982 with *Bronze Age America*. Fell's work led to the establishment of several amateur epigraphic associations such as the "Epigraphic Society" and the "Midwestern Epigraphic Society".

One example of Fell's claims is his contention that Irish monks reached North America centuries before Columbus. This is based on Fell's translation, published in the magazine *Wonderful West Virginia* in 1983, of two rock-cut inscriptions located at archaeological sites in Wyoming County, West Virginia. According to Fell, these inscriptions narrate the story of Christ's nativity and are written in an old Irish script called Celtic Ogham (also referred to as Ogam) dating back to the 6th or 8th century AD. This led to the publication of various articles in the journal *The West Virginia Archeologist* highly critical of Fell's conclusions and methodology, including a 1983 article by archaeologist and historian W. Hunter Lesser describing Fell's claims as pseudoscientific and unreliable, and a 1989 article by lawyers Monroe Oppenheimer and Willard Wirtz that relies on the opinions of academic archaeologists and linguists to dispute that the inscription is written in Ogam script, and which accuses Fell of deliberate fraud.

Fell's epigraphic work has not been well-received in academia. Critics of Fell's work have routinely dismissed him as an amateur, pointing out his lack of formal training in ancient scripts and languages. Criticism of Fell is not limited to academia, as some of Fell's critics themselves lack professional backgrounds in archaeology or linguistics, such as Oppenheimer and Wirtz.

Critics of Dr. Fell have pointed out that he seemed to jump to conclusions, and "to translate ancient languages to English with apparent ease" that was not typical of a critical analysis.

Richard D. Flavin wrote that:

"Fell often worked from material mailed to him, which he reacted to (read: "deciphered") without checking further. This seems to be a general complaint regarding his epigraphic work. He was an accomplished scholastic, well published, who knew the rigors of academic argument and presentation, yet with his epigraphic work Fell seldom stepped away from his desk to research an item or view it in person. Such pervasive carelessness (or, as some say, arrogance) marred his efforts and induced a negative reaction in most professionals. Which is unfortunate, as he had some interesting ideas.

David Kelley, an archaeologist at the University of Calgary who is credited with a major breakthrough in the decipherment of Mayan glyphs, complained about Fell in a 1990 essay:

"Fell's work [contains] major academic sins, the three worst being distortion of data, inadequate acknowledgment of predecessors, and lack of presentation of alternative views."

In the same essay, Kelley went on to acknowledge that, "I have no personal doubts that some of the inscriptions which have been reported [by Fell] are genuine Celtic ogham."

Having acknowledged Fell's shortcomings, Kelley concluded that, "Despite my occasional harsh criticism of Fell's treatment of individual inscriptions, it should be recognized that without Fell's work there would be no [North American] ogham problem to perplex us. We need to ask not only what Fell has done wrong in his epigraphy, but also where we have gone wrong as archaeologists in not recognizing such an extensive European presence in the New World."

BERNARD DAVIS

Bernard Davis (1916–1994) was a leading figure in biology, with his major contributions in microbial physiology and metabolism. Davis was a prominent figure at Harvard Medical School in microbiology and in national science policy.

Education

Davis was born in Franklin, Massachusetts, where his parents, Jewish immigrants from Lithuania, had settled. (Davis himself was nonobservant, and "insisted on atheism".) He was valedictorian at his high school, then attended Harvard University, where he majored in biochemistry. After earning his Bachelor of Science degree, he enrolled at Harvard Medical School, graduating in 1940 with a rare M.D., *summa cum laude.*

Moralistic Fallacy

Davis coined the term "moralistic fallacy" after calls for ethical guidelines to control the study of what could allegedly become "dangerous knowledge." The term is intended as a converse to the naturalistic fallacy, coined by David Hume in the 18th century, which occurs when reasoning jumps from statements about *what is* to prescription about *what ought to be.*

Sometimes a theory is rejected with a reference to the danger of misuse. In doing so, one fails to differentiate sufficiently clearly between its epistemological value and its practical value, or between the moral, value-free knowledge and – in consideration of moral valuations – the potentially negative consequences of the knowledge. From a perspective of scientific theory, the accuracy of a theory is relevant, not its practical value, its origin or history of use. No theory is protected against misuse, nor can a theory be falsified by misuse. Both misuse as well as renunciation of knowledge can have disadvantageous consequences.

An example of the naturalistic fallacy would be approving of all wars if scientific evidence showed warfare was part of human nature, whereas an example of the moralistic fallacy would be claiming that, because warfare is wrong, it cannot be part of human nature.

BENJAMIN SMITH BARTON

Benjamin Smith Barton (February 10, 1766-December 19, 1815) was an American botanist and physician.

Barton studied at the York Academy in Lancaster, Pennsylvania from 1780 to 1782, then attended the College of Philadelphia, studying medicine under Thomas Shippen from 1784, and accompanying David Rittenhouse on an expedition to survey the western boundary of Pennsylvania in 1785, which aroused his interest in Native Americans. In 1786 he transferred to the University of Edinburgh, where he stayed for two years before leaving as a result of disagreements with two professors. He then moved to the University of Gottingen, from which he obtained an M.D. in 1789.

Upon graduation, Barton returned to the College of Philadelphia as an instructor, which would soon (in 1781) merge with the University of Pennsylvania. In 1790 he was appointed professor of botany and natural history, and in 1795 chair of materia medica. In 1813 he became chair of the theory and practice of medicine following the death of Benjamin Rush, but continued to retain his position in natural history and botany. Concurrently with his academic position, he served as a physician at Pennsylvania Hospital from 1798 through his death in 1815.

In 1803 Barton published *Elements of botany, or Outlines of the natural history of vegetables*, the first American handbook of botany. From 1798-1804, he published a work on plants for medical use.

Barton was also interested in anatomy and zoology, and published *Memoir Concerning the Fascinating Faculty Which Has been Ascribed to the Rattle-Snake*. In 1803 he published a comparative study of linguistics, *Etymology of Certain English Words and one Their Affinity to Words in the Languages of Different European, Asiatic and American (Indian) Nations* and a test on the origin of the first American people, *New Views of the Origin of the Tribes and Nations of America* (1797). He was the editor of Philadelphia Medical and Physical Journal (1805-1808), one of the oldest scientific publications of the United States.

Barton made one significant contribution to the field of archaeology as well. Although his *Observations on Some Parts of Natural History* in 1787 incorrectly attributed the prehistoric mounds of Ohio to the Danish people, his 1797 book (mentioned above) correctly identifies the Mound builders as Native Americans. While he was not the first to make this claim, he may have been the first to suggest a significant age to the mounds, speculating that they may have been older than James Ussher's famous Biblical chronology. Barton also correctly guessed that Native Americans had an Asian origin.

In botany, his author abbreviation is **Barton**.

He was vice president of the American Philosophical Society from 1802 to his death, and president of the Philadelphia Medical Society from 1808 to his death. He died of tuberculosis in New York City.

His older brother, William Barton, was also a member of the American Philosophical Society. His maternal uncle, David Rittenhouse, served as the Society's second president after the death of founder Benjamin Franklin in 1790.

BRUCE AMES

Bruce Ames (born December 16, 1928), is a professor of Biochemistry and Molecular Biology at the University of California, Berkeley, and a senior scientist at Children's Hospital Oakland Research Institute (CHORI). He is the inventor of the Ames test, a system for easily and cheaply testing the mutagenicity of compounds. His research focuses on cancer and aging and he has authored over 500 scientific publications. He is among the few hundred most-cited scientists in all fields.

Ames' current research includes identifying agents that delay the mitochondrial decay of aging, understanding the role of mitochondrial decay in aging, particularly in the brain, optimizing micronutrient intakes in the population to prevent disease, malnutrition, and obesity. He is also interested in mutagens as they relate to cancer prevention and aging.

He is a recipient of the Tyler Prize for Environmental Achievement in 1985, the Japan Prize in 1997, the National Medal of Science in 1998 and the Thomas Hunt Morgan Medal in 2004, among many others. He was born and raised in New York City. He is a graduate of the Bronx High School of Science. His undergraduate studies were at Cornell University in Ithaca, New York, and his graduate studies were completed at the California Institute of Technology. He also worked in Germany at the University of Duisburg-Essen.

BRUCE ALBERTS

Dr. Bruce Alberts (b. 14 April 1938, Chicago) is an American biochemist. He is noted particularly for his extensive study of the protein complexes which enable chromosome replication when living cells divide. He was the president of the National Academy of Sciences from 1993 to 2005 and is a trustee of the Carnegie Corporation of New York. He is now the editor in chief of *Science.*

Career

Alberts graduated from Harvard College, with a degree in biochemical sciences, and earned a doctorate from Harvard University in 1965. He then went to the University of Geneva as a postdoctoral fellow to work with Richard Epstein on genes involved in DNA replication of phage T4. In 1966, Alberts joined the Department of Biochemical Sciences at Princeton University as an Assistant Professor. In 1972, he became an Associate Professor and in 1974 a full Professor. In 1976, he accepted a position as professor and vice-chair of the Department of Biochemistry and Biophysics at the University of California, San Francisco. In 1980, Alberts was awarded an American Cancer Society Lifetime Research Professorship. In 1985, he was named chair of the Department.

Alberts has long been committed to the improvement of science education, dedicating much of his time to educational projects such as City Science, a programme seeking to improve science teaching in San Francisco elementary schools. He has served on the advisory board of the National Science Resources Centre a joint project of the National Academy of Sciences and the Smithsonian Institution working with teachers, scientists, and school systems to improve teaching of science as well as on the National Academy of Sciences' National Committee on Science Education Standards and Assessment.

He has served in different capacities on a number of prestigious advisory and editorial boards, including as chair of the Commission on Life Sciences, National Research Council. Until his election as President of the National Academy of Sciences in 1995 he was president-elect of the American Society of Biochemistry and Molecular Biology. He currently serves on the advisory board of the Campaign to Defend the Constitution. December 17th, 2007, it was announced that Alberts had accepted the position of editor-in-chief of the American Association for the Advancement of Science's flagship publication, Science (journal).

Alberts is the Co-chair of the InterAcademy Council, a new advisory institution in Amsterdam governed by the presidents of fifteen science academies from around the world. Alberts served as the President of the National Academy of Sciences for two terms from 1993 until 2005.

BOYD ALEXANDER

Boyd Alexander (January 16, 1873-April 2, 1910) was an English British Army officer, explorer and ornithologist.

Lieutenant Boyd Francis Alexander was the oldest son of Lt Colonel Boyd Francis Alexander. On his mother's side he was the grandson of David Wilson the founder of one of the most famous hotels in India, the Great Eastern Hotel in Calcutta.

Lieutenant Alexander was a member of an expedition which travelled across Africa from the Niger to the Nile, exploring the Lake Chad area. Alexander was accompanied by his brother Claud, Captain G. B. Gosling and Jose Lopes. In February 1904 they set off from the mouth of the Niger, travelling upriver to Lokoja. Claud died in October of enteric fever after making a survey of the Murchison Range. Boyd and Gosling explored the area around Lake Chad. Gosling died in June 1906 at Niangara of blackwater fever. Boyd then followed the River Kibali, reaching the Nile late in the year and returning to England in February 1907. Alexander's account *From The Niger To The Nile* was published later that year. In 1908 he was awarded the Gold Medal of the Royal Geographical Society "for his three years' journey across Africa from the Niger to the Nile."

Alexander and Lopes sailed back to Africa in 1909. They visited Claud's grave at Maifoni in Bornu and then continued to Ouadai. Boyd was killed in a dispute with locals near Nyeri. His body was recovered by French soldiers and buried next to his brother in Maifoni.

C. V. RAMAN

Chandrasekhara Venkata Raman, (7 November 1888 – 21 November 1970) was an Indian physicist who was awarded the 1930 Nobel Prize in Physics for his work on the molecular scattering of light and for the discovery of the Raman effect, which is named after him.

Biography

Chandrasekhara Venkata Raman was born on November 7, 1888, in an Iyer family in Tiruchirapalli, Tamil Nadu. At an early age Raman moved to the city of Visakhapatnam, Andhra Pradesh. His father was a lecturer in mathematics and physics, so he grew up in an academic atmosphere. His nephew Subramanyan Chandrasekhar also won a Nobel prize in physics in 1983.

Middle Years

Raman entered Presidency College, Madras, in 1902, and in 1904 gained his BA, winning the first place and the gold medal in physics. In 1907 he gained his MA, obtaining the highest distinctions. He joined the Indian Finance Department as an Assistant Accountant General in Calcutta. As the story goes, one evening while returning from work, he spotted the sign of the Indian Association for the Cultivation of Science (IACS). He started visiting the laboratory after office hours and did experiments, which culminated with his Nobel Prize winning work.

In 1917 Raman resigned from his government service and took up the newly created Palit Professorship in Physics at the University of Calcutta. Simultaneously, he continued doing research at the IACS, where he became the Honourary Secretary. Raman used to refer to this period as the golden era of his career. Many talented students gathered around him at the IACS and the University of Calcutta. He was president of the 16th session of the Indian Science Congress in 1929.

Raman won the 1930 Nobel Prize in Physics for his work on the scattering of light and for the discovery of the Raman effect. Raman spectroscopy is based on this phenomenon. He was the first Asian and first non-White to get any Nobel Prize in Science. Before him Sir Rabindranath Tagore (also Indian) had received Nobel Prize for Literature.

Raman also worked on the acoustics of musical instruments. He worked out the theory of transverse vibration of bowed strings, on the basis of superposition velocities. He was also the first to investigate the harmonic nature of the sound of the Indian drums such as the tabla and the mridangam.

In 1934 Raman became the director of the Indian Institute of Science in Bangalore, where two years later he continued as a professor of physics. Other investigations carried out by Raman were: his experimental and theoretical studies on the diffraction of light by acoustic waves of ultrasonic and hypersonic frequencies (published 1934-1942), and those on the effects produced by X-rays on infrared vibrations in crystals exposed to ordinary light.

He also started a company called Travancore Chemical and Manufacturing Co. Ltd. in 1943 along with Dr. Krishnamurthy. The Company during its 60 year history, established 4 factories in Southern India. In 1947, he was appointed as the first National Professor by the new government of Independent India.

In 1948 Raman, through studying the spectroscopic behaviour of crystals, approached in a new manner fundamental problems of crystal dynamics. He dealt with the structure and properties of diamond, the structure and optical behaviour of numerous iridescent substances (labradorite, pearly felspar, agate, opal, and pearls). Among his other interests were the optics of colloids, electrical and magnetic anisotropy, and the physiology of human vision.

Old Age

He retired from the Indian Institute of Science in 1948 and a year later he established the Raman Research Institute in Bangalore Karnataka, serving as its director and remained active there until his death in 1970, in Bangalore, Karnataka, at the age of 82.

CARL HERMANN

Carl Hermann (17 June 1898 – 12 September 1961) was a German professor of crystallography. With Charles-Victor Mauguin, he invented an international standard notation for crystallographic groups known as the Hermann-Mauguin notation or International notation. Born in the north German port town of Wesermunde to parents both of long-time ministerial families, he got his doctorate from Gottingen in 1923, as a pupil of Max Born and a fellow student with Werner Heisenberg. With Paul P. Ewald at Stuttgart, he nurtured the growing field of crystallography, especially the study of space groups, and began what was later to become *Structure Reports*, a reference series giving every known crystal structure determination.

When the Nazi Party rose to power, he objected to its political restrictions on academic positions, leaving to take a position as a physicist with industrial dye firm I.G. Farbenwerke at Ludwigshafen, where he continued his crystallographic research and studied symmetry in higher-dimensional spaces.

During World War II, he and his wife Eva helped many Jews hide and escape the Holocaust, for which he was imprisoned and sentenced to death. As he was an eminent scientist with influential friends, the sentence was never carried out.

After the war, he lectured briefly at Darmstadt Polytechnic. Then, in 1947, he accepted a newly formed chair in crystallography at the University of Marburg, where he became director of the Crystallographic Institute and remained until his death.

An active Quaker, and having a gift for languages, he devoted much time to promoting international understanding.

In August 1994, the German Crystallographic Society (DGK) established the Carl Hermann Medal, its highest distinction, for outstanding contributions to the science of crystallography.

CHARLES H. HENRY

Charles H. Henry was born in Chicago, Illinois on May 6, 1937. He received an MS. degree in physics in 1959 from the University of Chicago, and a PhD degree in physics in 1965 from the University of Illinois, under the direction of Charles P. Slichter. In March, 2008, he was featured in an article in the Physics Illinois News, a publication of the Physics Department of the University of Illinois.

Henry's entire professional career was spent in the research area of Bell Laboratories in Murray Hill, New Jersey. He joined Bell Laboratories in 1965 as a member of technical staff. From 1971 to 1975, he was head of the Semiconductor Electronics Research Department. He retired from Lucent Technologies Bell Laboratories in 1997 as a Distinguished Member of Technical Staff. He has published 133 technical papers and holds 28 patents, including a 1976 patent covering what is now called the quantum well laser.

Throughout his career, Henry worked at the forefront of semiconductor-based optical technologies and science: light-emitting diodes, semiconductor lasers, and photonic integrated circuits. He was an inventor as well as an experimenter, with a particular interest in understanding the theory underlying semiconductor optical devices.

Quantum Wells

The idea of the quantum well occurred to Henry in late 1972. While thinking about optical waveguides, Henry suddenly realized that a double heterostructure is a waveguide for electrons, and that a heterostructure with a thin central active layer would have discrete electron modes. Such a heterostructure was later named a quantum well, and the modes are the electron states of the quantum well.

Henry further realized that these discrete electron states would greatly alter the optical absorption edge of the semiconductor. Instead of the absorption being a smooth curve steeply rising with optical energy, it would consist of a series of steps.

In early 1973, he proposed to R. Dingle that he look for these steps, and they were observed and reported in 1974 in a paper the pair wrote with W. Wiegmann.

After Dingle's experiment showed the reality of Henry's predicted quantum effects, Henry realized that the quantum well structure would alter the density of states of the semiconductor and result in an improved semiconductor laser. He also realized that the laser wavelength could be changed merely by changing the thickness of the thin quantum well layers, whereas in a conventional laser, a change in wavelength requires a change in layer composition.

On March 7, 1975, Henry and Dingle filed a patent entitled "Quantum Effects in Heterostructure Lasers," which was issued on Sept. 21, 1976. The story of the origin of the quantum well laser is told by Henry in the foreword to *Quantum Well Lasers*, edited by Peter S. Zory, Jr. (1993).

CARL FRIEDRICH GAUSS

Johann Carl Friedrich Gauss (30 April 1777 – 23 February 1855) was a German mathematician and scientist who contributed significantly to many fields, including number theory, statistics, analysis, differential geometry, geodesy, electrostatics, astronomy, and optics.

Sometimes known as the *princeps mathematicorum* (Latin, usually translated as "the Prince of Mathematicians", although Latin *princeps* also can simply mean "the foremost") and "greatest mathematician since antiquity", Gauss had a remarkable influence in many fields of mathematics and science and is ranked as one of history's most influential mathematicians.

Gauss was a child prodigy. There are many anecdotes pertaining to his precocity while a toddler, and he made his first ground-breaking mathematical discoveries while still a teenager. He completed *Disquisitiones Arithmeticae*, his magnum opus, in 1798 at the age of 21, though it would not be published until 1801. This work was fundamental in consolidating number theory as a discipline and has shaped the field to the present day.

Early Years (1777–1798)

Gauss was born in Braunschweig, in the Electorate of Brunswick-Luneburg, now part of Lower Saxony, Germany, as the only son of poor working-class parents. There are several stories of his early genius, all of them open to doubt; according to one, his gifts became very apparent at the age of three when he corrected, in his head, an error his father had made on paper while calculating finances.

Another famous story, and one that has evolved in the telling, has it that in primary school his teacher, J.G. Buttner, tried to occupy pupils by making them add a list of integers. The young Gauss reputedly produced the correct answer within seconds, to the astonishment of his teacher and his assistant Martin Bartels. Gauss's presumed method, which supposes the list of numbers was from 1 to 100, was to realise that pairwise addition of terms from opposite ends of the list yielded identical intermediate sums: $1 + 100 = 101$, $2 + 99 = 101$, $3 + 98 = 101$, and so on, for a total sum of $50 \times 101 = 5050$ (*see arithmetic series and summation*). However whilst the method works, the incident itself is probably apocryphal; some, such as Joseph Rotman in his book *A first course in Abstract Algebra*, question whether it ever happened.

As his father wanted him to follow in his footsteps and become a mason, he was not supportive of Gauss's schooling in mathematics and science. Gauss was primarily supported by his mother in this effort and by the Duke of Braunschweig, who awarded Gauss a fellowship to the Collegium Carolinum (now Technische Universitat Braunschweig), which he attended from 1792 to 1795, and subsequently he moved to the University of Gottingen from 1795 to 1798. While in university, Gauss independently rediscovered several important theorems; his breakthrough occurred in 1796 when he was able to show that any regular polygon with a number of sides which is a Fermat prime (and, consequently, those polygons with any number of sides which is the product of distinct Fermat primes and a power of 2) can be constructed by compass and straightedge. This was a major discovery in an important field of mathematics; construction problems had occupied mathematicians since the days of the Ancient Greeks, and the discovery ultimately led Gauss to choose mathematics instead of philology as a career. Gauss was so pleased by this result that he requested that a regular heptadecagon be inscribed on his tombstone. The stonemason declined, stating that the difficult construction would essentially look like a circle.

The year 1796 was most productive for both Gauss and number theory. He discovered a construction of the heptadecagon on March 30. He invented modular arithmetic, greatly simplifying manipulations in number theory. He became the first to prove the quadratic reciprocity law on April 8. This remarkably general law allows mathematicians to determine the solvability of any quadratic equation in modular arithmetic.

The prime number theorem, conjectured on May 31, gives a good understanding of how the prime numbers are distributed among the integers. Gauss also discovered that every positive integer is representable as a sum of at most three triangular numbers on July 10 and then jotted down in his diary the famous words, "Heureka! num = A + A + A." On October 1 he published a result on the number of solutions of polynomials with coefficients in finite fields, which ultimately led to the Weil conjectures 150 years later.

CHRISTIAN DOPPLER

Christian Andreas Doppler (November 29, 1803 – March 17, 1853) was an Austrian mathematician and physicist, most famous for the hypothesis of what is now known as the Doppler effect which is the apparent change in frequency and wavelength of a wave that is perceived by an observer moving relative to the source of the waves.

Christian Doppler was born in Salzburg, Austria as the son of a stone-mason. However he could not work in his father's business because of his generally weak physical condition. After completing high school he studied astronomy and mathematics in Vienna and Salzburg and started to work at the Prague Polytechnic (now Czech Technical University), where he was appointed professor for mathematics and physics in 1841. (Note: At that time, the present Czech Republic was ruled by the Empire of Austria.)

Only one year later at the age of 39 he published his most notable work on the Doppler effect (for instance to be noticed in the change of sound of a quickly passing vehicle). The German title was "Uber das farbige Licht der Doppelsterne und einige andere Gestirne des Himmels-Versuch einer das Bradleysche Theorem als integrirenden Theil in sich schliessenden allgemeineren Theorie" (English translation: On the coloured light of the binary refracted stars and other celestial bodies-Attempt of a more general theory including Bradley's theorem as an integral part). An English translation can be found in the book by Alec Eden together with the original German version (see reference). In this work, Doppler postulated his principle that the observed frequency depends on the speed of the source and the observer, and he tried to use it for explaining the colour of binary stars. The Doppler effect of sound was verified by Buys Ballot in 1845. In his time in Prague as professor he published more than 50 articles in mathematics, physics and astronomy.

His research career in Prague was interrupted by the revolutionary incidents of March 1848, when he fled to Vienna. There he was appointed head of the Institute for Experimental Physics at the University of Vienna in 1850. During his presence at the University of Vienna, Doppler, along with Franz Unger, played an influential role in the development of young Gregor Mendel, known as the founding father of genetics, who was a student at the University of Vienna from 1851 to 1853.

Doppler died on March 17, 1853 at age 49 from a pulmonary disease in Venice (also at that time part of the Austrian Empire). His tomb can be found just inside the entrance of the Venetian island cemetery of San Michele.

CLINTON DAVISSON

Clinton Joseph Davisson (22 October 1881 – 1 February 1958), was an American physicist who won the 1937 Nobel Prize in Physics for his discovery of electron diffraction. Davisson shared the Nobel Prize with George Paget Thomson, who independently discovered electron diffraction at about the same time as Davisson.

Life

Davisson was born in Bloomington, Illinois. He graduated from Bloomington High School in 1902, and entered the University of Chicago on scholarship. Upon the recommendation of Robert A. Millikan, in 1905 Davisson was hired by Princeton University as Instructor of Physics. He completed the requirements for his B.S. degree from Chicago in 1908, mainly by working in the summers. While teaching at Princeton, he did doctoral thesis research with Owen Richardson. He received his Ph.D. in physics from Princeton in 1911; in the same year he married Richardson's sister, Charlotte.

Davisson was then appointed as an assistant professor at the Carnegie Institute of Technology. In 1917 he took a leave from the Carnegie Institute to do war-related research with the Engineering Department of the Western Electric Company (later Bell Telephone Laboratories). At the end of the war, Davisson accepted a permanent position at Western Electric after receiving assurances of his freedom there to do basic research.

He had found that his teaching responsibilities at the Carnegie Institute largely precluded him from doing research. Davisson remained at Western Electric (and Bell Telephone) until his formal retirement in 1946. He then accepted a research professor appointment at the University of Virginia that continued until his second retirement in 1954.

Clinton and Charlotte Davisson had four children, including the American physicist Richard Davisson.

CHARLES-AUGUSTIN DE COULOMB

Charles Augustin de Coulomb (born June 14, 1736, Angouleme, France-died August 23, 1806, Paris, France) was a French physicist. He is best known for developing Coulomb's law: the definition of the electrostatic force of attraction and repulsion. The SI unit of charge, the coulomb, was named after him.

Life

Coulomb was born in Angouleeme, France, to a well-to-do family. His father, Henri Coulomb, was inspector of the Royal Fields in Montpellier. His mother, Catherine Bajet, came from a wealthy family in the wool trade. When Coulomb was a boy the family moved to Paris, and there Coulomb studied at the prestigious College des Quatre-Nations. The courses in mathematics there, under Pierre Charles Monnier, determined him to pursue mathematics and similar subjects as a career. From 1757 to 1759 he joined his father's family in Montpellier and took part in the work of the academy of the city, directed by the mathematician Augustin Danyzy. With his father's approval, Coulomb returned to Paris in 1759 where he was successful in the entrance examination for the military school at Mezieres.

After he left the school in 1761, he initially took part in the survey for the British coastal charts, and was then sent on a mission to Martinique in 1764 to take part in the construction of the Fort Bourbon under the orders of the lieutenant-colonel of Rochemore, as the French colony was insulated in the middle of the English and Spanish possessions following the Seven Years' War. Coulomb spent eight years directing the work, contracting tropical fever. He carried out several experiments on the resistance of masonries and the behaviour of the walls of escarpe (supportings), which were inspired by the ideas of Pieter van Musschenbroek on friction.

Upon his return, with the rank of Captain, he was employed at La Rochelle, the Isle of Aix and Cherbourg. He discovered an inverse relationship of the force between electric charges and the square of its distance, later named after him as Coulomb's law.

In 1781, he was stationed permanently at Paris. On the outbreak of the Revolution in 1789, he resigned his appointment as *intendant des eaux et fontaines*, and retired to a small estate which he possessed at Blois. He was recalled to Paris for a time in order to take part in the new determination of weights and measures, which had been decreed by the Revolutionary government. He was one of the first members of the National Institute; he was appointed inspector of public instruction in 1802. His health was already very feeble, and four years later he died in Paris, France.

Coulomb leaves a legacy as a hero in the field of geotechnical engineering for his contribution to retaining wall design.

C. H. D. BUYS BALLOT

Christophorus Henricus Diedericus Buys Ballot (October 10, 1817, Kloetinge – February 3, 1890, Utrecht) was a Dutch chemist and meteorologist after whom Buys-Ballot's law and the Buys Ballot table are named.

The son of a Dutch Reformed minister, Buys Ballot attended the Gymnasium at Zaltbommel and the Hogeschool (now University) of Utrecht. After receiving his doctorate in 1844, he became lecturer in mineralogy and geology at Utrecht; he added theoretical chemistry in 1846. In 1847 he was appointed professor of mathematics and from 1867 until his retirement he was professor of physics.

Buys Ballot tested the Doppler effect for sound waves in 1845 by using a group of musicians playing a calibrated note on a train in the Utrecht-Amsterdam line.

Buys Ballot is best known for his accomplishments in the field of meteorology, specifically the explanation of the direction of air flow in large weather systems. Furthermore, he founded the Royal Dutch Meteorological Institute in 1854 and he remained its chief director until his death. He was one of the first to see the need for international cooperation, and in 1873 became the first chairman of the International Meteorological Committee, a precursor of the World Meteorological Organization (WMO).

Buys-Ballot's law states that if a person in the Northern Hemisphere stands with his back to the wind, the low atmospheric pressure is found to his left. His main research effort in meteorology went into examining long-time series for regularities; he was more concerned with establishing the regularities than in explaining them. He made no contributions to the theory of meteorology which is perhaps surprising given his training in physics. The contrast with his American contemporary, William Ferrel, who discovered Buy-Ballot's law slightly earlier, is striking.

Buys Ballot devised a tabular method for investigating periodicity in time series. In 1847 he used the table now named after him to determine the period of the sun's rotation from daily observations of temperature in the Netherlands from 1729 to 1846.

CARL DAVID ANDERSON

Carl David Anderson (3 September 1905 – 11 January 1991) was an American physicist. He is best known for his discovery of the positron, an achievement for which he received the Nobel Prize in Physics in 1936.

Biography

Anderson was born in New York City, the son of Swedish immigrants. He studied physics and engineering at Caltech (B.S., 1927; Ph.D., 1930). Under the supervision of Robert A. Millikan, he began investigations into cosmic rays during the course of which he encountered unexpected particle tracks in his cloud chamber photographs that he correctly interpreted as having been created by a particle with the same mass as the electron, but with opposite electrical charge. This discovery, announced in 1932 and later confirmed by others, validated Paul Dirac's theoretical prediction of the existence of the positron. Anderson obtained the first direct proof that positrons existed by shooting gamma rays produced by the natural radioactive nuclide ThC" (^{208}Tl) into other materials, resulting in creation of positron-electron pairs. For this work, Anderson shared the Nobel Prize in Physics for 1936 with Victor Hess.

Also in 1936, Anderson and his first graduate student, Seth Neddermeyer, discovered the muon (or 'mu-meson', as it was known for many years), a subatomic particle 207 times more massive than the electron. Anderson and Neddermeyer at first believed that they had seen the pion, a particle which Hideki Yukawa had postulated in his theory of the strong interaction. When it became clear that what Anderson had seen was *not* the pion, theoretical physicist I. I. Rabi, puzzled as to how the unexpected discovery could fit into any logical scheme of particle physics, famously asked "Who ordered *that*?" (sometimes the story goes that he was dining with colleagues at a Chinese restaurant at the time).

The muon was the first of a long list of subatomic particles whose discovery initially baffled theoreticians who could not make the confusing 'zoo' fit into some tidy conceptual scheme. Willis Lamb, in his 1955 Nobel Lecture, joked that he had heard it said that "the finder of a new elementary particle used to be rewarded by a Nobel Prize, but such a discovery now ought to be punished by a $10,000 fine."

Carl Anderson spent all of his career at Caltech. During World War II he conducted research in rocketry. He died on 11 January 1991, and is interred in the Forest Lawn, Hollywood Hills Cemetery in Los Angeles, California.

CHARLES STEEN

Charles A. Steen (1919 – 2006-01-01), was a geologist who made and lost a fortune after discovering a rich uranium deposit in Utah during the Uranium boom of the early 1950s.

Early Years

Steen was born in Caddo, Texas and attended high school in Houston. He went on to study at John Tarleton Agricultural College in Stepenville and in 1940 transferred to the Texas College of Mines and Metallurgy (now named the University of Texas at El Paso), receiving a B.A. degree in geology in 1943.

Ineligible for the draft because of his poor eyesight, Steen spent World War II working as a geologist in Bolivia and Peru. Returning to Texas in 1945, he married Minnie Lee ("M.L.") Holland. He started graduate school at the University of Chicago but after a year returned to Houston to take a job doing field work for the Standard Oil Company of Indiana. However, within two years he had been fired for insubordination and had trouble getting any job as a geologist anywhere in the oil industry.

The Uranium Boom

Down on his luck, Steen read in the December 1949 issue of *The Engineering and Mining Journal* that the United States federal government had issued incentives for domestic uranium prospectors. Under the Atomic Energy Act of 1946, the U.S. Atomic Energy Commission had the authority to withdraw lands from the private sector in order to examine them as possible sites for uranium mining. During World War II, the Manhattan Project had received most of its uranium from foreign sources in Canada and the Belgian Congo. However, it had also received some from vanadium miners in the American Southwest, where uranium was often a by-product of mining (uranium was not, before the atomic bomb, a valuable metal). There was a concern that the United States would not have enough domestic supply of uranium for its nuclear weapons programme.

In the late 1940s and early 1950s the Atomic Energy Commission established itself as the only legal buyer of uranium in the U.S., and artificially manipulated prices to reflect their current uranium needs. By raising the price of uranium, they created an incentive for prospectors in the Four Corners region.

Despite the fact that his three sons, Johnny, Andy and Charles Jr., were all less than four years old, and his wife was expecting, Steen borrowed $1,000 from his mother and headed for the Colorado

Plateau, determined to strike it rich. Steen could not afford the standard radiation-detecting equipment used by uranium prospectors-the Geiger counter. Instead, he used a secondhand diamond drill rig and his geologic training for his prospecting. At the time, each prospector had his own idiosyncratic theory on where to find uranium. The uranium industry was composed primarily of individual prospectors and geologists who would attempt to find a large deposit and either mine it for themselves or mine it for a large company (such as Union Carbide) who would then transport the ore from the mine to the uranium mill where it could be converted into yellowcake. Steen's theory on uranium deposits was that they would collect in anticlinal structures in the same manner as oil, which others on the Plateau dismissed as "Steen's Folly."

His family moved into a small trailer at Dove Creek, Colorado, and then later into a tarpaper shack near Cisco, Utah. Steen fed his family on poached venison and cereal, in a highly marginalized state of existence, for two years.

Mi Vida

But on July 6, 1952, Steen hit it big, finding a massive, relatively highly-enriched uranium deposit in the Big Indian Wash of Lisbon Valley, southeast of Moab, Utah. He named it the "Mi Vida" mine (*My Life*), and it was the first big strike of the uranium boom. Steen made millions off his claims, and provoked a "Uranium Rush" of prospectors into the Four Corners region, similar to the Gold Rush of the 1850s in California.

In Moab, Steen built a $250,000 hilltop mansion to replace his tarpaper shack, with a swimming pool, greenhouse, and servants' quarters. He formed a number of companies to continue his uranium work, including the Utex Exploration Company, the Moab Drilling Company, the Mi Vida Company, Big Indian Mines, Inc., and later the Uranium Reduction Company. He made his money well known, inviting the entire population of Moab to annual parties in a local airport hangar, having his original worn prospecting boots bronzed, and flying to Salt Lake City in his private plane for weekly rumba lessons. He donated $50,000 towards a new hospital in Moab and gave land for churches and schools.

Steen was elected to the Utah State Senate in 1958, but quickly became disillusioned with politics. He resigned from office in 1961 and moved to a ranch near Reno, Nevada, building a 16,000 square foot (1500 m²) mansion near the residence of the Comstock millionaire miner, Sandy Bowers. He sold the Utex Exploration Company and the Uranium Reduction Company in 1962.

By the late 1950s, the U.S. government had enough uranium for its needs and had stopped supporting high prices of the ore, killing the market by 1960. Steen attempted to diversify his interests by investing in Arabian horse breeding, a marble quarry, an airplane factory, a pickle plant, and real estate. He met with financial losses and misfortune. In 1968 he declared bankruptcy after the Internal Revenue Service seized his assets to pay for back taxes. In 1971 he suffered a severe head injury working on a copper prospect.

Long suffering from Alzheimer's, Steen died on January 1, 2006, in Loveland, Colorado. Minnie Lee died in 1997.

CHARLES R. STELCK

Charles Richard Stelck (born 1917) is an award-winning Canadian petroleum geologist, paleontologist, stratigrapher and emeritus professor. His research has yielded many large oil and gas finds in western Canada. Stelck was born in Edmonton, Alberta. As a teenager he worked on summer geological field parties.

With the help of a Tegler Scholarship, Stelck attended the University of Alberta. He switched into the geology programme when his friend, Robert Folinsbee, convinced him that it was an exciting field. He obtained a BSc (1937) and a MSc (1941). He moved to California and obtained his PhD at Stanford University.

Career

In the early 1940s, he took a position at the University of Alberta. While there he hypothesized that coral reefs had once lived in what is now the Arctic. He further hypothesized that this would mean there would be oil there now. He discovered reef material while conducting geological research in a mountainous region near Norman Wells, Northwest Territories with a dog team. Most geologists were shocked by his findings as the theory of continental drift had yet to be proposed.

The next leap of discovery was to apply his knowledge to find if a reef had existed in Alberta. He worked with his students to develop an understanding of western Canada's sedimentary basin and the Leduc oilfields. Many of his former students discovered oil, including; Doug Layer (Leduc No. 1), and Arne Rudolph Nielsen and Tony Mason (Pembina oil field-the largest pool of oil in Canada).

CHARLES FRANCIS RICHTER

Charles Francis Richter (April 26, 1900 – September 30, 1985), was an American seismologist and physicist. Richter is most famous as the creator of the Richter magnitude scale which, until the development of the moment magnitude scale in 1979, quantified the size of earthquakes. Inspired by Kiyoo Wadati's 1928 paper on shallow and deep earthquakes, Richter first used the scale in 1935 after developing it in collaboration with Beno Gutenberg; both worked at California Institute of Technology, California, USA. The quote "logarithmic plots are a device of the devil" is attributed to Richter.

Career

Richter went to work at the Carnegie Institute in 1927 after receiving a job offer to be a research assistant there from Robert Millikan. Here he began a collaboration with Beno Gutenberg. The Seismology lab at the California Institute of Technology was hoping to begin publishing regular reports on earthquakes in southern California, and had a pressing need to have a system of measuring the strength of earthquakes for these reports.

Together they had devised the scale that would become known at the Richter scale to fill this need, based on measuring quantitatively the displacement of the earth due to seismic waves, as had been suggested by Kiyoo Wadati.

The pair designed a seismograph that measured this displacement, and developed a logarithmic scale to measure intensity. The name "magnitude" for this measurement came from Richter's childhood interest in Astronomy, where the intensity of stars is measured in magnitudes. Gutenberg's contribution was substantial, but his aversion to interviews contributed to his name being left off the scale. After publishing the proposed scale in 1935, it was quickly adopted for use in measuring the intensity of earthquakes.

He remained at the Carnegie Institute until 1936 when he obtained a post at the California Institute of Technology, where Beno Gutenberg worked. Gutenberg and Richter published *Seismicity of the Earth* in 1941. Its revised edition, published in 1954, is considered a standard reference in the field.

Richter became a full professor at the California Institute of Technology in 1952. In 1958, he published *Elementary Seismology* based on his undergraduate teaching notes. As Richter never published in peer reviewed journals, this is often considered his most important contribution to seismology. Richter spent 1959 and 1960 in Japan as a Fulbright scholar. Around this time in his career, he became involved in the development of building codes for earthquake prone areas.

The city government of Los Angeles removed many ornaments and cornices from municipal buildings in the 1960s as a result of Richter's awareness campaigns. After the 1971 Los Angeles Earthquake, the city cited Richter's warnings as important in preventing many deaths. Richter retired in 1970.

He was also a naturist, and travelled to many nudist communities with his wife.

Richter died of congestive heart failure on September 30, 1985 in Pasadena, California.

CHARLES LYELL

Sir Charles Lyell, 1st Baronet, (November 14, 1797 -- February 22, 1875) was a Scottish lawyer, geologist, and protagonist of uniformitarianism. He was the foremost geologist of his day, and an influence on the young Charles Darwin.

Life

Charles Lyell was born in Kinnordy, Forfarshire (now Angus), the eldest of ten children. Lyell's father, also named Charles, was a lawyer and botanist of minor repute and first exposed the younger Charles to the study of nature. Charles spent much of his childhood at the family's other home, Bartley Lodge in the New Forest, England, where his interest in the natural world was sparked.

After being sent down from Exeter College, Oxford in 1820, Lyell learnt geology under the wing of the naturalist William Buckland. After graduation he took up law as a profession, and completed a circuit through rural England, where he could observe geology. As his eyesight began to fail him he turned to geology as a full time profession. His first paper, "On a recent formation of freshwater limestone in Forfarshire", was presented in 1822. By 1827, he had abandoned the law and embarked on a geological career that would result in fame and the acceptance of ideas, mainly uniformitarianism, proposed by James Hutton a few decades earlier.

In 1832, Lyle married Mary Horner of Bonn, daughter of Leonard Horner (1785-1864), also associated with the Geological Society of London. The new couple spent their honeymoon in Switzerland and Italy on a geological tour of the area.

During the 1840s, he travelled to the United States and Canada, and wrote two popular travel-and-geology books: *Travels in North America* (1845) and *A Second Visit to the United States* (1849). After the Great Chicago Fire, Lyell was one of the first to donate books to help found the Chicago Public Library.

Lyell's wife Mary died in 1873, and two years later Lyell himself died as he was revising the twelfth edition of *Principles*. He is buried in Westminster Abbey. Lyell was rewarded by the State with a knighthood (KT), and later by a baronetcy (Bt), which is an hereditary honour. He was awarded the Copley Medal in 1858 and the Wollaston Medal in 1866. Lyell crater on the Moon and a crater on Mars were named in his honour. In addition, Mount Lyell in western Tasmania, Australia, located in a profitable mining area, bears Lyell's name.

CLARENCE KING

Clarence King (January 6, 1842 – December 24, 1901) was an American geologist and mountaineer. He was the first director of the United States Geological Survey, from 1879-1881. Clarence King was noted for his exploration of the Sierra Nevada. He was born in Newport, Rhode Island.

Career

In 1862, King graduated from the Sheffield Scientific School of Yale College with a Ph.B. in chemistry. While at Yale, he studied with James Dwight Dana. After graduation King travelled on horseback to California with his good friend and classmate, James Terry Gardiner. In California he joined the California Geological Survey without pay where he worked with William H. Brewer, Josiah D. Whitney and Richard D. Cotter. In October 1872, he uncovered a diamond and gemstone hoax perpetrated by Philip Arnold. In 1864, King and Richard Cotter reported the first ascent of Mount Tyndall, at the time labeling it mistakenly as the highest peak in the Sierra Nevada.

In 1867, King was named U.S. Geologist of the Geological Exploration of the Fortieth Parallel, commonly know as the Fortieth Parallel Survey, a position for which he strongly lobbied. King spent six years in the field exploring areas form Wyoming to the border of California. During that time he also published his famous "Mountaineering in the Sierra Nevada" (1872). After the completion of the field work, in 1878 King published "Systematic Geology."

While conducting field work for the Survey, King met and befriended Henry Brooks Adams. Their friendship lasted for the rest of King's life, and he is often mentioned by Adams in the autobiographical *The Education of Henry Adams* (1907). In 1879, the US Congress consolidated the number of geological surveys exploring the American West and created the United States Geological Survey. King was chosen its first director, however he served for only twenty months.

His common law marriage in 1888 to a black woman, Ada Copeland, was kept secret by his keeping a double identity. King didn't even reveal his true name to his wife until he was on his deathbed. He was survived by four children.

King died of tuberculosis in Phoenix, Arizona, and is buried in Newport, Rhode Island. Kings Peak in Utah and Mount Clarence King in Kings Canyon National Park are named in his honour.

CLAUDE HILLAIRE-MARCEL

Professor Claude Hillaire-Marcel FRSC (born April 1, 1944) is a Canadian geoscientist of great distinction and a world leader in Quaternary research. He is known for his groundbreaking research on the environment, climate change, and oceanography. He is a Fellow of the Royal Society of Canada and professor at l'Universite du Quebec a Montreal.

Dr. Hillaire-Marcel was born and educated in France. He received advanced degrees at the Sorbonne in 1968, and the University of Paris in 1979.

He moved to Canada and became a professor at l'Universite du Quebec a Montreal. From between 1970 and 2003, Claude Hillaire-Marcel authored or co-authored over 150 scientific papers. He supervised 20 doctoral dissertations and 37 M.Sc. & D.E.A. theses, and in addition he had 13 scientists working with him as postdoctoral fellows from Belgium, Canada, Denmark, France, Germany, Mexico, the UK & the U.S.

His early papers covered Pleistocene marine fauna and isostatic rebound near Montreal. Later he broadened his geographic scope to include Ungava Bay and Hudson Bay. In 1976, he began writing about oxygen and carbon isotopes. By 1980 he was involved in dating studies utilizing isotopes of uranium and thorium.

Between 1985 and 1991, Mr. Hillaire-Marcel participated in, or was chief scientist on various scientific marine expeditions, including six cruises on Canadian ships (CSS Dawson & CSS Hudson) and a cruise aboard the French research ship Marion-Dufresne in Greenland waters in 1999.

In 1994, a special issue of the Canadian Journal of Earth Sciences featured Labrador Sea studies. Nine of the 12 articles were co-authored by Claude Hillaire-Marcel. In 2001, he was lead author on a paper in Nature entitled "Absence of deep-water formation in the Labrador Sea during the last interglacial period", and he was one of several authors of an EOS article entitled "New Record Shows Pronounced Changes in Arctic Ocean Circulation and Climate".

Most of his work has been around the shores of Canada, but he has carried out field studies or been involved in research in Africa (Algeria, Burundi, Egypt, Ethiopia, Kenya, Libya, Mali, Niger, Tanzania and Tunisia, the Middle East (Israel and Syria, Latin America (Chile, Mexico, Peru, and Uruguay), and Europe (France, Greece and Spain (including the Balearic and Canary island.

Between 1977 and 2002 he co-authored 24 non-Quaternary scientific papers in the fields of agriculture, nutrition, and physical exercise. One involved testing the authenticity of maple syrup. All papers were peer-reviewed.

Professor Claude Hillaire-Marcel served on the following committees; the Royal Society of Canada, Canadian Quaternary Association, International Union for Quaternary Research, Ocean Drilling Programme, International Marine Global Change Study (IMAGES), the World Climate Research Programme (WCRP), and the Joint Global Oceans Flux Studies (JGOFS).

He is a member of the Consultative Committee for the Environment of Hydro-Quebec, the Canadian Scientific Committee for the Integrated ODP, the Scientific Committee of the Institut du

Sahel, and the Executive Committee of Fonds quebecois de la recherche sur la nature et les technologies (FONDS FCAR) and Vice-President of the Sub-commission for the Americas of the INQUA Commission on Shorelines.

Dr. Hillaire-Marcel performs editorial duties for GpQ, CJES and QSR.

Claude Hillaire-Marcel was the Founding Director (1981-1989, 1997-1999) of The Centre de recherche en geochimie et geodynamique, or GEOTOP. He served twice as Chairman of the Department of Earth Sciences at UQAM (1983-1985 and 1987-1989)

Dr. Hillaire-Marcel has held two endowed chairs: from 1989 to 2000 the Industrial Chair Hydro-Quebec-NSERC-UQAM and from 2000 on the International Chair UNESCO.

CLARENCE DUTTON

Clarence Edward Dutton (May 15, 1841 – January 4, 1912) was an American geologist and US Army officer. Dutton was born in Wallingford, Connecticut on May 15, 1841. He graduated from Yale College in 1860 and took postgraduate courses there until 1862, when he enlisted in the 21st Connecticut Volunteers; he fought at Fredericksburg, Suffolk, Nashville and Petersburg.

In 1875 he began work as a geologist for the U.S. Geological Survey. Working chiefly in the Colorado Plateau region, he wrote several classic papers, including geological studies of the high plateaus of Utah (1879-80), the Tertiary history of the Grand Canyon district (1882), and the Charleston, SC earthquake of 1886. As head of the division of volcanic geology at the USGS, he studied volcanism in Hawaii, California, and Oregon. He helped coordinate the scientific response to a large earthquake in Sonora, Mexico, in 1887. He was elected a member of the National Academy of Sciences in 1884.

In 1886, Dutton led a USGS party to Crater Lake, Oregon. His team carried a half-ton survey boat, the *Cleetwood*, up the steep mountain slope and lowered it 2,000 feet into the lake. From the

Cleetwood, Dutton used piano wire with lead weights to measure the depth of the lake at 168 different points. The survey team determined the lake was 1,996 feet deep. The currently-accepted maximum depth figure, measured by sonar, is 1,943 feet (592 meters).

In 1889, Dutton proposed the term "isostasy" for the concept of a general balance within the earth's crust, with lighter weight blocks coming to stand higher than adjacent blocks with higher density, an idea first expressed by Pratt and Airy in the 1850s.

Dutton was a close associate of John Wesley Powell and G.K. Gilbert at the USGS. He was an energetic and effective field geologist: in 1875-1877 Dutton's field party mapped 12,000 square miles of the high plateaus of southern Utah, an area of rugged topography and poor access.

Dutton had a distinctive flair for literary description, and is best remembered today for his colourful (and sometimes flamboyant) descriptions of the geology and scenery of the Grand Canyon region of Arizona. "Dutton first taught the world to look at that country and see it as it was... Dutton is almost as much the *genius loci* of the Grand Canyon as Muir is of Yosemite"—Wallace Stegner, *Beyond the Hundredth Meridian.*

In 1891 he retired from the USGS to serve as commander of the arsenal of San Antonio, Texas; then as ordnance officer of the department of Texas. After retiring from the Army in 1901, he returned to the study of geology. Dutton spent his last years at the home of his son in Englewood, New Jersey.

COLIN CAMPBELL

Colin J. Campbell, (born in Berlin, Germany in 1931) is a retired British petroleum geologist who predicts that oil production will peak by 2007. The consequences of this are uncertain but drastic, due to the world's dependence on fossil fuels for the vast majority of its energy. His theories have received wide attention, but are disputed by some in the oil industry and have not significantly changed U.S. governmental energy policies at this time. In order to deal with declining global oil production, he has proposed the Rimini protocol.

Influential papers by Campbell include *The Coming Oil Crisis*, which he wrote with Jean Laherrere in 1998, and is credited with convincing the International Energy Agency of the coming peak; and *The End of Cheap Oil*, which was published the same year in *Scientific American*. He was referred to as a "doomsayer" in the *The Wall Street Journal* in 2004.

Association for the Study of Peak Oil and Gas founded by Campbell is gaining recognition in the recent years. They have organized yearly international conferences since 2002. The last one was held in Cork, Ireland on 17th-18th September 2007. The next conference is scheduled for 20-22th October 2008 in Barcelona, Spain.

Background

The most famous peak oil petrogeologist is M. King Hubbert, who successfully predicted in 1956 that oil production would peak in the United States between 1965 and 1970. His theories became popular during the 1973 energy crisis, and during 1979 energy crisis when even the United States Secretary of Energy, James Schlesinger, announced that the peak had arrived.

In December 2000 Colin Campbell warned in a public lecture held in Clausthal University of a possible 'ill-conceived military intervention in the Middle East.'

CHRISTIAN LEOPOLD VON BUCH

Christian Leopold Freiherr von Buch (April 26, 1774-March 4, 1853) was a German geologist and paleontologist born in Stolpe (Brandenburg) and is remembered as one of the most important contributors to geology in the first half of the nineteenth century.

He studied together with Alexander von Humboldt under Abraham Gottlob Werner and travelled widely afterwards. His scientific interest was devoted to a broad spectrum of geological topics: volcanism, fossils, stratigraphy and more. His most remembered accomplishment is the scientific definition of the jurassic system. He died in Berlin.

In 1815, he visited the Canary Islands. During his time in the Canary Islands, he visited the Las Canadas Caldera on Tenerife and the Caldera de Taburiente on La Palma. When he published his memoirs and observations about his excursion, he introduced the Spanish word "Caldera" for "*Bowl*" into the geological and scientific vocabulary. The German Geological Society (DGG) named its Leopold-von-Buch-Plakette after him.

Regarding personal names: *Freiherr* is a title, translated as *Baron*, not a first or middle name. The female forms are *Freifrau* and *Freiin*.

CONRAD HAL WADDINGTON

Conrad Hal Waddington (1905–1975) was a developmental biologist, paleontologist, geneticist, embryologist and philosopher who laid the foundations for systems biology. He had wide interests that included poetry and painting, as well as left-wing political leanings.

Life

Waddington was educated at Clifton College and Cambridge University, where he was a lecturer in zoology and a Fellow of Christ's College until 1942, where his friends included Walter Gropius, C. P. Snow, and J. D. Bernal. His interests began with palaeontology but moved on to the heredity and development of living things. He also studied philosophy.

During World War II he was involved in operational research with the Royal Air Force and became scientific advisor to the Commander in Chief of Coastal Command from 1944 to 1945. After the war he became Professor of Animal Genetics at the University of Edinburgh. He would stay at Edinburgh for the rest of life. His personal papers are largely kept at the University of Edinburgh library.

Waddington was married twice. His first marriage produced a son, C. Jake Waddington, now professor of physics at the University of Minnesota, but ended in 1936. He then married Justin Blanco White, daughter of the writer Amber Reeves, with whom he had two daughters, noted mathematician Dusa McDuff and noted anthropologist Caroline Humphrey.

In the early 1930s, Waddington and many other embryologists looked for the molecules that would induce the amphibian neural tube.

The search was, of course, beyond the technology of that time, and most embryologists moved away from such deep problems. Waddington, however, came to the view that the answers to embryology lay in genetics, and in 1935 went to Thomas Hunt Morgan's *Drosophila* laboratory in California, even though this was a time when most embryologists felt that genes were unimportant and just played a role in minor phenomena such as eye colour.

In the late 30's, Waddington produced formal models about how gene regulatory products could generate developmental phenomena, showed how the mechanisms underpinning Drosophila development could be studied through a systematic analysis of mutations that affected developmental anatomy (this was the essence of the approach that won the 1995 Nobel prize in medicine for Christiane Nusslein-Volhard and Eric F. Wieschaus) and wrote his first textbook of developmental epigenetics, a term that then meant the external manifestation of genetic activity.

Waddington also coined other essential concepts, such as canalisation, which refers to the ability of an organism to produce the same phenotype in various different environments. He also invented a mechanism called genetic assimilation which would allow an animal's response to an environmental stress to become a fixed part of its developmental repertoire, and then went on to show that the mechanism would work. He thus demonstrated that the ideas of inheritance put forward by Jean-Baptiste Lamarck could, in principle at least, occur.

Epigenetic Landscape

Waddington's epigenetic landscape is a metaphor for how gene regulation modulates development. One is asked to imagine a number of marbles rolling down a hill towards a wall. The marbles will compete for the grooves on the slope, and come to rest at the lowest points. These points represent the eventual cell fates, that is, tissue types. This idea was actually based on experiment: Waddington found that one effect of mutation (which could modulate the epigenetic landscape was) was to affect how cells differentiated.

Waddington as Organiser

Waddington was very active in advancing biology as a discipline. He contributed to a book on the role of the sciences in times of war, and helped set up several professional bodies representing biology as a discipline.

A remarkable number of his contemporary colleagues in Edinburgh became Fellows of the Royal Society during his time there, or shortly thereafter.

Waddington was an old-fashioned intellectual who lived in both the arts and science milieus of the 1950s and wrote widely. His 1960 book "Behind Appearance; a Study Of The Relations Between Painting And The Natural Sciences In This Century" (MIT press) not only has wonderful pictures but is still worth reading.

Waddington was, without doubt, the most original and important thinker about developmental biology of the pre-molecular age and the medal of the British Society for Developmental Biology is named after him.

CEDRIC SMITH

Cedric Austen Bardell Smith (February 5, 1917 – January 10, 2002) was a British statistician and geneticist. Born in Leicester, he was educated at Wyggeston Boys' School until 1929 when the family moved to London. His education continued at Bec School, Tooting for three years then at University College School, London. In 1935, having failed his Higher School Certificate, he was awarded an exhibition to Trinity College, Cambridge. He graduated in the Mathematical Tripos, with a First in Part II in 1937 and a Distinction in Part III in 1938. Following graduation he began postgraduate research, taking his Ph.D. in 1942.

While a student at Cambridge, Smith became close friends with three other students at Trinity College, R. L. Brooks, A. H. Stone and W. T. Tutte. Together they tackled a number of problems in the mathematical field of combinatorics and devised an imaginary mathematician, 'Blanche Descartes', under which name to publish their work. The group studied dissections of rectangles into squares, especially the 'perfect' squared square, a square that is divided into a number of smaller squares, no two of which are the same size. Publications under the name of 'Blanche Descartes' or 'F. de Carteblanche' continued to appear into the 1980s. The group also published more mainstream articles under their own names, the final one being R.L. Brooks, C.A.B. Smith, A.H. Stone and W.T. Tutte, 'Determinants and current flows in electric networks', Discrete Math., Vol. 100 (1992).

During the Second World War, as a Quaker, Smith joined the Friends Relief Service. He worked as a Porter at Addenbrooke's Hospital in Cambridge. Smith's pacifist views saw him develop an interest in peace studies. Among other responsibilities for the Society of Friends, he was a member of the Quaker Peace Studies Trust which established the chair of Peace Studies at the University of Bradford. Smith was also a founder member (and Chairman) of the Conflict Research Society.

In 1946 he was appointed Assistant Lecturer at the Galton Laboratory at University College London. He remained at UCL for the rest of his career, becoming successively Lecturer and Reader, before appointment as Weldon Professor of Biometry in 1964. On his arrival at UCL Smith was influenced by J. B. S. Haldane, who introduced him to problems of linkage in human genetics in which field he was able to bring his skills as a statistician to bear.

Smith was elected a Fellow of the Royal Statistical Society in 1945. He was a member of the Genetical Society (serving as Treasurer), the Biometric Society (British Region), serving as President 1971-1972, and the International Statistical Institute. In 1957 he married Piroska Vermes (1921-2000), known as 'Piri'. They had one son, who survived them. Piri's father, Dr. Paul Vermes (1897-1968), was a Hungarian refugee who became a professional mathematician at the age of 50.

CRODOWALDO PAVAN

Crodowaldo Pavan (b. Campinas, December 1, 1919) is a Brazilian biologist and geneticist, and an influential scientific leader in Brazil.

Life

Pavan was born to a family of second-generation immigrants from Italy in 1919, in the city of Campinas, Sao Paulo state, Brazil. His great-grandfather was an expert in textile paints and a fanatical anarchist, who was frequently persecuted and imprisoned in Italy as well in Brazil for his political activism. As a boy, he wished first to follow a career in engineering, by influence of his father's porcelain manufacturing plant at Mogi das Cruzes, but changed radically when he had the opportunity, in high school, to attend a lecture by noted French physician and professor Andre Dreyfus and the projection of the movie "The Story of Louis Pasteur", with Oscar Awards-winning actor Paul Muni in the main role. Following Dreyfus' advice, he enrolled in 1938 in the course of natural history at the University of Sao Paulo, continuing to work in biological research under his mentor. His doctoral thesis was also completed in the same institution, on the subject of the blind cave fish *Typhlobagrus kronci.* He also accepted in 1942 a position as assistant professor at the University of Sao Paulo, becoming shortly thereafter a full professor, a position he held until his retirement in 1978.

In 1942, Pavan became involved in a pioneering research project on the genetics, taxonomy and ecology of *Drosophila* fruit flies, financed by the Rockefeller Foundation under the direction of the noted Russian-American biologist Theodosius Dobzhansky. Both subjects became Pavan's lifelong research interest and the source of his international recognition. In particular, Dr. Pavan introduced into biology the cytogenetical study of *Rhynchosciara angelae*, a fly which is noted for its giant chromosomes, thus facilitating the determination of the loci of genes. He and his collaborators were among the first to prove that the structure of genes and chromosomes was not fixed and could be changed by infections.

In 1966, the Oak Ridge National Laboratory, in Tennessee, U.S., invited Dr. Pavan to establish a laboratory for further investigations on cellular genetics, and Dr. Pavan moved to the States, where he remained until 1975. In 1968 he accepted an invitation to become a tenured full professor at the University of Texas at Austin, in Austin, Texas. He returned to Brazil in 1975, and, after officially retiring from his post at the University of Sao Paulo, he accepted a position of full professor at the recently founded State University of Campinas, in Campinas, working as departmental chairman and dean of the Instituto de Biologia da Universidade Estadual de Campinas (Institute of Biology) until a second retirement. He is an emeritus professor at both universities.

As a scientific leader, Dr. Pavan has been very influential and became involved in the main developments of science and technology in Brazil in the second half of the 20th century. He was a president of the National Research Council (CNPq) from 1986 to 1990, a president of the Brazilian Society for the Advancement of Science from 1980 to 1986 (a critical period for the redemocratization of the country, when the Society played a very important role in the civil resistance to the military government).

Dr. Pavan has been internationally recognized by many memberships to learned societies, decorations, medals and awards from several countries. He is one of the few Brazilians who is a member of the Pontifical Academy of Sciences. Internationally he is also a member of the Third World Academy of Sciences, Academy of Sciences of Lisbon, Physiographic Academy of Lund, and Academy of Sciences of Chile. In Brazil, he is a member of Brazilian Academy of Sciences, one of the founders of the Academy of Sciences of Sao Paulo, the Academy of Medicine of Sao Paulo, Academy of Letters of Sao Paulo and Academy of Education of Sao Paulo.

He was one of the founders of the Brazilian Society of Genetics and one of its presidents.

Currently Dr. Pavan lives in the city of Sao Paulo and is involved in several activities related to the public understanding of science. He is one of the founders and director of the Associacao Brasileira de Divulgacao Científica, and scientifically is still active in research on the biological control of agricultural plagues.

CARL NEUBERG

Carl Alexander Neuberg (1877-1956) was an early pioneer in biochemistry, and often referred to as the "Father of Biochemistry".

He was the first editor of the journal *Biochemische Zeitschrift.* This journal was founded in 1906 and is now known as the *FEBS Journal.* Neuberg was born in Hanover, Germany and studied chemistry at the University of Berlin. In his early work in Germany, he worked on solubility and transport in cells, the chemistry of carbohydrates, photochemistry, as well as investigating and classifying different types of fermentation. He was also a pioneer in the study of the chemistry of amino acids and enzymes.

Neuberg was head of the biochemistry section of one of the first Kaiser Wilhelm Institutes (that of August von Wasserman). In the 1910s, after announcing the discovery of an enzyme he called "carboxylase" (which catalyzed the decarboxylation of pyruvic acid), he developed a theory of the alcoholic fermentation of glucose. Support for his theory was bolstered when he helped develop an industrial process that contributed materially to the German war effort in World War I, manufacturing glycerol—for the production of explosives—by the fermentation of sugar.

Neuberg made a particularly important discovery in 1916: hydrotropy, a solubilization process where the addition of large amounts of a second solute causes an increase in the aqueous solubility of a different solute. Due to his Jewish faith, Neuberg was forced to end his work at the Kaiser Wilhelm Institute for Biochemistry in 1936 and leave Germany by the Nazis in 1937 and moved to the United States, where he continued to work on enzymes and cell transport processes. Succesor for the position at the Kaiser Wilhelm Institute for Biochemistry became Adolf Butenandt.

CESAR MILSTEIN

Cesar Milstein (October 8, 1927 – March 24, 2002) was an Argentine biochemist in the field of antibody research. Milstein shared the Nobel Prize in Physiology or Medicine in 1984 with Niels K. Jerne and Georges Kohler.

Biography

Milstein was born in Bahia Blanca, Argentina. He graduated from the University of Buenos Aires and obtained a PhD under Professor Stoppani (Professor of Biochemistry) in the Medical School on kinetic studies with the enzyme aldehyde dehydrogenase. In 1958, funded by the British Council, he joined the Biochemistry Department at the University of Cambridge to work for a PhD under Malcolm Dixon on the mechanism of metal activation of the enzyme phosphoglucomutase. During this work he collaborated with Frederick Sanger whose group he joined with a short-term Medical Research Council appointment.

Career

The major part of Milstein's research career was devoted to studying the structure of antibodies and the mechanism by which antibody diversity is generated. It was as part of this quest that in 1975 he, together with Georges Kohler (a postdoctoral fellow in his laboratory), developed the hybridoma technique for the production of monoclonal antibodies-a discovery recognised by the award of the 1984 Nobel Prize for Physiology or Medicine. This discovery led to an enormous expansion in the exploitation of antibodies in science and medicine.

Milstein himself made many major contributions to improvements and developments in monoclonal antibody technology-especially focusing on the use of monoclonal antibodies to provide markers that allow distinction between different cell types. He also foresaw the potential wealth of ligand-binding reagents that could result from applying recombinant DNA technology to monoclonal antibodies and inspired the development of the field of antibody engineering.

Milstein's early work on antibodies focused on the nature of their diversity at the amino acid level as well as on the disulphide bonds by which they were held together. Part of this work was done in collaboration with his wife, Celia. The emphasis of his research then shifted towards the mRNA encoding antibodies where he was able to provide the first evidence for the existence of a precursor for these secreted polypeptides that contained a signal sequence.

The development of the hybridoma technology coupled to advances in nucleic acid sequencing then allowed Milstein to chart the changes that occurred in antibodies following antigen encounter. He demonstrated the importance of somatic hypermutation of immunoglobulin V genes in antibody affinity maturation.

In this process, localised mutation of the immunoglobulin genes allows the production of improved antibodies which make a major contribution to protective immunity and immunological memory.

Much of his work in recent years was devoted to characterising this mutational process with a view to understanding its mechanism and, indeed, he contributed a manuscript for publication on this topic less than a week before he died. Quite apart from his own achievements, Milstein acted as a guide and inspiration to many in the antibody field as well as devoting himself to assisting science and scientists in less well developed countries.

He was elected a Fellow of the Royal Society in 1975, was a fellow of Darwin College, Cambridge from 1980 to 2002, awarded the Louisa Gross Horwitz Prize from Columbia University in 1980, won the Copley Medal in 1989, and became a Companion of Honour in 1995.

Milstein died early on 24 March 2002 in Cambridge, England at age 74 as a result of a heart condition from which he had suffered for many years.

CLEMENT MARKERT

Clement Lawrence Markert (April 11, 1917 – October 1, 1999) was an American biologist credited with the discovery of isozymes (different forms of enzymes that catalyze the same reaction). He was a member of the National Academy of Science and American Academy of Arts and Sciences, and served as president of several biology societies.

Markert was born in Las Animas, Colorado and raised in Pueblo, Colorado. He attended the University of Colorado, and in 1937, left college to fight in the Spanish Civil War—stowing away aboard a freighter to circumvent government travel restrictions. After returning to college, Markert completed his bachelor's degree in 1940; upon graduation, he married Margaret Rempfer, and they moved to UCLA for graduate work. He enrolled in the United States Merchant Marine to take part in World War II; by 1954 they would have three children.. After the war, he finished a master's degree at UCLA followed by a Ph.D. from Johns Hopkins University in 1948.

Markert's Ph.D. research, and subsequent postdoctoral work at Caltech, focused on the sexuality and other physiological and genetic aspects of *Glomerella*, a genus of pathogenic plant fungi. At Caltech, he also worked with George Beadle on corn and *Neurospora* genetics.

In 1950 he began teaching at the University of Michigan, part of the new wave of what would become molecular biology. In 1954, Markert became a victim of McCarthyism; he was suspended from teaching because he refused to testify before the House Un-American

Activities Committee. He was later reinstated, and continued at the University of Michigan until moving to Johns Hopkins in 1957, followed by Yale University—as head of the Department of Biology. In 1966, he served as president of the American Institute of Biological Sciences. He remained at Yale until retiring in 1986 to North Carolina State University, where he continued researching until 1993.

Early in his career, Markert developed the concept of isozymes based on electrophoresis and histochemical staining of enzymes. He found that often what had been assumed to be a single enzyme catalyzing a specific reaction was in fact multiple enzymes, with different proteins present in different tissues. In biochemistry, this forced a re-evaluation of some basic assumptions of enzyme kinetics; in genetics, it contributed to the shift from the "one gene-one enzyme hypothesis" to the "one gene-one polypeptide" concept. Markert's early work with isozymes, many of which are formed by gene duplication, was a precursor to the concept of gene families. Markert's later career focused on developmental biology, particularly developmental genetics in experiments with mosaic animals.

Markert was Editor-in-Chief of the *Journal of Experimental Zoology* from 1963 to 1985. He also edited the *Journal of Developmental Biology*. In 1990, the University of Michigan created the annual "Davis, Markert, Nickerson Lecture on Academic and Intellectual Freedom" series, in honour of Markert and two other Michigan faculty suspended for refusing to testify in 1954.

CRAIG MELLO

Craig Cameron Mello (born October 18, 1960) is an American biologist and Professor of Molecular Medicine at the University of Massachusetts Medical School in Worcester, Massachusetts. He was awarded the 2006 Nobel Prize for Physiology or Medicine, along with Andrew Z. Fire, for the discovery of RNA interference. This research was conducted at the University of Massachusetts Medical School and published in 1998. Mello has been a Howard Hughes Medical Institute investigator since 2000.

Early Life

Mello was born in New Haven, Connecticut on October 18, 1960. He was the third child of James and Sally Mello. His father, James Mello, was a paleontologist and his mother, Sally Mello, was an artist. His paternal grandparents immigrated to the US from the Portuguese islands of Azores.

His parents met while attending Brown University and were the first children in their respective families to attend college. His grandparents on both sides withdrew from school as teenagers to work for their families. James Mello completed his Ph.D. in paleontology from Yale University in 1962. The Mello family moved to Falls Church in northern Virginia so that James could take a position with the United States Geological Survey (USGS) in Washington, DC.

After a brief stay in Falls Church, the family moved to Fairfax, Virginia, when James Mello switched from the USGS to a position as assistant director at the Smithsonian Museum of Natural History. Among his fondest early memories were field trips with his father and the whole family to Colorado and Wyoming and more frequent trips to the Blue Ridge mountains in Virginia.

The Mello family had a very strong tradition of discussions around the dinner table and this experience was very important to young Mello. He learned to argue, to listen, and to admit it when he was wrong about something. At a time when young Mello was not performing so well in school, these daily discussions helped to build his confidence and self esteem. Mello struggled during the first few years of grade school. He started first grade at the age of five in a local private school because he was too young to enter first grade in the public system. He doesn't know if he was a slow learner, or just not interested, but he did not do well in school until the seventh grade. In second grade, Mello only pretended that he could read and he was embarrassed of being called on in class. He much preferred playing outdoors, in the woods and creeks, to time spent in the classroom. Meanwhile, his older siblings were model students, raising the teacher's expectations for him. During these eaily years, Mello had no doubt that he would be a scientist when he grew up.

Education

Mello attended Fairfax High School (Fairfax, Virginia). He took all of the science courses offered except advanced physics. Mello liked his earth science, chemistry and biology teachers.

After receiving his high school diploma, Mello attended Brown University. Mello pursued biochemistry and molecular biology as his major at Brown. Some of his teachers at Brown were Frank Rothman, Ken Miller, Susan Gerbi and Nelson Fausto. He received his Sc.B. from Brown University in 1982.

After completing his studies at Brown, Mello went to Boulder, Colorado for graduate studies. He took courses in molecular, cellular and developmental biology. Some of his instructors were David Hirsh, Dick McIntosh, Mike Yarus, Larry Gold, and Bill Wood. Mello joined David's lab in 1982. David's lab was filled with people, such as Dan Stinchcomb (who introduced Mello to the practice of molecular biology), who would prove to be important in Mello's future training.

During his first year in Boulder, David Hirsh decided to take a position in industry. Because of this, Mello moved to Harvard University where he could continue his research with Dan Stinchcomb, who was starting up an independent lab there.

Mello enjoyed his time at Harvard. He worked on the project and worked long hours in the lab. He took advantage of opportunities to attend lectures on a wide range of subjects. He completed his Ph.D. from Harvard in 1990. He was a postdoctoral fellow at the Fred Hutchinson Cancer Research Centre in the laboratory of Dr. James Priess.

COLIN MUNRO MACLEOD

Colin Munro MacLeod (January 28, 1909 — February 11, 1972) was a Canadian-American geneticist.

Biography

Born in Port Hastings, Nova Scotia, Canada MacLeod entered McGill University at the age of 16 (having skipped three grades in primary school), and completed his medical studies by age 23.

In his early years as a research scientist, MacLeod, together with Oswald Avery and Maclyn McCarty, discovered that genes are made of DNA. In 1941, Avery and MacLeod had separated a crude extract from the pneumonia-causing S ('smooth') strain of the bacteria. The S strain extract could convert the far more benign R ('rough') strain of pneumocci to the disease-causing S form. Later that year, McCarty joined the Avery laboratory, and in 1942, the group began to focus on DNA as the elusive ingredient in the S strain extract that could transform R pneumococcus into S pneumococcus. By early 1943, Avery, MacLeod, and McCarty had shown that DNA was indeed the transforming principle. In February 1944, the trio published the first of a series of scientific papers in the *Journal of Experimental Medicine* demonstrating that DNA was the transforming principle. Subsequent experiments confirmed DNA as a universal bearer of genetic information. Despite the scientific importance of this work, Avery, MacLeod, and McCarty were never awarded a Nobel Prize for their discovery.

MacLeod, meanwhile, had been diverted to health and science issues related to the Second World War. At the time, microbial diseases such as typhus fever, malaria, and pneumonia posed significant threats to the health of U.S. military personnel. During the war, MacLeod was one of many university-based scientists and physicians who advised the Federal government on medical matters "when asked." In 1941, he had been appointed Chairman of the Department of Microbiology at New York University (NYU) School of Medicine, and also worked as a consultant to the U.S. Secretary of War.

He became an official member of the Army Epidemiological Board, which in 1949 was enlarged to include all the armed forces and renamed the Armed Forces Epidemiological Board (AFEB).

MacLeod became president of the Army board in 1947, a position he held until 1955. The organization of the AFEB into 12 disease-related commissions foreshadowed the organization of the USJCMSP into its disease-related panels.

At the end of World War II, Congress gave the National Institutes of Health (NIH) the authority to make external research awards, thereby creating its extramural programmes, which today constitute almost 90 percent of NIH funding. The NIH took over the funding of various research projects that had begun during the war, and MacLeod, from 1946 – 1949, served as a member of the first NIH study section, the Antibiotics Study Section. Given his background with the newly renamed Department of Defense, MacLeod grew into the role of informal advisor to several NIH directors and served on various grant committees, commissions, and task forces.

Thus, MacLeod had entered the third phase of his highly successful career—the first two being a laboratory research scientist and academic department head—with multiple forays into the realm of science policy and international health.

MacLeod was elected to membership in the National Academy of Sciences in 1955. In 1956, he gave up his position as head of microbiology at NYU, spent several years at the University of Pennsylvania, and then returned in 1960 to NYU as a professor of medicine. The same year, NIH Director James Shannon asked MacLeod to work with the Southeast Asia Treaty Organization (SEATO) to find ways to address the problem of cholera.

Other scientists on the project were Joseph Smadel of the NIH, and Theodore Woodward and Fred L. Soper. (Woodward served as a U.S. Delegation Member from 1965–1995 and is now emeritus member.) MacLeod, Smadel, Woodward, Soper, and the other scientific advisors to SEATO recommended the establishment of a laboratory in Dacca, East Pakistan (now Dhaka, Bangladesh), that could conduct field research on cholera. Soper became the first director of the facility, initially called the Cholera Research Laboratory, and later renamed the International Centre of Diarrhoeal Diseases Research, Bangladesh (ICDDR, B). Several years later, the newly formed USJCMSP Cholera Panels coordinated their cholera research and treatment activities with the Cholera Research Laboratory.

C. C. LITTLE

Clarence Cook "C.C." Little (October 6, 1888 – December 22, 1971) was an American genetics, cancer, and tobacco researcher and academic administrator.

He was born in Brookline, Massachusetts and attended Harvard University. While studying under W. E. Castle, Little began his work with mice, focused on inheritance, transplants, and grafts. He also was an assistant dean and secretary to the president. His most important research occurred at Harvard, including what some call his most brilliant work, "A Mendelian explanation for the inheritance of a trait that has apparently non-Mendelian characteristics". His observations on transplant rejection became codified into the "five laws of transplant immunology" by George Snell. Little developed the "DBA (Dilute, Brown and non-Agouti)" strain of mice while at Harvard.

During World War I Little served in the U.S. Army Signal Corps, attaining the rank of Major. Following the war he spent three years at the Cold Spring Harbour Laboratory. In 1921 he helped found the American Birth Control League with Margaret Sanger and Lothrop Stoddard.

Little accepted the post of President of the University of Maine in 1922, becoming at age 33 the youngest university president in the country. While there he started a summer laboratory in Bar Harbour. In 1925 he left to become the President of the University of Michigan. His tenure at the university was controversial due to his outspokenness in favour of eugenics, birth control, and euthanasia. He left Michigan in 1929 in order to devote himself to his research at Bar Harbour. With funding from Detroit car manufacturers he was able to improve the facility for year-round use. He renamed it the "Jackson Laboratory" in honour of one donor, Roscoe B. Jackson of the Hudson Motor Car Corporation, who had died in a car accident. Also in 1929 he took on a part-time job as managing director of the American Society for the Control of Cancer (later became the American Cancer Society (ACS)) and served as President to the American Eugenics Society.

Funding for the Jackson Laboratory was extremely limited during the Great Depression, but it received one of the first grants from the newly formed National Cancer Institute in 1938. Little energetically developed both the lab and the ACS, and by 1944 they were shipping 9000 mice a week to other laboratories. A brush fire destroyed the laboratory and all of the livestock in 1947, but it was quickly rebuilt and most mouse strains were recovered from other labs around the world. By 1950 the lab was maintaining 60 inbred strains, and had developed the F_1 hybrid that became widely used for chemical testing. Little resigned in 1954.

His last major post, from 1954 to 1969, was as the Scientific Director of the Scientific Advisory Board of the Tobacco Industrial Research Committee (renamed Council for Tobacco Research in 1964). In that role he was a leading scientific voice of the tobacco industry and oversaw a USD$1 million research budget that gave grants to hundreds of scientists. In 1959 he refuted his earlier assertion, made as Director of the ACS, that inhaling fine particles is unhealthy, and stated that smoking does not cause lung cancer and is at most a minor contributing factor. A decade later he said, "there is no demonstrated causal relationship between smoking or any disease." In keeping with his earlier research he believed that the main cause of cancer was genetic, not environmental.

He died of a heart attack in 1971 at the age of 83.

CHARLES LEONARD HUSKINS

Charles Leonard Huskins (1897-1953) was an English-born Canadian geneticist who specialized in the field of cytogenetics. He is also sometimes referred to as C. Leonard Huskins or C.L. Huskins.

Huskins was born in Walsall, England and moved with his family at the age of 9 to Red Deer, Alberta, Canada. He served in the Canadian Infantry and as an aviator in the Royal Flying Corps (which became the RAF) in World War I.

After the war Huskins returned to Canada and enrolled in the University of Alberta from which he received his Bachelor's degree in 1923 and his Master's degree in 1925. With the aid of a scholarship for graduate study abroad, he went to England where he obtained his Ph.D. from King's College London in 1927. Huskins stayed on in England from 1927 to 1930 to do research with the renowned geneticist William Bateson at what is now the John Innes Centre.

In 1930 Huskins returned to Canada to teach at McGill University in Montreal. He taught initially (1930-1934) in the Department of Botany and then (1934-1945) as Professor in the Department of Genetics, the first head of a Department of Genetics in Canada. In 1945 he left McGill for the University of Wisconsin-Madison where he was Professor of Botany until his death. In 1942-1943 Huskins spent a year at Columbia University on a Guggenheim Fellowship he was awarded "to prepare a book on the cytology and genetics of plants, animals and man." Except for that year, he spent essentially all of his career at McGill and Wisconsin.

Huskins worked at first on mutations in oats and wheat. At the Innes Centre he studied a species of the grass Spartina (cordgrass) and showed that a suspected hybrid had undergone chromosome doubling in the course of evolution, one of the first demonstrations of this phenomenon.

He then went on to do research on chromosome synapsis and crossing-over in higher plants, grasshoppers and mice. Huskins and F. M. Hearne published the first studies on the cytology of the grasshopper in 1935 and in 1936 they published on animal cytology (on chiasma frequencies in mice). The Genetics Society of Canada established the Huskins Memorial Lecture in his honour and there is the C. Leonard Huskins Professor of Botany at University of Wisconsin-Madison.

CHRISTIAN DE DUVE

Christian Rene de Duve (born October 2, 1917) is an internationally acclaimed cytologist and biochemist. De Duve was born in Thames-Ditton, Britain, as a son of Belgian immigrants. They returned to Belgium in 1920. De Duve was educated by the Jesuits at Onze-Lieve-Vrouwecollege in Antwerp, before studying at the Catholic University of Leuven, where he became a professor in 1947. He specialized in subcellular biochemistry and cell biology and discovered peroxisomes and lysosomes, cell organelles. Amongst other subjects, de Duve studied the distribution of enzymes in rat liver cells using rate-zonal centrifugation. De Duve's work on cell fractionation provided an insight into the function of cell structures.

In 1960, De Duve was awarded the Francqui Prize for Biological and Medical Sciences. He was awarded the shared Nobel Prize for Physiology or Medicine in 1974, together with Albert Claude and George E. Palade, for describing the structure and function of organelles in biological cells. His later years have been mostly devoted to origin of life studies, which he admits is still a speculative field (see thioester). His work has contributed to the emerging consensus that the endosymbiotic theory is correct; this idea proposes that mitochondria, chloroplasts, and perhaps other organelles of eukaryotic cells originated as prokaryote endosymbionts, which came to live inside eukaryotic cells.

De Duve proposes that peroxisomes may have been the first endosymbionts, which allowed cells to withstand the growing amounts of free molecular oxygen in the Earth's atmosphere. Since peroxisomes have no DNA of their own, this proposal has much less evidence than the similar claims for mitochondria and chloroplasts.

C. D. DARLINGTON

Cyril Dean Darlington (19 December 1903-26 March 1981) was an English biologist, geneticist and eugenicist, who discovered the mechanics of chromosomal crossover, its role in inheritance, and therefore its importance to evolution.

Biography

Cyril Darlington was born in Chorley, a small cotton town in Lancashire, England in 1903. His father, William was a teacher at a small school. He had one brother six years older. When he was eight, the family moved to London. His childhood was an unhappy one, characterized by a stern, bitter and frustrated father, who struggled mightily against poverty. He enjoyed neither sports, nor studies. He began to cultivate a disdain for authority. He decided to become a farmer in Australia, so he applied to the South Eastern Agricultural College at Wye, known later as Wye College. He was a rather indifferent student, but his social life took a decided turn for the better when he took up boxing, with some success. He was now six feet three inches tall, and an imposing figure. One subject that captured his imagination, however, was Mendelian genetics, taught by a Mr. Brade-Birks. He discovered Thomas Hunt Morgan's *The Physical Basis of Heredity*. He graduated with a London University degree in 1923.

Early Professional Years

After being turned down for a scholarship to go to Trinidad as a farmer, Cyril was induced in 1923 by one of his professors to apply for a scholarship at the John Innes Horticultural Institution in Merton. He wrote at once to its director, William Bateson, famous for having introduced the word "genetics" into biology. His application was unsuccessful, but he wrangled a temporary post as an unpaid technician. It was an interesting time for the Innes. Bateson had spent the last two decades fighting against the notion that chromosomes were the seat of what he had been calling "heredity factors" and had only very recently capitulated. He had just hired a cytologist, Frank Newton, who now began to take Cyril under his wing. Darlington published his first scientific paper, on the tetraploidy of the sour cherry, and he was hired as a permanent employee.

Shortly after, both of his mentors, Bateson and Newton, died within a year of each other and J.B.S. Haldane came to the Innes. Although neither an experimentalist nor cytologist, Haldane formed a close friendship with Darlington, whose self-confidence grew. He began to make significant contributions to the understanding of the relationship of genetic crossing-over and the microscopically observed events that the chromosome passed through during mitosis (It seems that meiosis should be mentioned here rather than mitosis). In 1931 he began writing the book that would establish his reputation, *Recent Advances in Cytology*. It was published in 1932, and created a firestorm of controversy at first, then nearly universal acceptance as a work of the first rank. He showed that the mechanisms of evolution that acted at the level of the chromosome created possibilities far more rich than the simple mutations and deletions that affect single genes.

His now remarkable determination and achievement saw him become Director of the cytology department in 1937 and became director of the Innes two years later, just 15 years after his arrival as an unpaid volunteer. He was elected a Fellow of the Royal Society on 20 March 1941. A few months after that, he was awarded the prestigious Darwin Medal. He was elected president of the Genetical Society. In 1947 he co-founded with Ronald Fisher the highly successful journal "Heredity: An International Journal of Genetics."

CYRIL CLARKE

Sir Cyril Astley Clarke (Hon) (22 August 1907–21 November 2000) was a British physician, geneticist and lepidopterist. He was honoured for his pioneering work on prevention of Rh disease of the newborn, and also for his work on the genetics and evology of the Lepidoptera (butterflies and moths).

Cyril Clarke's school education was at Wyggestson Grammar School in Leicester and Oundle School near Peterborough. His interest in butterflies and moths began at school. His studied natural science at Gonville and Caius College, University of Cambridge and then medicine at Guy's Hospital, London. During the Second World War, he worked as a medic in the Royal Naval Volunteer Reserve. Clarke helped to developed the technique of giving Rh-negative women inter-muscular injections of anti-RhD antibodies during pregnancy to prevent Rh disease in their newborn babies. This was one of the major advances in preventive medicine in the second half of the 20th century.

Clarke answered an advert in an insect magazine for swallowtail butterfly pupae that had been placed by Philip Sheppard. They met and began working together in their common interest of lepidoptery. From 1959 they started running a moth trap in Caldy Common near West Kirby, Wirral, England. They studied the peppered moth, the scarlet tiger moth and swallowtail butterfly.

They published papers on the genetics of lepidoptera and also on Rh disease. Clarke continued research in his retirement and in 1988 he rediscovered a Scarlet Tiger Moth colony on the Wirral Way, West Kirby, that had been started in 1961 by Philip Sheppard. The colony was useful for study of the genetics of changes in populations.

He was married Frieda (or Feo) in 1934. Lady Feo Clarke died in 1998. Cyril Clark died in 2000. They had three sons.

DEREK ABBOTT

Derek Abbott (3 May 1960, in South Kensington, London, UK) is a physicist and electronic engineer. He is a Professor of Electrical and Electronic Engineering at the University of Adelaide, Australia. He is notable for leading theoretical work in the development of Parrondo's paradox, contributions to the field of stochastic resonance, and experimental contributions to T-ray imaging.

Early Years

In the period 1963-1965 Abbott attended the famous Norland College pre-school, Chislehurst, Kent, UK, as a boarder. Then during 1965-1967 he attended Oakfield School, Dulwich, UK, at the same time as the singer Kim Wilde. In 1968, he attended the Ecole de Ferney-Voltaire, France, and the Ecole Seminaire de Collonges-sous-Saleve, France. In 1969 he did a stint at Bassett House School, London, UK. In the 1969-1971 period, he was a boarder at Copthorne Preparatory School, Sussex, UK. He attended Copthorne Preparatory

School at the same time as the deputy editor of *Private Eye,* Francis Wheen.

During 1971-1978 he attended the infamous Holland Park School, London, UK, known as the "socialist Eton." At Holland Park School, the singer Yazz was one of his classmates. Here, he was taught English Literature by the comedian Mike Walling and music by Andy Mackay who later became the saxophonist of Roxy Music. In the early 1970s he lived next door to Cat Stevens' drummer Gerry Conway in Holland Park, London.

Career

In 1978, he began work at GEC Hirst Research Centre, Wembley, UK, performing research in the area of CCD and microchip design for imaging systems. Whilst working, he graduated in 1982 with a BSc in Physics from Loughborough University, where his key intellectual influence was Nicholas J. Phillips. In 1986, at the time when the mysterious GEC deaths started, he began work as a microchip designer at Austek Microsystems in Adelaide, Australia. In 1987, he joined the University of Adelaide completing his PhD thesis in Electrical & Electronic Engineering in 1995, entitled *GaAs MESFET Photodetectors for Imaging Arrays*, under Kamran Eshraghian and Bruce R. Davis.

Teaching

He is currently a full professor at the University of Adelaide, where he has won a number of teaching awards. In the late 1990s, Abbott wore two watches, one on each wrist. When asked why, he would reply, "It is a way of identifying the best students—to check their powers of observation." In the 1990s, during undergraduate lectures, if a student raised a hand and spotted a mistake in the lecture material, Abbott would open his wallet and give the student the lowest coin or note that he happened to be carrying. On occasion, if he forgot to bring coins, he had to part with a high denomination. Around 1998, he also adopted the same prize money approach for the "most perceptive question" asked in a lecture.

DAVID STRANGWAY

David William Strangway, is a Canadian geophysicist and university administrator. Strangway is the founder and Chancellor of Quest University Canada, a private non-profit liberal arts and sciences university in Squamish, British Columbia which opened in September 2007.

Strangway studied at the University of Toronto, earning a B.A. in physics and geology in 1956, an M.A. in physics and a Ph.D in physics in 1960. After work in the field of geology and three years on the faculty at M.I.T, in 1970, he joined NASA as the Chief of the Geophysics Branch and was responsible for the geophysical aspects of the Apollo missions. In 1972, he was awarded the NASA Exceptional Scientific Achievement Medal for his scientific contribution to NASA. He was a vice-president at the University of Toronto and the chairman of its geology department from 1973 to 1983. Upon the retirement of James Ham in 1983, Strangway was appointed the acting president of the University of Toronto. He was unexpectedly elevated to become the university's eleventh president after the designated successor, Donald Forster, suddenly died of a heart attack in August of that year.

From 1985 to 1997, he was the tenth President of the University of British Columbia. From 1998 to 2004, he was the President and Chief Executive Officer of the Canada Foundation for Innovation, an independent corporation created by the Government of Canada to fund research infrastructure.

DAVID M. RAUP

David M. Raup is a University of Chicago paleontologist. Raup studied the fossil record and the diversity of life on Earth. Raup contributed to the knowledge of extinction events along with his colleague Jack Sepkoski. They suggested that the extinction of dinosaurs 65 mya was part of a cycle of mass extinctions that may have occurred every 26 million years. In addition to his time at the University of Chicago, Raup has taught at Caltech, Johns Hopkins, and the University of Rochester. He was also a curator and Dean of Science at the Field Museum of Natural History in Chicago as well as a visiting professor in Germany at Tubingen and on the faculty of the College of the Virgin Islands. Raup was heavily involved through his career in joint programmes with biology and in promoting training of paleontologists in modern marine environments. In 1994, he retired to Washington Island in northern Lake Michigan. Currently, he assists the Santa Fe Institute to develop methods and approaches to dealing with the evolutionary exploration of morphospace.

Early Life

Born in 1933 and raised in Boston, Raup's interest in the fossil record did not begin at a young age, having had very little contact with such things until later in life. He focused instead on leisure activities such as skiing and camping. His first mentor was John Clark, a vertebrate paleontologist and sedimentologist at the University of Chicago while starting his education. Raup began his academic career at Colby College in Maine before transferring two years later to the University of Chicago where he earned his Bachelor of Science degree. From there, he went to Harvard for graduate studies where he majored in geology while focussing on palaeontology and biology; he earned his MA and PhD degrees there.

DAN MCKENZIE

Daniel (Dan) Peter McKenzie, (b. 1942) is a Professor of Geophysics at Cambridge University, and one-time head of the Bullard Laboratories. He wrote the first paper defining the principles of plate tectonics, and his early work on mantle convection created the modern discussion of planetary interiors.

Early Life

Born in Cheltenham 1942, the son of an Ear Nose and Throat surgeon, he first attended Westminster Under School and later Westminster School, London.

Education and Career

Dan McKenzie attended King's College, Cambridge where he read Physics, obtaining a 2:1 in his final degree. As a graduate student, he worked with Edward "Teddy" Bullard who suggested he work on the subject of thermodynamic variables. He was awarded a Research Fellowship at King's College at the beginning of his second year which enabled him to study anything he wanted. As such, he gave up doing what Teddy had suggested and became interested in how the interior of the earth convects, something completely speculative at that time. McKenzie taught himself fluid mechanics and then went to the Scripps Oceanography Institute at the University of California, San Diego, on the invitation of Freeman Gilbert and Walter Munk. After eight months he returned to the Cambridge, submitting his PhD in 1966. He has since said that nothing in his early life as a scientist had such a profound effect on him as those eight months in California.

Plate Tectonics

Spending time between Cambridge and a Fellowship held in Caltech, Dan was invited, along with with Teddy Bullard, to a conference in New York which initiated his revolutionary work on plate tectonics. After listening to separate talks from Fred Vines and Lynn Sykes he came back to Cambridge and started work on the first paper to be published on plate tectonics, looking at the thermal structure of oceanic plates as they formed and cooled.

Following this, he published a seminal paper with Bob Parker, which employed the Euler Theorem, in conjunction with magnetic anomalies and earthquakes to determine a precise mathematical theory on plate tectonics. This work was published some 3-4 months after the same work had been carried out by Jason Morgan at Princeton. Allegations were subsequently made suggesting that McKenzie was at Morgan's spring AGU talk where he presented his plate tectonics work. Later in 1968 he went to Princeton where he found that he and Morgan had solved two or three problems using identical mathematics in exactly the same way – plate tectonics was one, another was the thermal structure of the oceans and another was looking at earthquake mechanisms in a different way to seismologists.

Working with John Sclater, McKenzie determined the entire geological history of the Indian Ocean, the publication of which eventually resulted in them both receiving Fellowships at the Royal Society.

Mantle Convection and Sedimentary Basins

McKenzie was awarded a University position and took it up in 1971. At this point he decided to move away from plate tectonics, choosing instead to focus on the behavior of fluids below the plates. He studied cellular convection and motions in the mantle whilst at the same time pursuing yet another new avenue of research; the development of sedimentary basins. It was from this work that he produced a classic paper that has been widely accepted by oil companies as the "McKenzie Model of Sedimentary Basins."

McKenzie was elected a Fellow of the Royal Society in 1976 at just 34 years of age, and by 1978 was awarded a University Readership position.

Later Career

Dan McKenzie continues to work at the Bullard Laboratories in Cambridge where he holds a Royal Society Research Professorship, awarded in 1996. Most recently his research has provided new insights into the tectonic evolution of Mars and Venus.

In 2002 he was awarded the prestigious Crafoord Prize from the Royal Swedish Academy of Sciences for his contributions to research in the field of plate tectonics, sedimentary basin formation and mantle melting.

DIGBY MCLAREN

Dr. Digby Johns McLaren (December 11, 1919 – December 8, 2004) was a Canadian geologist and palaeontologist.

Born in Carrickfergus, Ireland and educated at Sedbergh School, he received a Bachelor of Arts in geology from the University of Cambridge. During World War II, he fought in the Middle East and Europe with the Royal Regiment of Artillery. After the war, he received a Master of Arts in geology from the University of Cambridge in 1948. In 1948, he moved to Canada and joined the Geological Survey of Canada (GSC). In 1951, he received a Ph.D. from the University of Michigan.

From 1959 to 1967, he was the head of the palaeontology section of the GSC. In 1967, he became the first director of the Institute of Sedimentary and Petroleum Geology of the GSC and in 1973 he was appointed Director of the Geological Survey of Canada. In 1981, he became Assistant Deputy Minister of Science and Technology for Energy, Mines and Resources Canada.

He was the author of over 100 publications and maps in the fields of palaeontology, biostratigraphy and regional geology. He was one of the early theorist of the Cretaceous-Tertiary extinction event.

From 1987 to 1990, he was the president of the Royal Society of Canada. He was also President of the Geological Society of America.

In 1942, he married to Phyllis Matkin with whom he had three children: Ian, Patrick, and Alison.

DOUGLAS MAWSON

Sir Douglas Mawson,(5 May 1882 – 14 October 1958) was an Australian Antarctic explorer and geologist. With Roald Amundsen, Robert Falcon Scott, and Ernest Shackleton, Mawson was a key expedition leader during the Heroic Age of Antarctic Exploration.

He was appointed geologist to an expedition to the New Hebrides (now Vanuatu) in 1903; his report *The geology of the New Hebrides*, was one of the first major geological works of Melanesia. Also that year he published a geological paper on Mittagong, New South Wales. His major influences in his geological career were

Professor Edgeworth David and Professor Archibald Liversidge. He then became a lecturer in petrology and mineralogy at the University of Adelaide in 1905. He identified and first described the mineral Davidite, named for Edgeworth David.

In 1907, Mawson joined the *British Antarctic Expedition* led by Ernest Shackleton as an expedition geologist. With his mentor and fellow geologist, Edgeworth David, he was on the first ascent of Mount Erebus. Later, he was a member of the first team to reach the South Magnetic Pole, assuming the leadership of the party from David on their perilous return.

Mawson's Australian Antarctic Expedition

Dawson turned down an invitation to join Robert Falcon Scott's Terra Nova Expedition in 1910; Australian geologist Griffith Taylor went instead. Dawson chose to lead his own expedition, the *Australian Antarctic Expedition*, to King George V Land and Adelie Land, the sector of the Antarctic continent immediately south of Australia, which at the time was almost entirely unexplored. The objectives were to carry out geographical exploration and scientific studies, including visiting the South Magnetic Pole.

The expedition, using the ship *Aurora* commanded by Captain John King Davis, departed Hobart on 2 December 1911, and landed at Cape Denison on Commonwealth Bay on 8 January 1912 and established the Main Base. A second camp was located to the west on the ice shelf in Queen Mary Land. Cape Denison proved to be unrelentingly windy; the average wind speed for the entire year was about 50 mph (80 km/h). They built a hut on the rocky cape and wintered through nearly constant blizzards. On pg. 133 in "The Home of the Blizzard Mawson wrote "...on the evening of May 24, in the form of Herculean gusts....the momentary velocity of these doubtlessly approached two hundred miles per hour."

Mawson's exploration programme was carried out by five parties from the Main Base and two from the Western Base. Mawson's team, which was to trek east, consisted of Xavier Mertz, Lieutenant B. E. S. Ninnis and himself. Nearing the end of this team's trek, Ninnis, his dog team and sledge with most of the provisions fell through a crevasse and were lost.

Mawson and Mertz turned back immediately. Mertz died during the return journey and Mawson continued alone. On one occasion during his return trip to the Main Base, he fell through the lid of a crevasse and was saved only by his sledge wedging itself into the ice above him. When he finally made it back to Cape Denison, the ship Aurora had left only a few hours before. Using wireless communication the ship was recalled only to have bad weather thwart the rescue effort. Mawson, and six men who had remained behind to look for him, wintered a second year until December 1913. In Mawson's book, *Home of the Blizzard*, he describes his experiences. His party, and those at the Western Base, had explored large areas of the Antarctic coast, describing its geology, biology and meteorology, and more closely defining the location of the south magnetic pole.

Dog Livers and Hypervitaminosis

The dogs became a food resource after Ninnis, his dog team and the sledge they were pulling fell into a crevasse and were lost, along with most of the food supply. The liver of one dog contains enough vitamin A to produce the condition called hypervitaminosis A. Mawson did not know this and fed more of the dog livers to Mertz, as the latter was the weaker of the two men, thus causing vitamin A poisoning and facilitating Mertz's demise.

The words of his first rescuer upon finding Mawson were "My God, which one are you?"

DUNCAN R. DERRY

Duncan R. Derry (1906–1987) was an internationally known Canadian economic geologist. He was largely responsible for the creation of the *World Atlas of Geological and Mineral Deposits*.

Derry was born in England. He obtained an honour science degree from University of Cambridge before moving to Canada. He attended the University of Toronto and obtained his M.A. and Ph.D. degrees in geology.

In 1935, he started work at Ventures Ltd., which later became Falconbridge Ltd.. Derry worked closely with Thayer Lindsley. He supervised exploration and mining programmes in Canada and many other countries, including South Africa, Greece, Guyana, Chile, Peru, and Greenland. His work at Venture was interrupted by World War II. He enlisted and served as a squadron leader navigation training officer.

In 1950, he compiled a tectonic map of Canada with John Sinclair Stevenson. It was the first time in Canada that structural data from government, university, and industry sources were combined and synthesized.

In 1954, Derry became president of Rio Tinto Exploration. He was apart of the acquisition and development of the Rio Algom's bit uranium mines in the Elliot Lake area of Ontario. In 1960, he left Rio to be a founding partner of the consulting firm Derry Michener Booth & Wahl.

Dr. Derry spent three years researching, compiling, funding and publishing the *World Atlas of Geological and Mineral Deposits*. In reference to his work on this textbook and his induction, the representative of the Canadian Mining Hall of Fame expressed that he, "added immeasurably not only to the advancement of the geological sciences and their practical application to mining development in Canada and elsewhere, but to the publication of world literature in the field."

Dr. Derry was a past-president of the Society of Economic Geologists. He was a part of founding Geological Association of Canada, the Canadian Geological Foundation, and the Canadian Geoscience Council.

DAVID SLOAN WILSON

David Sloan Wilson (1949-) is an American evolutionary biologist. Son of the author Sloan Wilson, David Sloan Wilson is a distinguished professor at Binghamton University. He is a prominent proponent of the concept of group selection (aka multi-level selection) in evolution. He has, along with Elliott Sober in their book *Unto Others* proposed a framework called multilevel selection theory, which incorporates the more orthodox approach of gene-level selection and individual selection. This framework argues that while genes serve as the means by which organisms' designs are transmitted across generations, individuals and groups are vehicles for those genes and both are arenas for genes to act on. Indeed, genes themselves can be affected by selection, not just because of their effects on the design of their vehicle (the organism) but also because of their effect on the functioning of the DNA on which they reside. Hence, the notion of multilevel selection. Wilson has also coined the concept of a trait-group, a group of organisms linked not permanently as a group but having a shared fate due to interactions that they have.

Wilson's book *Darwin's Cathedral* proposes that religion is a multi-level adaptation, a product of cultural evolution developed through a process of multi-level selection. His latest book *Evolution for Everyone: How Darwin's Theory Can Change the Way We Think About Our Lives* attempts to give an introduction to evolution for a broad audience, detailing the various ways in which evolution can be applied to everyday affairs.

Wilson started the Evolutionary Studies (EvoS) programme at Binghamton University to provide a programme that unifies diverse disciplines under the theory of evolution. Students in the programme take evolution-themed courses in a variety of disciplines including biology, anthropology, psychology, bioengineering, and philosophy. SUNY New Paltz has started a similar programme.

DAVID WEATHERALL

Sir David John Weatherall (born 9 March 1933) is a British physician and researcher in molecular genetics, haematology, pathology and clinical medicine. His research concentrated on the genetics of the haemoglobinopathies and, in particular, a group of inherited haematological disorders known as the thalassemias that are associated with abnormalities in the production of globin (the protein component of haemoglobin). Weatherall is one of the world's experts on the clinical and molecular basis of the thalassemias and the application of this information for the control and prevention of these diseases in the developing countries.

Weatherall was educated at Calday Grange Grammar School and then graduated from the Medical School at the University of Liverpool in 1956. After house staff training, he joined the Army for 2 years. Returning from military service, he took a fellowship at Johns Hopkins University before returning to Liverpool, where he rose to the rank of Professor of Haematology.

In 1974 Weatherall was appointed Nuffield Professor of Clinical Medicine at the University of Oxford, and, in 1992, he assumed the most prestigious chair, that of Regius Professor of Medicine, from 1992 to 2000.

He was knighted in 1987.

In 1989 Weatherall founded the Institute of Molecular Medicine at Oxford, which was renamed the Weatherall Institute of Molecular Medicine in his honour in the year 2000 upon his retirement. He then became Chancellor of Keele University.

In 2002 Weatherall wrote a major report on the application of genomics for global health for the World Health Organization. Sir David is a Distinguished Supporter of the British Humanist Association.

In 2006 a working group report under the Chairmanship of Professor David Weatherall concludes that there is a strong scientific case to maintain biomedical research activities using non-human primates in carefully selected areas.

DAVID SUZUKI

David Takayoshi Suzuki (born March 24, 1936), is a Canadian science broadcaster and environmental activist. Since the mid-1970s, Suzuki has been known for his TV and radio series and books about nature and the environment. He is best known as host of the popular and long-running CBC Television science magazine, *The*

Nature of Things, seen in syndication in over 40 nations. He is also well known for criticizing governments for their lack of action to protect the environment.

A long time activist to reverse global climate change, Suzuki co-founded the David Suzuki Foundation in 1990, to work "to find ways for society to live in balance with the natural world that sustains us." The Foundation's priorities are: oceans and sustainable fishing, climate change and clean energy, sustainability, and David Suzuki's Nature Challenge. He also served as a director of the Canadian Civil Liberties Association from 1982-1987.

Early Life

Suzuki had a twin sister named Marcia, as well as two other siblings, Geraldine (now known as Aiko) and Dawn. They were born to Setsu Nakamura and Kaoru Carr Suzuki in Vancouver, Canada. Suzuki's maternal and paternal grandparents had immigrated to Canada at the beginning of the 20th century.

A third-generation Japanese-Canadian ("Canadian Sansei"), Suzuki and his family suffered internment in British Columbia during the Second World War from when he was six (1942) until after the war ended. In June 1942, the government sold the Suzuki family's dry-cleaning business, then interned Suzuki, his mother, and two sisters in a camp at Slocan in the British Columbia Interior. His father had been sent to a labour camp in Solsqua two months earlier. Suzuki's sister, Dawn, was born in the internment camp.

After the war, Suzuki's family, like other Japanese Canadian families, was forced to move east of the Rockies. The Suzukis moved to Islington, Leamington, and London, Ontario. David Suzuki, in interviews, has many times credited his father for having interested and sensitized him to nature.

Suzuki attended Mill Street Elementary School and Grade 9 at Leamington Secondary School before moving to London, where he attended London Central Secondary School, eventually winning the election to become Students' Council President in his last year there by more votes than all of the other candidates combined. In 2006, David Suzuki was the recipient of the Bradford Washburn Award presented at the Museum of Science in Boston, Massachusetts.

DAVID STATES

David J. States is a Professor of Human Genetics at the University of Michigan. His research group is using computational methods to understand the human genome and how it relates to the human proteome. He is the Director of the Michigan NIH Bioinformatics Training Programme and a Senior Scientist in the National Centre for Integrative Biomedical Informatics.

Dr. States earned his BA ('75), MD ('83) and PhD ('83) degrees at Harvard University. He was a Staff Scientist at the National Magnet Laboratory at MIT and a resident in internal medicine at UCSD Medical Centre.

He then moved to the NIH as a Clinical Associate and Senior Staff Fellow where he joined the National Centre for Biotechnology Information (NCBI). While at NCBI, he and Warren Gish enhanced BLAST, one of the most widely used programmes in bioinformatics. In 1992, Dr. States was recruited to Washington University as Director of the Institute for Biomedical Computing, and in 2001, he moved to the University of Michigan to establish the University of Michigan Bioinformatics Programme. He was a member of the founding Board of Directors and Treasurer of the International Society for Computational Biology and Chair of the 1996 and 2005 Intelligent Systems for Molecular Biology Conferences.

Dr. States is also known for his work in nuclear magnetic resonance where he developed pure absorption phase multi-dimensional spectroscopy, a technique now widely used in protein structure determination. Dr. States also contributed to computational biophysics as an author of the CHARMM molecular dynamics simulation programme. He combined NMR spectroscopy and modeling to demonstrate for the first time the presence of native-like structure in the folding intermediates of bovine pancreatic trypsin inhibitor and the first demonstration of a conformationally trapped folding intermediate.

DAVID T. LYKKEN

David Thoreson Lykken (June 18, 1928-September 15, 2006) was a behavioural geneticist and Professor Emeritus of Psychology and Psychiatry at the University of Minnesota. He is best known for his work on twin studies.

Life

Born in Minneapolis, Minnesota, at 17, Lykken joined the United States Navy, then attended University of Minnesota on the G.I. Bill, earning his bachelor of arts (psychology, philosophy and mathematics) 1949, his masters degree in psychology and statistics in 1952, and his doctorate in clinical psychology and neuropsychiatry in 1955. He remained on Minnesota's permanent faculty for his entire career and taught as a visiting professor at Deep Springs College. He was an emeritus professor from 1998 until his death.

Work

Lykken was also known for his work on twins, which he began in 1970. He was a principal investigator on the Minnesota Twin Family Study, which examines heritability of certain psychological traits based on evidence found in identical and fraternal twins. He was a signatory of a collective statement in response to *The Bell Curve* titled "Mainstream Science on Intelligence", written by *Intelligence* editor Linda Gottfredson and published in the *Wall Street Journal* in 1994 and in *Intelligence* in 1997.

Lykken was the proponent of a set-point theory of happiness, which argues that one's sense of well-being is half determined by genetics and half determined by circumstances, and has been the subject of international media attention. His research findings suggest that a person's baseline levels of cheerfulness, contentment, and psychological satisfaction are largely a matter of heredity. He was elected a Fellow of the American Psychological Association

(Division 1), a Charter Fellow of the American Psychological Society and a Fellow of the American Association for the Advancement of Science. He was also a member of the Behaviour Genetics Association and the International Society for Twin Research. Throughout his career, he consulted with government and industry. He frequently testified as an expert witness on polygraph testing and personality assessment in the wake of Daubert standard requirements.

DOROTHY CROWFOOT HODGKIN

Dorothy Mary Hodgkin, (12 May 1910 – 29 July 1994) was a British chemist, credited with the discovery of protein crystallography

She pioneered the technique of X-ray crystallography, a method used to determine the three dimensional structures of biomolecules. Among her most influential discoveries are the determination of the structure of penicillin and vitamin B12, for which she was awarded the Nobel Prize in Chemistry. In 1969, after 35 years of work and five years after winning the Nobel Prize in Chemistry, Hodgkin was able to decipher the structure of insulin. She is regarded as one of the foremost scientists in the field of X-Ray crystallography studies of natural molecules. Besides her extraordinary scientific abilities, she was unassuming, very communicative, and passionate about social inequalities and peace.

Early Years

She was born Dorothy Mary Crowfoot in May 12, 1910 in Cairo, Egypt, to John Crowfoot, excavator and scholar of classics, and Grace Mary Crowfoot *nee* Hood. For the first four years of her life she lived as an English expatriate in Asia Minor, returning to England only a few months each year. She spent the period of World War I in the UK under the care of relatives and friends, but separated from her parents. After the war, her mother decided to stay home in England and educate her children, a period that Hodgkin later described as the happiest in her life.

In 1921, she entered the Sir John Leman Grammar School in Beccles, Suffolk. She travelled abroad frequently to visit her parents in Cairo and Khartoum. Both her father and her mother had a strong influence with their Puritan ethic of selflessness and service to humanity which reverberated in her later achievements.

Education and Research

She developed a passion for chemistry from a young age, and her mother fostered her interest in science in general. Her excellent early education prepared her well for university. At age 18 she started studying chemistry at Somerville College, Oxford, then one of the University of Oxford colleges for women only.

She also studied at the University of Cambridge under the tutelage of John Desmond Bernal, where she became aware of the potential of X-ray crystallography to determine the structure of proteins. In 1934, she moved back to Oxford and two years later, in 1936, she became a research fellow at Somerville College, a post which she held until 1977. In 1960 she was appointed Wolfson Research Professor at the Royal Society.

DEAN HAMER

Dr. Dean Hamer (born 1951) is a geneticist, who, as of 2007 is the director of the Gene Structure and Regulation Unit at the U.S. National Cancer Institute (part of the National Institutes of Health). He obtained his BA at Trinity College, CT, U.S. and his Ph.D from Harvard Medical School. In the 1990s Hamer began studies of the role of genes in human behaviour. In 1993 he published a paper suggesting the existence of genes that predispose men towards homosexuality, and presented evidence that one of these genes was associated with the Xq28 marker on the X chromosome. Subsequently, several additional linked regions on other chromosomes have been described, and the heritability of sexual orientation has been confirmed via improved twin studies.

In 1996, Hamer and colleagues investigated the genetic roots of anxiety, and found that the gene for the serotonin transporter, which is the target of antidepressant drugs such as Prozac, is partially responsible. This polymorphism has been extensively investigated in over 300 scientific studies (as of 2006), and its activity has been confirmed by direct brain imaging studies. More recently, Hamer has postulated the existence of a God gene for religious experience. This work, which was featured on the cover of Time magazine, has been predictably controversial.

Currently Hamer is conducting research into the field of Human Immunodeficiency Virus (HIV) microbicides and HIV latency. This work involves engineering and animal model testing of a live microbial microbicide. By engineering a non-pathogenic endrogenous strain of E. coli (nissle 1917) to secrete HIV fusion inhibiting peptides on the sexual mucosa of patients Hamer hopes to create a long lasting, transparent, barrier to HIV infection.

In addition to his scientific work, he has published a number of popular science books aimed at a general readership and is the holder of a number of patents.

DAVID BOTSTEIN

David Botstein (born 1942 in Switzerland) is an American biologist who has been the director of the Lewis-Sigler Institute for Integrative Genomics at Princeton University since 2003.

He graduated from Harvard in 1963 and received a Ph.D. from the University of Michigan in 1967. He then taught at the Massachusetts Institute of Technology, where he became a Professor of Genetics. In 1990, he became Chairman of the Department of Genetics at Stanford University. He has also worked for Genentech, as the Vice President-Science. Dr. Botstein was elected to the U.S. National Academy of Sciences in 1981 and to the Institute of Medicine in 1993.

Professor Botstein is known for his commitment to education. He is the director of the Integrated Science Programme at Princeton University. Many of his students have gone on to be very successful in the field of molecular biology.

In 1980, David Botstein and his colleagues Ray White, Mark Scolnick, and Ron Davis proposed a method for mapping genes that was used in subsequent years to identify several human disease genes including Huntington's and BRCA1. Variations of this method were used in the mapping efforts that predated and enabled the sequencing phase of the Human Genome Project.

In 1998, David Botstein and his postdoctoral fellow Michael Eisen, together with graduate student Paul Spellman and colleague Patrick Brown, developed a statistical method and graphical interface that is widely used to interpret genomic data including microarray data. Dr. Botstein has won the Eli Lilly and Company Award in Microbiology (1978), the Genetics Society of America Medal (1988), the Allen Award of the American Society of Human Genetics (1989) and the Gruber Prize in Genetics (2003).

He is the brother of Leon Botstein. Both of Botstein's parents were physicians and Holocaust survivors.

DANIEL RUTHERFORD

Daniel Rutherford (3 November 1749 – 15 November 1819) was a Scottish chemist and physician who was most famous for the isolation of nitrogen in 1772.

Daniel Rutherford was born in Edinburgh and was educated at the University of Edinburgh where his father John Rutherford (1695–1779) was a professor of medicine. As a student, he isolated nitrogen in 1772 and described oxygen, or "vital air" as he called it, in 1778. In 1786, he was appointed Regius Professor of Botany in Edinburgh and as Keeper of the Royal Botanic Garden Edinburgh, after the death of Professor John Hope (1725–86). Rutherford held these posts until his death. His daughter Margaret, a very pretty young lady, married James Haldane and he was also a maternal uncle of Sir Walter Scott.

Isolation of Nitrogen

When Joseph Black was studying the properties of carbon dioxide, he found that a candle would not burn in it. When a candle was burned in a closed container of air, the candle would go out eventually, and the remaining air would not support a flame. This was normal, but when the carbon dioxide (caused by the candle) was absorbed by chemicals, some air was not absorbed. The air that remained did not support a flame. He turned this problem over to his student at the time, Daniel Rutherford. Rutherford kept a mouse in a space with a confined quality of air until it died. Then, he burned a candle in the remaining air until it went out. Afterwards, he burned phosphorus in that, until it would not burn. Then the air was passed through a carbon dioxide absorbing solution. The remaining air did not support combustion, and a mouse could not live in it. Rutherford called the gas (which we now know would have consisted primarily of nitrogen) "noxious air" or "phlogisticated air".

Rutherford reported the experiment in 1772. He and Black were convinced of the validity of the phlogiston theory, so they explained their results in terms of the theory. They said that as mice breathed and combustion was created, phlogiston was given off and entered the air, along with the carbon dioxide. When the carbon dioxide was later absorbed, the air still contained phlogiston. In fact, the air was saturated with it. That was why candles and other objects would not burn in it. Rutherford believed that, in like manner, a living creature gives up phlogiston while breathing and when placed in air that is already saturated with phlogiston, can no longer breathe and must die.

DMITRI MENDELEEV

Dmitri Ivanovich Mendeleev (8 February [O.S. 27 January] 1834 – 2 February [O.S. 20 January] 1907), was a Russian chemist and inventor. He is credited as being the creator of the first version of the periodic table of elements. Unlike other contributors to the table, Mendeleev predicted the properties of elements yet to be discovered.

Life

Dmitri Mendeleev was born in Tobolsk, Siberia, to Ivan Pavlovich Mendeleev and Maria Dmitrievna Mendeleeva (born

Kornilieva). His grandfather was Pavel Maximovich Sokolov, a Russian priest. Ivan, along with his brothers, obtained new family names while attending Tver theological seminary.

Mendeleev was the youngest of 17 siblings, but the exact number differs among sources. At the age of 13, after the passing of his father and the destruction of his mother's factory by fire, Mendeleev attended the Gymnasium in Tobolsk.

In 1849, the now poor Mendeleev family relocated to St. Petersburg, where he entered the Main Pedagogical Institute in 1850. After graduation, an illness that was diagnosed as tuberculosis caused him to move to the Crimean Peninsula on the northern coast of the Black Sea in 1855. While there he became chief science master of the Simferopol gymnasium. He returned with fully restored health to St. Petersburg in 1857.

Between 1859 and 1861, he worked on the capillarity of liquids and the workings of the spectroscope in Heidelberg. In the late august of 1861 he wrote his first book on the spectroscope in which it received high acclaim. In 1862, he married Feozva Nikitichna Leshcheva. Mendeleev became Professor of Chemistry at the Saint Petersburg Technological Institute and the University of St. Petersburg in 1863 he achieved tenure in 1867, and by 1871 had transformed St. Petersburg into an internationally recognized centre for chemistry research. In 1865 he became Doctor of Science for his dissertation "On the Combinations of Water with Alcohol". In 1876, he became obsessed with Anna Ivanova Popova and began courting her; in 1881 he proposed to her and threatened suicide if she refused. His divorce from Leshcheva was finalized one month after he had married Popova in early 1882.

Even after the divorce, Mendeleev was technically a bigamist; the Russian Orthodox Church required at least 7 years before lawful re-marriage. His divorce and the surrounding controversy contributed to his failure to be admitted to the Russian Academy of Sciences (despite his international fame by that time). His daughter from his second marriage, Lyubov, became the wife of the famous Russian poet Alexander Blok. His other children were son Vladimir (a sailor, he took part in the notable Eastern journey of Nicholas II) and daughter Olga, from his first marriage to Feozva, and son Ivan and a pair of twins from Anna. Though Mendeleev was widely honoured by scientific organizations all over Europe, including the Copley Medal from the Royal Society of London, he resigned from St. Petersburg University on August 17, 1890.

In 1893, he was appointed Director of the Bureau of Weights and Measures. It was in this role that he was directed to formulate new state standards for the production of vodka. His fascination with molecular weights led him to conclude that to be in perfect molecular balance, vodka should be produced in the ratio of one molecule of ethyl alcohol diluted with two molecules of water, giving a dilution by volume of approximately 38% alcohol to 62% water. As a result of his work, in 1894 new standards for vodka were introduced into Russian law and all vodka had to be produced at 40% alcohol by volume.

Mendeleev also investigated the composition of oil fields, and helped to found the first oil refinery in Russia.

Mendeleev died in 1907 in St. Petersburg, Russia from influenza. The Mendeleev crater on the Moon, as well as element number 101, the radioactive mendelevium, are named after him.

DUDLEY R. HERSCHBACH

Dudley Robert Herschbach (born June 18, 1932) is an American chemist at Harvard University. He won the 1986 Nobel Prize in Chemistry jointly with Yuan T. Lee and John C. Polanyi "for their contributions concerning the dynamics of chemical elementary processes." Herschbach and Lee specifically worked with molecular beams, performing so-called "crossed molecular beam" experiments that enabled a detailed molecular-level understanding of many elementary reaction processes.

Herschbach was born in San Jose, California. After graduating from Campbell High School, Herschbach received a B.S. in mathematics in 1954 and an M.S. in chemistry in 1955 from Stanford University, and an A.M. in physics in 1956 and a Ph.D. in chemical physics in 1958 from Harvard University under the direction of Edgar Bright Wilson. His recent work includes a collaboration with Steven Brams studying approval voting.

Herschbach's research has ranged broadly over the field of chemical physics, including much theoretical work in dimensional scaling. Hershbach's teaching ranges from graduate seminars on chemical kinetics to an introductory undergraduate course in general chemistry that he taught for many years at Harvard and described as his "most challenging assignment."

Herschbach has been a strong proponent of science education and science among the general public, and frequently gives lectures to students of all ages, imbuing them with his infectious enthusiasm for science and his playful spirit of discovery. Herschbach has also lent his voice to the animated television show *The Simpsons* for the episode "Treehouse of Horror XIV" where he is seen presenting the Nobel Prize in Physics to Professor Frink.

Although still an active research professor at Harvard, he joined the Texas A&M University faculty September 1, 2005 as a Professor of Physics.

He is a board member of the Centre for Arms Control and Non-Proliferation. He is also an Eagle Scout and recipient of the Distinguished Eagle Scout Award (DESA).

Herschbach is a member of the Board of Sponsors of The Bulletin of the Atomic Scientists.

His wife, Georgene Herschbach, is the Associate Dean of Harvard College for Undergraduate Academic Programmes. She chairs Harvard's influential Committee on Undergraduate Education.

DAVID VAN GOORLE

David van Goorle also known under his Latinized name *David Gorlaeus* (15 January 1591, Utrecht-21 April 1612, Cornjum) was a Dutch scientist, and in the seventeenth century one of the first early modern atomists. Van Goorle was born as the son of a Protestant refugee from Antwerp, who at the time was treasurer for the Count of Moers, and a Frisian noblewoman. Although he called himself *Ultrajectinus* after his birthplace Utrecht, he grew up with his maternal grandparents in the Frisian village of Cornjum. In 1606 he enrolled as a student in arts at the University of Franeker. From April 1611, Van Goorle studied theology at the University of Leiden, and expressed his theories regarding the theories of atoms in his Ideae Physicae, in which he disputes the theories of Aristotle and claims that there is something as a "smallest, undevidable, paricle".

For the early seventeenth century these were revolutionary thoughts, and hence Van Goorle is sometimes seen as one of the founders of the particle-atom theory. He died at the very early age of 21; on his tombstone in the church of Cornjum he is mourned as an "erudite and very intelligent young man". His larger work, *Exercitationes philosophicae*, was only printed posthumously in 1620. It is thought that especially this last work has influenced Henricus Regius and Descartes.

The University of Leiden has named the Gorlaeus Laboratoria after Van Goorle, in which the both education is given to students in chemical studies and chemical research is performed.

DEREK BARTON

Sir Derek Harold Richard Barton (8 September 1918-16 March 1998) was a British organic chemist and Nobel Prize laureate.

Barton was to William Thomas and Maude Henrietta Barton. In 1938 he entered Imperial College, University of London, where he graduated in 1940 and obtained his Ph.D. degree in Organic Chemistry in 1942. From then to 1944 he was a government research chemist, from 1944 to 1945 he was with Albright and Wilson in Birmingham. He then became assistant lecturer in the Department of Chemistry of Imperial College, and from 1946 to 1949 he was ICI Research Fellow. During 1949 and 1950 he was Visiting Lecturer in the Chemistry of Natural Products, at Harvard University, and was then appointed Reader in Organic Chemistry and, in 1953, Professor at Birkbeck College. In 1955 he became Regius Professor of Chemistry at the University of Glasgow, in 1957 he was appointed Professor of Organic Chemistry at Imperial College.

In 1950, Professor Barton showed that organic molecules could be assigned a preferred conformation based upon results accumulated by chemical physicists, in particular by Odd Hassel. Using this new technique of "conformational analysis", he later determined the geometry of many other natural product molecules. In 1969, Barton was awarded the Nobel Prize in Chemistry for "contributions to the development of the concept of conformation and its application in chemistry."

In 1958 Prof. Barton was Arthur D. Little Visiting Professor at Massachusetts Institute of Technology, and in 1959 Karl Folkers Visiting Professor at the Universities of Illinois and Wisconsin.

In 1954 he was elected to Fellowship of the Royal Societyand the International Academy of Science, in 1956 he became Fellow of the Royal Society of Edinburgh; in 1965 he was appointed member of the Council for Scientific Policy. He was knighted in 1972 but chose to be known as Sir Derek only in Britain. In 1978 he became Director of the Institut de Chimie des Substances Naturelles (ICSN-Gif Sur-Yvette) in France.

In 1986 he became Distinguished Professor at Texas A&M and held this position for 12 years until his death.

As well as for his work on conformation, his name is remembered in a number of reactions in organic chemistry such as the Barton-McCombie deoxygenation.

He married three times, and had a son by his first marriage. He died in College Station Texas.

DEEPAL WARAKAGODA

Deepal Warakagoda (born 1965) is a prominent Sri Lankan ornithologist. His early working career was in electronics, but for many years he has studied birds and also works as a professional guide for birding tours of the island. He discovered a new species of bird endemic to Sri Lanka, the Serendib Scops Owl. His expertise in vocalizations had enabled him to realize that an owl be heard calling near Kitulgala was an unknown species, and he later saw this bird in January 2001 in the Sinharaja rainforest..

He has also identified (each for the first time) 15 new migrant species of birds in Sri Lanka, and has published a large number of articles on the avifauna of Sri Lanka.

Warakgoda is Sri Lanka's foremost sound recordist in natural history subjects, and has produced and published the only comprehensive audio guide to the island's birds (on tape and CD). He has an unmatched knowledge of Sri Lanka's bird songs and calls. His recordings of the island's distinct bird species have played a major role in the recognition of several of them as endemic to Sri Lanka in the book Birds of South Asia. The Repley Guide (2005) by Pamela C. Rasmussen and John C. Anderton. Although best known for his knowledge of the avifauna of Sri Lanka, and expertise in finding and identifying birds, his knowledge extends to the island's mammals and butterflies.

Warakagoda founded the Drongo Nature Sounds Library, the only one of its kind in Sri Lanka, and is joint secretary of the Ceylon Bird Club. He is a national coordinator in Sri Lanka for the Asian Waterbird Census. He is a founder of Bird and Wildlife Team.

He is currently working on several new publications in the print and audio/video media, including Field Guide to the Birds of Sri Lanka, of which he is co-author with three authorities on the avifauna of Asia.

DANIEL SOLANDER

Daniel Carlsson Solander or *Daniel Charles Solander* (19 February 1733– 13 May 1782) was a Swedish botanist.

Solander was born in Pitea, Norrland, Sweden and was the son of a Lutheran principal. He enrolled at Uppsala University in July 1750 and studied languages and the humanities. The professor of botany was the celebrated Carolus Linnaeus who was soon impressed by young Solander's ability and accordingly persuaded his father to let him study natural history. He travelled to England in 1760 to promote Linnaeus' new system of classification. He was an assistant librarian at the British Museum from 1763 onwards, and elected as Fellow of the Royal Society in the following year. Afterwards he held the position of Keeper of Printed Books at the British Museum.

In 1768 Solander and his fellow scientist Dr. Herman Sporing were employed by Joseph Banks, to join him on James Cook's first voyage to the Pacific Ocean on board the *Endeavour.* They were the botanists who inspired the name *Botanist Bay* (which later became Botany Bay), Cook's expedition's first landing place in Australia. Solander helped make and describe an important collection of Australian plants while the Endeavour was beached at the site of present-day Cooktown for nearly 7 weeks, after being damaged on the Great Barrier Reef. These collections later formed the basis of Banks' Florilegium.

On their return in 1771 he became Banks' secretary and librarian and lived in his house at Soho Square. In 1772 he accompanied Banks on his voyage to Iceland, the Faroes and the Orkney Islands. Between 1773 and 1782 he was Keeper of the Natural History Department of the British Museum.

Solander invented the book-form box known as the Solander box which is still used in libraries and archives as the most suitable way of storing prints, drawings, herbarium materials and some manuscripts.

He died at Banks' home in Soho Square of a stroke, aged 49, at 9.30pm on 13 May 1782. An autopsy was performed the next day, and revealed a brain haemorrhage.

Solander Gardens in the east end of London is named after him, as are the Solander Islands off New Zealand's South Island. One of the many plants named in his honour is *Nothofagus solandri.* He was associated with Banks in *Illustrations of the Botany of Captain Cook's Voyage Round the World,* and his *The Natural History of Many*

Curious and Uncommon Zoophytes, Collected by the late John Ellis, was published posthumously in 1786.

The standard author abbreviation *Sol.* is used to indicate this individual as the author when citing a botanical name.

DAVID ANDREW PHOENIX

David Andrew Phoenix was born in 1966 in Greater Manchester, England. After attending school in Bolton he progressed to study Biochemistry at Liverpool University where he graduated with a Bachelor of Science. He remained at Liverpool to complete his Doctorate on penicillin binding proteins and after postdoctoral work in England and the Netherlands he began work at the University of Central Lancashire where he is now Deputy Vice Chancellor responsible for areas of strategic planning and performance across the University group.

Academic Background

David Phoenix read Biochemistry and obtained his Bachelor of Science degree from the University of Liverpool in 1987. This was followed by completion of his Doctor of Philosophy, again in Biochemistry in 1991. In 1993 he obtained a Bachelor of Arts degree from the Open University which focused on mathematics. This was followed by a Masters in Education (1999) and a Masters in Business Administration (2005). He has published widely on the structure-function relationship of amphiphilic biomolecules, obtaining his Chair in Biochemistry in 2002. In addition to research monographs he has also been recognised for publication of undergraduate textbooks. In addition to sitting on the editorial boards for a range of international scientific journals he has been Editor in Chief of The Journal of Biological Education and of periodicals such as Biologist which are aimed at a broader readership.

Career History

His PhD work engaged his interest in the role amphipilicity plays in driving the interaction of bioactive molecules with cell membranes. He was awarded a Long Term Fellowship by the European Molecular Biology Organisation which enabled him to investigate the importance of amphiphilicty in protein translocation at Utrecht University Centre for Biomembranes and Lipid Enzymology. He continued to work on amphiphilic helices, being one of the first to help characterise their role as membrane protein anchors. He later expanded this work to investigate the importance of structure-function relationships in the design of antimicrobial peptides. He was made a Reader in Biochemistry in 1998 and in 2000 was awarded a Chair in Biochemistry at the University of Central Lancashire. From 1996-1999 he was a Visiting Professor in Bioinformatics at Moscow Engineering Physics Institute (MEPhI) where he began developing his interest in algorithms for identification of low homology repeat sequences.

In 1993, as a founder member of the Lancashire Centre for Medical Studies, his work with local NHS Trusts was recognised by the award of a Visiting Consultants title by the Health Authority. He also continued to act as a consultant to pharmaceutical companies such as SmithKline Beecham.

In 2000 he launched a new Department of Forensic and Investigative Science at the University of Central Lancashire and became its inaugural head. For his work in this area, and support given, he was made a Distinguished Visiting Professor by the University of Ontario Institute of Technology in 2004. He was successful in obtaining funds from the Higher Education Funding Council (HEFCE) in the UK to set up a National Knowledge Exchange focused on crime reduction in partnership with other Universities and business. He also provided the Regional Crime Lead for the Northwest on a HEFCE funded regeneration bid and advised the Sector Skills Council for Science Engineering, Manufacturing and Technology (SEMTA) on issues related to developing degrees in Forensic Science.

During 2002 he became Dean of Science and launched a new School of Pharmacy. At this time he began developing links overseas with the aim of expanding higher education opportunity, especially in India. He was invited to become a member of the D Y Patil Academic Council supporting a range of educational institutes in India such as the D. Y. Patil college of Engineering and Technology, Kolhapur. During this time he also remained the UK representative on the European Committee of Biological Associations (ECBA) and for a while was a Commissioner for Biotechnology.

In 2008 he became Deputy Vice-Chancellor with responsibility for strategic planning and performance across the University of Central Lancashire group.

DONALD C. PEATTIE

Donald Culross Peattie (June 21, 1898-November 16, 1964) was a U.S. botanist, naturalist and author. He was described by Joseph Wood Krutch as "perhaps the most widely read of all contemporary American nature writers" during his heyday.

Biography

Peattie was born in Chicago and initially studied French poetry for two years at the University of Chicago. He then transferred to, and graduated (1922) from, Harvard University where he studied with the noted botanist Merritt Lyndon Fernald. After field work in the Southern and Mid-West United States, he worked as a botanist for the U.S. Department of Agriculture (1922-1924).

He was nature columnist for the *The Washington Star* from 1924 to 1935.

His nature writings are distinguished by a poetic and philosophical cast of mind and are scientifically scrupulous. His best known works are the two books (out of a planned trilogy) on North American trees which he wrote in the late 1940s and early '50s. These were published as a single volume for the first time in April 2007 as *A Natural History of North American Trees.* (Unfortunately, this hardbound volume reduces the two books' original 257 mini-essays to only 112 and includes only 135 of Paul Landacre's original 365 woodcut illustrations.) Peattie also produced children's and travel books, altogether totalling almost forty volumes.

DESMOND MORRIS

Desmond John Morris (born 24 January 1928 in the village of Purton, north Wiltshire, UK) is most famous for his work as a zoologist and ethologist, but is also known as a surrealist artist and author.

Early Life and Career

He was educated at Dauntsey's School, an independent school in West Lavington, Wiltshire. After military service, he attended the University of Birmingham where he graduated in 1951 with a First Class Honours Degree in Zoology. In 1954, he was awarded a D.Phil. from Oxford University for his doctoral thesis on the *Reproductive Behaviour of the Ten-spined Stickleback*, supervised by Niko Tinbergen. He then was employed by the Zoological Society of London as Curator of Mammals at the London Zoo, which he left in 1966 in frustration about stagnation at the zoo.

He is sometimes wrongly stated to be a relative of Welsh zoologist, Johnny Morris, but this is not the case.

Writer and Broadcaster

He first came to public attention in the 1950s as a presenter of the ITV television programme *Zoo Time*, but achieved worldwide fame in 1967 with his book "The Naked Ape". The book is an unabashed look at the human species, notable for its focus on humanity's animal-like qualities and our similarity with apes, and for explaining human behaviour as largely evolved to meet the challenges of prehistoric life as a hunter-gatherer. Reprinted many times and in many languages, it continues to be a best-seller.

His later studies, books and television shows have continued this focus on human behaviour, explained from a bluntly zoological point of view. This approach itself, and his specific conclusions, have often attracted controversy.

Morris' theories explaining elements of human behaviour via a zoological lens, in particular via natural evolutionary mechanisms, have been attacked in some quarters of the popular media and by religious fundamentalists and extremists as incomplete, incorrect, or simplistic, though no alternative is ever given or cited. Some explanations have also been criticised for being allegedly male-centred or supporting a sexist view of sexual behaviour. Some contend that his comments are often untestable, and as a result unscientific.

However, it is generally a given by more objective scientific minds that his explanations are balanced, well thought out and more liable to be correct. Religious objectors to Darwinism reject on principle the idea humans are dominated by strictly animal instincts. Nevertheless, supporters defend him for starting, or at least bringing into mainstream discussion, the approach of applying principles of animal behaviourism to explaining human behaviour.

Art

In addition to his scientific pursuits, he is an artist in the Surrealist tradition. Morris has exhibited with Joan Miro and contributed significantly to the British Surrealist movement. He had his first solo show in 1948, and has shown regularly ever since. In 1957, he curated an exhibition of chimpanzee paintings and drawings at the Institute of Contemporary Arts, London, including paintings by a young chimpanzee called Congo.

DAVID LACK

David Lambert Lack (16 July 1910 – 12 March 1973) was a British ornithologist and biologist.

Early Life

Lack was born in London and educated at Gresham's School, Holt, Norfolk, and Magdalene College, Cambridge, where he studied Natural Sciences. He was the oldest of four children of Harry Lambert Lack MD FRCS, who later became President of the British Medical Association. The name 'Lack' is derived from 'Lock'. His father grew up in a farming family from Norfolk and became a leading ear, nose and throat surgeon at the London Hospital.

Although his father had some interest in birds as a boy it does not appear that he influenced David's interest. His mother Kathleen was the daughter of Lt. Col. McNeil Rind of the Indian army. Kathleen's father was Scottish and on her mother's side was part Irish, Greek and Georgian.

Until the age of fifteen, Lack lived in a large house in Devonshire Place, London. By the age of nine, he had learnt the names of most birds and had written out an alphabetically arranged life-list.

Career

After Cambridge, he became a schoolmaster at Dartington Hall School, Devonshire until Summer 1938 when he took a year off to study bird behaviour on the Galapagos Islands. He was only in the Galapagos for part of that year, starting August 1938. April to August 1939 was spent at the California Academy of Sciences and at Ernst Mayr's home in New Jersey. He returned home in September 1939, after the outbreak of war.

During World War II Lack served in the British Army working on radar research. After hostilities ended he was made Director of the Edward Grey Institute of Field Ornithology at Oxford University (1945-1973). His wartime experience enabled him to make radar observations of bird migration.

Lack's work in ornithology was almost entirely based on studies of the *living bird.* He was one of the pioneers of life-history studies in Britain, especially those based on quantitative approaches, when some traditional ornithologists of the time were focussing their studies on morphology and geographic distribution. Lack's major scientific research included work on population biology and density dependent regulation. His work suggested that natural selection favoured clutch sizes that ensured the greatest number of surviving young. This interpretation was however debated by V.C. Wynne-Edwards who suggested that clutch-size was density-independent.

This was one of the earliest debates on group selection. Lack's studies were based on nidicolous birds and some recent studies have suggested that this may not hold for other groups such as seabirds.

He wrote numerous papers in ornithological journals, and had a knack of choosing memorable titles: he once claimed to have single-handedly caused the renaming of a group of birds through the submission of a scientific paper, his 1935 publication, "Territory and polygamy in a bishop bird, *Euplectes hordeacea hordeacea* (Linn.)" in the journal *Ibis*.

Up to that point birds in the genus *Euplectes* had been referred to simply as bishops, but the journal editor felt that with that form the title might cause misunderstanding.

DAVID STARR JORDAN

David Starr Jordan, (January 19, 1851 – September 19, 1931) was a leading eugenicist, ichthyologist (the study of fish), educator and peace activist. He was president of Indiana University and Stanford University.

Jordan was born in Gainesville, New York, and studied at Cornell University, Butler University, and the Indiana University School of Medicine. In 1885, he was named President of Indiana University, becoming the nation's youngest university president at age 34.In 1891, he became president of Stanford, serving there as president until 1913 and chancellor until his retirement in 1916.

Although highly regarded as an ichthyologist, Jordan was best known for being a peace activist. He argued that war was detrimental to the human species because it removed the strongest organisms from the gene pool. Jordan was president of the World Peace Foundation from 1910 to 1914 and president of the World Peace Conference in 1915, and opposed U.S. involvement in World War I.

In 1925, Jordan was an expert witness for the defense in the Scopes Trial.

Jordan's papers are housed at Swarthmore College.

DANIEL JANZEN

Daniel Hunt Janzen (born 1939 in Milwaukee, Wisconsin, U.S.) is an evolutionary ecologist, naturalist, and conservationist. He divides his time between his professorship in biology at the University of Pennsylvania (Philadelphia, USA), where he has been since 1976, and his research and field work in Costa Rica, where he is an *ad honorem* (without remuneration) technical advisor for two long-term and long-range projects, which he conceived and initiated in the early 1970s: Area de Conservacion Guanacaste, probably the oldest, largest and most successful habitat restoration project in the world, 1.430 km^2, located just south of the Costa Rica-Nicaragua border, between the Pacific Ocean and the Cordillera de Tilaran; and the Instituto Nacional de Biodiversidad (INBio), a research organisation that has taken the task of inventorying, cataloguing and describing the country's gigantic natural endowment.

Janzen obtained his B.Sc. degree from the University of Minnesota, Minneapolis in 1961, and his Ph.D. from the University of California, Berkeley, in 1965. In 1964 he attended as a student a two-month course in tropical biology taught in several field sites throughout Costa Rica, offered by the Organization for Tropical Studies (OTS), a consortium of several North American and Costa Rican universities. He went back in 1965 as an instructor and has lectured in at least one of the three yearly courses every year since. Before joining the faculty at the University of Pennsylvania he taught at the University of Kansas (1965–1968), the University of Chicago (1969–1972) and at the University of Michigan (1972–1976). Janzen has also held teaching positions in Venezuela (Universidad de Oriente, Cumana in 1965-66; Universidad de los Los Andes, Merida in 1973), and in Puerto Rico (Universidad de Puerto Rico, Rio Piedras, 1969). From these teaching positions, because of his continuous association with OTS, through his numerous publications and mostly from his exemplary dedication, Janzen has been in close contact and influenced the thinking and ideas of just about every researcher and student of tropical ecology and conservation in the western hemisphere during the last 40 years.

Research, from Theory to Praxis and Back to Theory

Janzen's work exemplifies the dialectic method of research applied to the biology of the natural world. For him it has not been the passive analysis of documents and data about ecological processes in order to formulate theories, but rather the active creation of life size scenarios of ecological change and their careful and meticulous documentation from which he then formulates theories which inspire new grand experiments in an ever expanding spiral of knowledge based on the keen observation of nature. The following three sections are an attempt to synthesise the three main themes of his lifelong quest and work.

ERNST MACH

Ernst Mach (February 18, 1838 – February 19, 1916) was an Austrian physicist and philosopher and is the namesake for the "Mach number" (also known as Mach speed) and the optical illusion known as Mach bands.

Biography

Ernst Mach was born in Chrlice (then part of the Austrian empire, now part of Brno, Czech Republic). His father was tutor to the Brethon noble family in Zlin having graduated from Prague University]. Some sources state that Mach' birthplace was Tuoany, but this was where the Chrlice registry office was situated.

Up to the age of 14 he was educated at home by his parents. He then joined a Gymnasium in Kromioiz where he studied for three year. In 1855 he entered the University of Vienna. There he studied physics and for one semester medical physiology, receiving his doctorate in physics in 1860 and his Habilitation the following year. His early work focused on the Doppler effect in optics and acoustics. In 1864 he took a job as Professor of Mathematics in Graz, and in 1866 he was appointed as Professor of Physics.

During that period Mach continued his work in psycho-physics and in sensory perception. In 1867 he took the chair of Professor of Experimental Physics at Charles-Ferdinand University, Prague, where he stayed for 28 years.

Mach's main contribution to physics was his description and photographs of spark shock waves and then ballistic shock waves. He described how passing the sound barrier compressed air in front of bullets and shells. Using a so-called "schlierenmthod" he and his son Ludwig were able to photograph the shadows of the invisible shock waves.

During the early 1890's Ludwig was able to invent an interferometer which allowed for much clearer photographs. But Mach also made many contributions to psychology and physiology including his anticipation of gestalt phenomena, his discovery of Mach bands an inhibition influenced type of visual illusion, and especially his discovery of a non-acoustic function of the inner ear which helped control human balance.

Mach is also well-known for his philosophy, which was a type of phenomenalism as if only sensations were real. Unfortunately, this position was not compatible with the reality of atoms and molecules, and from about 1908 to 1911 his views were criticized by Max Planck as being incompatible with physics. Some of Mach's criticisms of Newton's position on space and time influenced Einstein, but later Einstein realized that Mach was basically opposed to Newton's philosophy and that his physical criticism was not sound. As an experimental physicist Mach tended to think that scientific theories were only provisional and had no lasting place in physics. This attitude made it hard for him to accept Einstein's special theory of relativity, especially since the second axiom seemed like an absolute of the kind Mach opposed, which was criticized in the preface to a posthumously published book on light which appeared in 1921.

In 1898 he suffered a stroke and in 1901 retired from the University of Vienna and was appointed to the upper chamber of the Austrian parliament. On leaving Vienna in 1913 he moved to his son's home in Vaterstetten, near Munich where he continued writing and corresponding until his death in 1916.

EVGENY LIFSHITZ

Evgeny Mikhailovich Lifshitz (February 21, 1915 – October 29, 1985) was a leading Soviet physicist from a Jewish origin and the brother of Ilya Mikhailovich Lifshitz.

(Some commonly encountered alternative transliterations of his names include Yevgeny or Evgenii and Lifshits or Lifschitz.)

Lifshitz is well known in general relativity for coauthoring the BKL conjecture concerning the nature of a *generic curvature singularity*. As of 2006, this is widely regarded as one of the most important open problems in the subject of classical gravitation.

With Lev Landau, Lifshitz co-authored an ambitious series of physics textbooks, in which the two aimed to provide a graduate-level introduction to the entire field of physics. These books are still considered invaluable and continue to be widely used. Lifshitz was the second of only 43 people ever to pass Landau's "Theoretical Minimum" examination.

The wife of Lev Landau strongly criticized his scientific abilities, hinting at how much of the two of them was done by Lifshitz, and how much by Landau. (Of their textbooks, the joke is made, "Not one word of Landau, not one thought of Lifshitz.") Despite the sniping, he is well known for many invaluable contributions, in particular to quantum electrodynamics, where he calculated the Casimir force in an arbitrary macroscopic configurations of metals and dielectrics.

ERNEST LAWRENCE

Ernest Orlando Lawrence (August 8, 1901 – August 27, 1958) was an American physicist and Nobel Laureate best known for his invention, utilization, and improvement of the cyclotron beginning in 1929, and his later work in uranium-isotope separation in the Manhattan Project. He had a long career at the University of California, Berkeley where he was a professor of physics. In 1939, Lawrence was awarded the Nobel Prize in Physics for his work on the cyclotron and its applications. Chemical element number 103 is named "lawrencium" in his honour. He was also the first recipient of the Sylvanus Thayer Award. His brother John H. Lawrence is known for pioneering the field of nuclear medicine.

Early Life

Born in Canton, South Dakota, Lawrence attended St. Olaf College in Minnesota, but transferred to the University of South Dakota after his first year. He earned his bachelor's degree in 1922. He received his Master's Degree in Physics from the University of Minnesota in 1923. He spent a year at the University of Chicago, and received his Ph.D. in physics at Yale University in 1925, making him somewhat unusual in his field—a very promising young scientist who had received his entire education in the United States, in a day when study at one of the great science institutions of Europe was considered essential for someone who truly wished to make a significant contribution. He remained at Yale as a researcher on the photoelectric effect, becoming an assistant professor in 1927. In 1928 he was appointed Associate Professor of Physics at the University of California, Berkeley, and two years later he became a full Professor, being the youngest at Berkeley. There, he was called the "Atom Smasher,"; the man who "held the key" to atomic energy. "He wanted to do 'big physics,' the kind of work that could only be done on a large scale with a lot of people involved," said Herbert York, the first director of the Lawrence Livermore laboratory, as quoted on the lab's official Web site.

ERWIN FUES

Erwin Richard Fues (January 17, 1893 in Stuttgart, Germany – 1970 in Germany) was a German theoretical physicist who made contributions to atomic physics and molecular physics, quantum wave mechanics, and solid-state physics.

Education and Career

During the period 1912 to 1914, Fues studied at the University of Berlin and then the University of Munich. He served in the military 1914 to circa 1915, and then attended the University of Tubingen from 1916 to 1918. During 1918, he became a student of Arnold Sommerfeld, and he received the *doctor rerum naturalium* from the University of Munich in 1920. From 1922 he did postgraduate work at the Stuttgart Technische Hochschule, under Paul Peter Ewald, also a former student of Arnold Sommerfeld, and he completed his Habilitation in 1924. At Stuttgart he served as a Privatdozent and assistant to Ewald until 1929, during which time he worked on atomic and molecular structure and spectroscopy based on the Sommerfeld-Bohr theory.

During his tenure under Ewald, he was absent during the period 1925 to 1927, when, as an International Education Board fellow, he was first an assistant to Erwin Schrodinger at the University of Zurich, and then a research assistant at the University of Copenhagen at Neils Bohr's Institute of Theoretical Physics. At that time three major centres for the development of quantum mechanics were the Theoretical Physics Institute at the University of Munich, under Arnold Sommerfeld, the Institute of Theoretical Physics at the University of Gottingen, under Max Born, and the Institute of Theoretical Physics, under Niels Bohr.

From 1929 to 1934, he served as ordinarius professor at the Hanover Technische Hochschule. From 1934 to 1943, he served as ordinarius professor jointly at the University of Breslau and the Breslau Technische Hochschule, after which, he went to the Vienna Technische Universitat, where he remained until 1947.

In that year, he went back to the Stuttgart Technische Hochschule, where the Institute for Theoretical and Applied Physics (Institut fur Theoretische und Angewandte Physik) had been formed with two chairs. Fues became ordinarius professor for theoretical physics as well as director of the institute; the other joint director was Ulrich Dehlinger.

The institute followed the tradition of both Sommerfeld and Ewald in carrying on with both theoretical and experimental research and teaching. After the death of Sommerfeld in 1951, Fues edited and supplemented multiple editions of two volumes of Sommerfeld's six-volume *Vorlesungen uber theoretische Physik.*

In his career, Fues made contributions to theoretical physics, especially in atomic structure, quantum wave mechanics, and solid-state physics. In 1960, Hermann Haken took over from Fues at the Institute for Theoretical and Applied Physics.

ENRICO FERMI

Enrico Fermi (September 29, 1901 – November 28, 1954) was an Italian physicist most noted for his work on the development of the first nuclear reactor, and for his contributions to the development of quantum theory, nuclear and particle physics, and statistical mechanics. Fermi was awarded the Nobel Prize in Physics in 1938 for his work on induced radioactivity and is today regarded as one of the top scientists of the 20th century. He is acknowledged as a unique physicist who was highly accomplished in both theory and experiment. Fermium, a synthetic element created in 1952 is named after him.

Biography

Enrico Fermi was born in Rome, Italy. His father was Alberto Fermi, a Chief Inspector of the Ministry of Communications, and his mother was Ida de Gattis, an elementary school teacher. As a young boy he enjoyed learning physics and mathematics and shared his interests with his older brother, Giulio. When Giulio died unexpectedly of a throat abscess in 1915, Enrico was distraught, and immersed himself into scientific study to distract himself. According to his own account, each day he would walk in front of the hospital where Giulio died until he became inured to the pain. Later, Enrico befriended another scientifically inclined student named Enrico Persico, and the two together engaged in scientific projects such as building gyroscopes, and measuring the magnetic field of the earth. Fermi's interest in physics was further encouraged when a friend of his father's gave him several books on physics and mathematics, which he read and assimilated.

Fermi received his undergraduate and doctoral degree from the Scuola Normale Superiore in Pisa. There was an entrance exam which candidates had to take in order to enter the prestigious institute, which included an essay. For his essay on the given theme *Characteristics of Sound*, 17-year-old Fermi chose to derive and solve the Fourier analysis based partial differential equation for waves on a string. The examiner interviewed Fermi and concluded that his essay would have been commendable even for a doctoral degree. At the Scuola Normale Superiore, Fermi teamed up with a fellow student named Franco Rasetti with whom he used to indulge in light hearted pranks. Later, Rasetti became Fermi's close friend and collaborator.

Fermi's Ph.D advisor was Luigi Puccianti. In 1924 Fermi spent a semester in Gottingen, and then stayed for a few months in Leiden with Paul Ehrenfest. From January 1925 to the autumn of 1926 he stayed at the University of Florence. In this period he wrote his work on the Fermi-Dirac statistics. When he was only 24 years old, Fermi took a professorship in Rome (the first for atomic physics in Italy, which he won in a competition created by Professor Orso Mario Corbino, director of the Institute of Physics). Corbino helped Fermi in selecting his team, which soon was joined by notable minds like Edoardo Amaldi, Bruno Pontecorvo, Franco Rasetti and Emilio Segre.

For the theoretical studies only, Ettore Majorana also took part in what was soon nicknamed "the Via Panisperna boys" (after the name of the road in which the Institute had its labs). The group went on with its now famous experiments, but in 1933 Rasetti left Italy for Canada and the United States, Pontecorvo went to France and Segre left to teach in Palermo.

During their time in Rome, Fermi and his group made important contributions to many practical and theoretical aspects of physics. Some of these include the theory of beta decay, and the discovery of slow neutrons, which was to prove pivotal for the working of nuclear reactors. His group also systematically bombarded elements with slow neutrons, and during their experiments with uranium, narrowly missed observing nuclear fission.

At that time, fission was thought to be improbable, if not impossible, mostly on theoretical grounds. While people expected elements with higher atomic number to form from neutron bombardment of lighter elements, nobody expected neutrons to have enough energy to actually split a heavier atom into two light element fragments. However, the chemist Ida Noddack had criticised Fermi's work and had suggested that some of his experiments could have produced lighter elements. At the time, Fermi dismissed this possibility on the basis of calculations.

Fermi was well-known for his simplicity in solving problems. He began his inquiries with the simplest lines of mathematical reasoning, then later produced complete solutions to the problems he deemed worth pursuing. His abilities as the greatest combined theoretical and applied nuclear physicist of all time were acknowledged by and influenced many physicists who worked with him, such as Hans Bethe, who spent two semesters working with Fermi in the early 1930s. From the time he was a boy, Fermi meticulously recorded his calculations in notebooks, and later used to solve many new problems that he encountered based on these earlier known problems.

When Fermi submitted his famous paper on beta decay to the prestigious journal *Nature*, the journal's editor turned it down because "it contained speculations which were too remote from reality". Thus, Fermi saw the theory published in Italian and in German before it was published in English. *Nature* eventually did publish Fermi's report on beta decay on January 16, 1939.

ERNEST COURANT

Ernest Courant (born 1920) has been called the "father of modern particle accelerators". A fundamental contributor to the field, he has also been mentor to several generations of students. In this kind of generative academic influence, he can be compared to his father, the mathematician Richard Courant.

Currently, Ernest Courant is a member the National Academy of Sciences, and remains active as a distinguished scientist emeritus at Brookhaven National Laboratory. He has played a part in the work of Brookhaven for sixty years.

Early Life

The first of their four children, he was born in Gottingen, Germany in 1920, to Richard Courant and Nerina Runge Courant, a year after their marriage.

He has written that he "came by science naturally". His mother's father, Carl Runge, is credited with the Runge-Kutta method for numerical solutions of differential equations. A maternal great-grandfather (Runge's father-in-law) was Emil DuBois-Reymond, a pioneer in electrophysiology. Affinity for science and mathematics extended further than his biological family. Ernest Courant's childhood neighbours included the mathematician David Hilbert (his father's thesis director, in whose honour Ernest received the middle name of David) and the physicists Max Born and James Franck. Further, his father's students and colleagues became friends of the family, and frequented their home.

Ernest's early interests centred on chemistry. "I had a lab at home full of test tubes, Bunsen burners, and chemicals. Once there was a small fire (easily put out), but I got a sense of how things were put together."

Adolf Hitler came to power in 1933, and the neighborhood and its intellectual society were disrupted-along with the mathematics department at the University. Ernest's father had been born to a Jewish family of small businessmen, and he was now now identified as a Jew, and an undesirable, by the new regime. Expelled from his position at the University of Gottingen, Richard Courant took a temporary teaching position in England, and the family abandoned Gottingen in favour of Cambridge for a few months. Forewarned by a Nazi acquaintance that the anti-Semetic storm would not settle-but intensify, the family made plans to emigrate permanently. They returned only briefly to Germany before embarking to New York

City, where his father had secured a post at New York University- and immigration visas to the USA.

Fluent in English from both early lessons and the recent period enrolled at the Perse School in Cambridge, Ernest was accepted at the Fieldston School of the School for Ethical Culture, with scholarship, thanks to intervention by family friend (and Fieldston alumnus), J. Robert Oppenheimer.

Career

Courant graduated from the Fieldston School in 1936, received a physics degree from Swarthmore College, and earned a Ph.D. in physics from the University of Rochester in 1943. Courant has worked at Brookhaven National Laboratory from 1948 to the present, first as an associate scientist in the Proton Synchrotron Division. He received tenure in 1955, and was promoted to senior scientist in 1960. In addition, he taught as an Adjunct Professor at SUNY Stony Brook from 1966 to 1986.

His most notable discovery is his 1952 work with M Stanley Livingston and Hartland Snyder on the Strong Focusing Principle, a critical step in the development of modern particle accelerators.

EDWARD CONDON

Edward Uhler Condon (March 2, 1902 – March 26, 1974) was a distinguished American nuclear physicist, a pioneer in quantum mechanics, a participant in the development of radar and nuclear weapons in World War II, research director of Corning Glass, director of the National Bureau of Standards, and president of the American Physical Society (as well as, late in his life, professor of physics at the University of Colorado, where he directed a controversial Air Force-funded scientific study of UFOs). He was born in Alamogordo, New Mexico, United States, and earned a Ph.D. from University of California, Berkeley in 1926.

In 1943, Condon joined the Manhattan Project; however, within six weeks, he resigned as a result of conflicts with General Leslie R. Groves, the project's military leader.

Condon was one of the physicists whose loyalty to the United States was challenged by members of Congress — including Congressman Richard M. Nixon, who called for the revocation of his security clearance — in the late 1940s and early 1950s. The superpatriotic chairman of the House Committee on Un-American Activities (HUAC), Rep. J. Parnell Thomas, would call the physicist "Dr. Condon," the "weakest link" in American security, and even the "missing link."

In 1948, U.S. President Harry Truman — at the Annual Meeting of the American Association for the Advancement of Science, and with Condon sitting beside him — denounced Rep. Thomas and HUAC on the grounds that vital scientific research "may be made impossible by the creation of an atmosphere in which no man feels safe against the public airing of unfounded rumours, gossip and vilification." He called HUAC's activities "the most un-American thing we have to contend with today. It is the climate of a totalitarian country."

Carl Sagan, once a student of Condon, documented Condon's own account of being brought up before a loyalty review board: *"Dr. Condon, it says here that you have been at the forefront of a revolutionary movement in physics called" — and here the inquisitor read the words slowly and carefully — "quantum mechanics. It strikes this hearing that if you could be at the forefront of one revolutionary movement...you could be at the forefront of another."*

Condon replied that the accusation was unfounded, since he most emphatically was *not* a "revolutionary". He raised his right hand and solemnly declared, "I believe in Archimedes' Principle, formulated in the third century B.C. I believe in Kepler's laws of planetary motion, discovered in the seventeenth century. I believe in Newton's laws...." He continued in this vein, listing a long sequence of scientists whose work, done centuries before, was still valid and respected: The Bernoulli family, Fourier, Ampere, Boltzmann, and Maxwell. HUAC did not appreciate his sense of humour; however, fortunately for Condon, the most severe charge they could confirm was that in high school he had a paper route delivering a socialist newspaper.

From 1966 to 1968, Condon directed the University of Colorado UFO Project. Though plagued with infighting and controversy, the project's conclusion—that all unidentified flying objects had prosaic explanations—have been cited as a key factor in the generally low levels of interest in UFOs among most mainstream scientists and academics. See Condon Report. In his negative critique of the Condon Report, astronomer J. Allen Hynek hoped that Condon's reputation would not be soured by the Condon Report, writing, "It is unfortunate that, almost certainly, popular history will henceforth link Dr. Condon's name with UFOs, and only the arcane history of physics will accord him his true place and record his brilliant career in contributing to the understanding... of the nature of the physical world. These contributions UFOs cannot take away from him, even though his work with this problem is analogous to that of a Mozart producing an uninspired pot-boiler, unworthy of his talents." (Clark, 605)

Following his death, Condon crater on the Moon was named after him.

ERNST CHLADNI

Ernst Florens Friedrich Chladni (November 30, 1756–April 3, 1827) was a German physicist and musician. Chladni was born in Wittenberg. His important works include research on vibrating plates and the calculation of the speed of sound for different gases. For this some call him the "Father of Acoustics". He also did pioneering work in the study of meteorites, and therefore is regarded by some as the "Father of Meteoritics" as well.

Personal Life

Although Chladni was born in Wittenberg, Germany, Chladni's family was from Kremnica, a mining town now in central Slovakia, then part of the Kingdom of Hungary. This has led to Chladni as being identified in the literature as German, Hungarian and Slovak.

Chladni came from an educated family of academics and learned men. Chaldni's great-grandfather, Georg Chladni (1637-92), a

Lutheran clergyman, had to flee Kremnica on October 19, 1673 during the Counter Reformation. Chaldni's grandfather, Martin Chladni (1669-1725), was also a Lutheran theologian, and in 1710 became professor of theology at the University of Wittenberg, and from 1720-1721 was dean of the faculty of theology and later rector of the university. Chaldni's uncle, Justus Georg Chladni (1701-1765), was a law professor at University of Wittenberg.

Another uncle, Johann Martin Chladni (1710-1759), was a theologian and historian, and professor at the University of Erlangen and the University of Leipzig. Chladni's father, Ernst Martin Chladni (1715-1782), was a law professor and rector of the University of Wittenberg, where he joinied the law faculty in 1746. Chaldni's father disapproved of his son's interest in science and insisted that Chaldni become a lawyer.

Chladni studied law and philosophy in Wittenberg and Leipzig, and obtained a law degree in 1782 from the University of Leipzig. When his father died in 1782, Chladni began his research in physics in earnest.

Chladni died in 1827 in Wrocaw, Lower Silesia, an area that is now in southwestern Poland. When Chladni died, this town was called Breslau, and was part of the Kingdom of Prussia, which was a member of the German Confederation.

EDWARD VICTOR APPLETON

Sir Edward Victor Appleton, (September 6, 1892 – April 21, 1965) was an English physicist.

Biography

Appleton was born in Bradford, West Yorkshire and educated at Hanson Grammar School. At the age of 18 he won a scholarship to St. John's College, Cambridge. He graduated with a first class degree in Natural Sciences.

During the First World War he joined the West Riding Regiment, and later transferred to the Royal Engineers.

After returning from active service in World War I, Appleton became assistant demonstrator in experimental physics at the Cavendish Laboratory in 1920. He was professor of physics at King's College London (1924–36) and professor of natural philosophy at Cambridge University (1936–39). From 1939 to 1949 he was secretary of the Department of Scientific and Industrial Research. Knighted in 1941, he received the 1947 Nobel Prize in Physics for his contributions to the knowledge of the ionosphere, which led to the development of radar.

In 1902 Oliver Heaviside and Arthur Edwin Kennelly independently proposed the idea of there being a conducting layer that reflected radio signals. Guglielmo Marconi had been able to make his historic transatlantic transmissions; to achieve this, refraction of the signals was necessary to reach its destination.

In his work, Appleton had observed that the strength of the radio signal from a transmitter on a frequency such as the medium wave band and over a path of a hundred miles or so was constant during the day but that it varied during the night.

This led to him to believe that it was possible that two radio signals were being received. One was travelling along the ground, and another was reflected by a layer in the upper atmosphere. The fading or variation in strength of the overall radio signal received resulted from the interference pattern of the two signals.

To prove his theory, in 1924 Appleton used the British Broadcasting Corporation (BBC) radio broadcast transmitter at Bournemouth, England. This transmitted a signal towards the upper reaches of the atmosphere. He received the radio signals near Cambridge, proving they were being reflected. By making a periodic change to the frequency of the broadcast radio signal he was able to measure the time taken for the signals to travel to the layers in the upper atmosphere and back. In this way he was able to calculate that the height of the reflecting layer was 60 miles above the ground.

From 1949 until his death in 1965, he was Principal and Vice-Chancellor of the University of Edinburgh.

In 1974 the Radio and Space Research Station was renamed the Appleton Laboratory in honour of the man who had done so much to establish the UK as a leading force in ionospheric research, and had been involved with the station first as a researcher and then as secretary of its parent body, the Department of Scientific and Industrial Research.

EDUARD SUESS

Eduard Suess (August 20, 1831 London – April 26, 1914 Vienna) was a geologist who was an expert on the geography of the Alps. He is responsible for hypothesising two major former geographical features, the supercontinent Gondwana (proposed 1861) and the Tethys Ocean.

Born in London to a Saxon merchant, when he was three his family relocated to Prague, then to Vienna when he was 14. Interested in geology at a young age, he published his first paper (on the geology of Carlsbad, now in the Czech Republic) when he was 19.

By 1857 he was a professor of geology at the University of Vienna, and from there he gradually developed views on the connection between Africa and Europe; eventually he came to the conclusion that the Alps to the north were once at the bottom of an ocean, of which the Mediterranean was a remnant. While not quite correct (mostly because plate tectonics had not yet been discovered — he used the earlier geosyncline theory), this is close enough to the truth that he is credited with postulating the earlier existence of the Tethys Ocean, which he named in 1893.

His other major theory involved glossopteris fern fossils occurring in South America, Africa, and India (as well as Antarctica, though Suess did not know this). His explanation was that the three lands were once connected in a supercontinent, which he named Gondwanaland. Again, this is not quite correct: Suess believed that the oceans flooded the spaces currently between those lands, when in fact the lands drifted apart. Still, it is so similar to what is currently believed that his naming has stuck.

Suess is considered one of the early practitioners of ecology. He published a comprehensive synthesis of his ideas in 1885-1901, entitled *Das Antlitz der Erde* (translated as "The Face of the Earth"), which was a popular textbook for many years. In this work Suess also introduced the concept of the biosphere, which was later extended by Vladimir I. Vernadsky in 1926.

> *"... one thing seems to be foreign on this large celestial body consisting of spheres, namely, organic life. But this life is limited to a determined zone at the surface of the lithosphere. The plant, whose deep roots plunge into the soil to feed, and which at the same time rises into the air to breathe, is a good illustration of organic life in the region of interaction between the upper sphere and the lithosphere, and on the surface of continents it is possible to single out an independent biosphere"-Eduard Suess*

He won the Copley Medal of the Royal Society in 1903.

Suess crater on the Moon and a crater on Mars are named after his son, Franz Eduard Suess (1867-1942), who was superintendent and geologist at the *Imperial Geological Institute* in Vienna.

EMILIANO MUTTI

Emiliano Mutti is a geologist who has made significant contributions to petroleum geosciences, especially to sedimentary dynamics of turbidites and their reservoir characterization.

Emiliano Mutti was born in 1933 near the small lake Orta in northern Italy. During WW II his father Ido moved the family to the small mountain village of Nociveglia in the Northern Apennines. Surrounded by rocks and forests, Emiliano developed a love for the mountains that he has never lost. Later, when he realized that the rocks in this valley were turbidites, he returned to study them and produce classic papers on deep-water depositional systems.

Emiliano completed a Masters degree in geology at the University of Milan in 1959. His thesis was on the stratigraphy and structure of Tertiary Macigno turbidites in the Northern Apennines. From 1960-65 Emiliano was assistant professor of sedimentology at the

University of Milan. In 1965, interest in research led him to accept a job with the Esso Production Research Lab in Bordeaux, the European affiliate of Exxon Production Research Company in Houston. Through this connection, Emiliano met Chuck Campbell, and the two of them did field work in Italy.

After several weeks, Chuck invited Emiliano to the US for additional training. The time spent with Chuck was a turning point in Emiliano's career. He describes the experience this way: "At that time I had a lot of experience in field mapping and knew turbidites quite well.

Chuck realized that I didn't know anything else. He took me into the field in the States and taught me how to recognize fluvial and shallow-marine. Most importantly he taught me his stratigraphic approach" In 1969 Emiliano resigned from Esso to become a professor at the University of Torino. In 1971 he received his PhD and in 1975 he became a full professor. In 19sn Emiliano moved to the University of Parma where he is currently a full professor of sedimentary geology.

During his career Emiliano has mainly worked on stratigraphy and sedimentology of turbidite basins in fold-thrust belts, notably in the Spanish Pyrenees, the northern Apennines, and Greece. Much of his work is summarized in classic papers co-authored with Franco Ricci Lucchi, and Bill Normark. Since 1989 his work has focused on stratigraphy and facies analysis of flood-dominated fluvio-deltaic deposits and their relationships to turbidite systems in many tectonically mobile basins worldwide.

Emiliano is a field geologist with a very strong passion for sedimentary rocks. Anyone who has been in the field with him knows that he is a master of observation and description. He always carries a sketchpad in the field; his sketches of outcrops are extraordinary for their detail and ability to sort out complex sedimentary relationships. All of' his papers are characterized by superb photographs, which are the result for his love of photography. Emiliano has received numerous awards and honorary memberships in geological societies. He has written over 100 scientific papers and several books on stratigraphy and turbidite systems.

FREDERICK SEITZ

Frederick Seitz (2008-07-04–2008-03-02) was an American physicist and a pioneer of solid state physics. Seitz studied under Eugene Wigner at Princeton University, graduating in 1934. He, along with Wigner, came up with the concept of the Wigner-Seitz unit cell. He also founded the Frederick Seitz Materials Research Laboratory at the University of Illinois at Urbana-Champaign as well as several other material research laboratories across the United States.

Biography

Born in San Francisco on 2008-07-04, Seitz graduated from Lick-Wilmerding High School in the middle of his senior year. He went on to study physics at Standford University obtaining his bachelor's degree in three years, and then moved to Princeton University to study metals under Eugene Wigner. He and Wigner pioneered one of the first quantum theory of crystals, and developed concepts such as the Wigner-Seitz unit cell.

After his graduate studied, Seitz continued to work on solid state physics, publishing *The Modern Theory of solids* in 1940, motivated by a desire to "write a cohesive account of the various aspects of solid-state physics in order to give the field the kind of unity it deserved". *The Modern Theory of Solids* helped unify and understand the relations between the fields of metallurgy, ceramics, and electronics. He was also a consultant on many World War II related projects in metallurgy, radiation damage to solids and electronics amongst others. He, along with Hillard Huntington, made the first calculation of the energies of formation and migration of vacancies and interstitials in copper, inspiring many works on point defects in metals. He was the president of Rockefeller University from 1968 to 1978 during which he helped to launch new research programmes in molecular biology, cell biology, and neuroscience as well as creating a joint MD-PhD programme with Cornell University. Shortly before his retirement from Rockefeller University in 1979, Seitz began working as a paid permanent consultant for the R.J. Reynolds Tobacco Company, advising their research programme.

In 1994, Seitz authored *Global warming and ozone hole controversies. A challenge to scientific judgment.*, a report published by the George C. Marshall Institute, of which he was a founder and chairman of the board, titled "" In a broader discussion of environmental toxins, he concluded "there is no good scientific evidence that passive inhalation is truly dangerous under normal circumstances."

Seitz questioned whether global warming is anthropogenic. He supported the position of the Oregon Institute of Science and Medicine (OISM) on global warming and in an open letter invited scientists to sign the OISM's global warming petition. He also signed the 1995 Leipzig Declaration and questioned the view that CFCs "are the greatest threat to the ozone layer". Seitz died March 2, 2008 in New York. He was said to have a "wry sense of humour" and to be "a kind and generous person, giving untold and unacclaimed time and energy to help young scientists and young science along their way".

FULVIO MELIA

Fulvio Melia (born 2 August 1956) is an Italian-American physicist/astrophysicist and author. He is Professor of Physics and Astronomy at the University of Arizona and Associate Editor of the Astrophysical Journal Letters. A former Presidential Young Investigator and Sloan Research Fellow, he is the author of six books and more than 230 articles on theoretical astrophysics.

Career

Melia was educated at Melbourne University and The Massachusetts Institute of Technology, and held a post-doctoral research position at the University of Chicago before taking an assistant professorship at Northwestern University in 1987. Moving to the University of Arizona as an associate professor in 1991, he became a full professor in 1993. From 1988 to 1995, he was a Presidential Young Investigator (under President Ronald Reagan), and then an Alfred P. Sloan Research Fellow from 1989 to 1992. He became a Fellow of the American Physical Society in 2002. He is also a Professorial Fellow in the School of Physics, Melbourne University.

From 1996 to 2002, he was a Scientific Editor with the Astrophysical Journal, and since then has been an Associate Editor with the Astrophysical Journal Letters. He is also the Chief Editor of the Theoretical Astrophysics series of books at the University of Chicago Press.

In a career that has seen him publish over 230 research papers and several books, Melia has made important contributions in High Energy Astronomy and the physics of supermassive black holes. He is especially known for his work on the Galactic centre, particularly developing a theoretical understanding of the central supermassive black hole, known as Sagittarius A*.

With his students and collaborators, he was the first to propose imaging this object with millimeter-interferometry, which should be feasible within a few years, proving beyond any doubt that it possesses an event horizon, as predicted by Einstein's theory of general relativity. He is also a well-respected and popular publicist of astronomy and science in general, delivering many lectures at public venues, including museums and planetariums. His books have won several awards of distinction, including the designation of Outstanding Academic Books by the American Library Association, and selection as world-wide astronomy books of the year by Astronomy (magazine).

FRITZ HOUTERMANS

Friedrich Georg "Fritz" Houtermans (January 22, 1903 – March 1, 1966) was an atomic and nuclear physicist born in Zoppot (today Sopot, Poland) near Danzig (today Gdansk, Poland). Houtermans made important contributions to geochemistry and cosmochemistry.

Education

Houtermans began his studies at the Georg-August University of Gottingen in 1921, and he received his doctorate under James Franck in 1927, the same year Robert Oppenheimer received his doctorate under Max Born. He completed his Habilitation under Gustav Hertz at the Technische Hochschule Berlin, in 1932. Hertz and Franck were Nobel Prize laureates; they shared the 1925 Nobel Prize in Physics.

While at Gottingen, Houtermans met Enrico Fermi, George Gamow, Werner Heisenberg, Wolfgang Pauli, and Victor Frederick Weisskopf. Houtermans and Gamow did pioneering work on quantum tunneling in 1928. Houtermans, in 1929, with Robert d'Escourt Atkinson, made the first calculation of stellar thermonuclear reactions. Their pioneering calculations were the impetus for Carl Friedrich von Weizsacker and Hans Bethe, in 1939, to put forth the correct theory of stellar thermonuclear energy generation.

Charlotte Riefenstahl, who received her doctorate in physics at the University of Gottingen in 1927, the same year as Houtermans and Robert Oppenheimer, was courted by both men. She was no relation to Leni Riefenstahl, the notable German filmmaker. In 1930, she left her teaching position at Vassar College and went back to Germany. During a physics conference at the Black Sea resort of Batumi, Riefenstahl and Houtermans were married in August 1930, in Tbilisi, with Wolfgang Pauli and Rudolf Peierls as witnesses to the ceremony. (Three other references cite the year as being 1931.)

Career

From 1932 to 1933, Houtermans taught at the Technische Hochschule Berlin and was an assistant to Hertz. While there, he met Patrick Blackett, Max von Laue, and Leo Szilard.

Houtermans was a Communist; he had been a member of the German Communist Party since the 1920s. After Adolf Hitler came to power in 1933, Charlotte Houtermans insisted that they leave Germany. They went to Great Britain, near Cambridge, where he worked for the EMI (Electrical and Musical Instruments, Ltd.) Television Laboratory. In 1935 Houtermans emigrated to the Soviet Union, as the result of a proposal by Alexander Weissberg, who had emigrated to there in 1931. Houtermans took an appointment at the Khar'kov Physico-Technical Institute and worked there for two years with the Russian physicist Valentin P. Fomin. In the Great Purge, Houtermans was arrested by the NKVD in December 1937. He was tortured and confessed to being a Trotskyist plotter and German spy, out of fear from threats against Charlotte.

However, Charlotte had already escaped from the Soviet Union to Denmark, after which she went to England and finally the USA. After the Hitler-Stalin Pact of 1939, Houtermans was turned over to the Gestapo in May 1940 and imprisoned in Berlin. The Gestapo subjected him to brutal interrogation, accused of being a Soviet spy. Through efforts of Max von Laue, Houtermans was released in August 1940, whereupon he took a position at *Forschungslaboratoriums fur Elektronenphysik*, a private laboratory of Manfred Baron von Ardenne, in Lichterfelde, a suburb of Berlin. In 1944, Houtermans took a position as a nuclear physicist at the Physikalisch-Technische Reichsanstalt.

While imprisoned in the Soviet Union, a cellmate of Houtermans was the Kiev University historian Konstantine F. Shteppa. They would later write a book together, "Russian Purge and the Extraction of Confession", under the pseudonyms of Beck and Godin to protect their many friends and colleagues back in the USSR.

At the Forschunsinstitut Manfred von Ardenne, Houtermans showed that transuranic isotopes, such as neptunium and plutonium, could be used as fissionable fuels in substitution for uranium. Houtermans sent a telegram from Switzerland to Eugene Wigner at the Met Lab warning the USA's Manhattan Project of German work on fission: "Hurry up. We are on the track."

During Houtermans' employment at the Physikalisch-Technische Reichsanstalt (PTR), he got himself into serious trouble as a result of his habit of being a chain-smoker and suffering great distress if he did not have a supply of tobacco. On official PTR stationery, he wrote to a Dresden cigarette manufacturer to obtain a kilogram of Macedonian tobacco, claiming the tobacco was "kriegswichtig", *i.e.*, important for the war effort.

When he had smoked the tobacco, he again wrote for more, however, the letter fell into the hands of an official at the PTR, who fired him. Werner Heisenberg and Carl Weizsacker came to the rescue of Houtermans and arranged an interview for him with Walter Gerlach, the plenipotentiary (Bevollmachtiger) for German nuclear research under the Reich Research Council. As a result, Houtermans moved to Gottingen in 1945, where Hans Kopferman and Richard Becker got him positions at the Institut fur Theoretische Physik and II. Physikalischen Institut der Universitat Gottingen. From 1952, Houtermans took a position as ordinarius professor of physics at the University of Bern. During his tenure there, he founded the internationally renowned *Berner Schule*, whose thrust was the application of radioactivity to astrophysics, cosmochemistry, and geosciences.

FRED HOYLE

Sir *Fred Hoyle* (24 June 1915 – 20 August 2001) was an English astronomer primarily remembered today for his contribution to the theory of stellar nucleosynthesis and his often controversial stance on other cosmological and scientific matters, in particular his rejection of the Big Bang hypothesis.

Hoyle was born in Gilstead, West Yorkshire, England, near Bradford, where his father, George Hoyle, worked in the wool trade. His mother, Mabel Pickard, had studied music at the Royal College of Music in London. Hoyle was educated at Bingley Grammar School and read mathematics at Emmanuel College, Cambridge. In addition to his work as an astronomer, Hoyle was a writer of science fiction, including a number of books co-authored with his son Geoffrey Hoyle. Hoyle spent most of his working life at the Institute of Astronomy at Cambridge and served as its director for a number of years. He died in Bournemouth, England, after a series of strokes.

Contribution to Cosmology

An early paper of Hoyle's made an interesting use of the anthropic principle. In trying to work out the routes of stellar nucleosynthesis, he observed that one particular nuclear reaction, the triple-alpha process, which generated carbon, would require the carbon nucleus to have a very specific energy for it to work. The large amount of carbon in the universe, which makes it possible for carbon-based lifeforms (*e.g.* humans) to exist, demonstrated that this nuclear reaction must work. Based on this notion, he made a prediction of the energy levels in the carbon nucleus that was later borne out by experiment. However, those energy levels, while needed in order to produce carbon in large quantities, were statistically very unlikely. Hoyle later wrote:

> *Would you not say to yourself, "Some super-calculating intellect must have designed the properties of the carbon atom, otherwise the chance of my finding such an atom through the blind forces of nature would be utterly minuscule." Of course you would... A common sense interpretation of the facts suggests that a superintellect has monkeyed with physics, as well as with chemistry and biology, and that there are no blind forces worth speaking about in nature. The numbers one calculates from the facts seem to me so overwhelming as to put this conclusion almost beyond question.*

Hoyle, an atheist until that time, said that this suggestion of a guiding hand left him "greatly shaken." Consequently, he began to believe in a god and panspermia. Those who advocate the intelligent design hypothesis sometimes cite Hoyle's work in this area to support the claim that the universe was fine tuned in order to allow intelligent life to be possible.

His co-worker William Alfred Fowler eventually won the Nobel Prize for Physics in 1983 (with Subramanyan Chandrasekhar), but for some reason Hoyle's original contribution was overlooked, and many were surprised that such a notable astronomer missed out. Fowler himself in an autobiographical sketch affirmed Hoyle's pioneering efforts:

The concept of nucleosynthesis in stars was first established by Hoyle in 1946. This provided a way to explain the existence of elements heavier than helium in the universe, basically by showing that critical elements such as carbon could be generated in stars and then incorporated in other stars and planets when that star "dies". The new stars formed now start off with these heavier elements and even heavier elements are formed from them. Hoyle theorized that other rarer elements could be explained by supernovas, the giant explosions which occasionally occur throughout the universe, whose temperatures and pressures would be required to create such elements.

FRIEDRICH HASENOHRL

Friedrich Hasenohrl (November 30, 1874-October 7, 1915), was an Austro-Hungarian physicist.

Friedrich Hasenohrl was born in Vienna, Austria-Hungary in 1874. His father was a lawyer and his mother belonged to a prominent aristocratic family. After his elementary education, he studied natural science and mathematics at the University of Vienna under Stephan and Boltzmann. He worked under H. A. Lorentz in Leiden at the low temperature laboratory. In 1907 he became Boltzmann's successor at the University of Vienna as the head of the Department of Theoretical Physics. He had a number of illustrious pupils there and had an especially significant impact on Erwin Schrodinger, who later won the Nobel Prize for Physics for his contributions to Quantum Mechanics.

When the war broke out in 1914, he volunteered at once into the Austria-Hungarian army. He fought as Oberleutnant against the Italians in Tyrol. He was wounded, recovered and returned to the front. He was then killed by a grenade in an attack on Mount Plaut on October 7, 1915 at the age of 40.

$E = mc^2$

In 1904 and 1905 he published two papers on the inertia of a cavity containing radiation. This was an entirely classical derivation (no use of special relativity) and used Maxwell's equation for the pressure of light. In the first paper, Hasenohrl specifically associated mass via inertia with the energy concept through an equation. Hasenohrl first concluded that $m = (8 / 3)E / c^2$. The same formula appeared on the page 363 in his paper. The title of this paper, which in English is *On the radiation of the bodies in motion*, is very similar to the title of the Einstein's paper published a year later *On the electrodynamics of the bodies in motion.*

In the later paper Hasenohrl re-calculated this result and arrived at $m = (4 / 3)E / c^2$. Hasenohrl indicated that if the internal energy of a system consists of radiation, then, in general, the inertial mass of the system would depend upon that energy.

Thus, this new Hasenohrl calculation establishes that due to the radiant energy E contained in his system, to that inertial mass must be added an apparent mass m. Indeed, in 1914 Cunningham showed that Hasenohrl had made an error in that he did not include the shell. If he had included the shell in his calculations in a way consistent with relativity, the pre-factor would have been 1, so yielding $m = E / c^2$. He could not have done this, since he did not have relativistic mechanics, with which he could model the shell.

FEZA GURSEY

Feza Gursey (April 7, 1921-April 13, 1992) was a Turkish mathematician and physicist. His best known contribution to theoretical physics is his work on the Nonlinear Chiral Lagrangian.

Biography

Feza Gursey was born on April 21, 1921 in Istanbul, to Reoit Sureyya Gursey, a military physician, and Remziye Hisar (tr:Remziye Hisar), a chemist and a pioneering female Turkish scientist. He graduated from Galatasaray Lisesi in 1940, and received his degree in Mathematics – Physics from Istanbul Fen Fakultesi in 1944.

Through a scholarship of the Turkish Ministry of Education he received while he was an assistant in Istanbul University, he pursued a doctorate degree at the Imperial College London in the

United Kingdom. He completed his work on Application of Quaternions to Quantum Field Theory in 1950. After spending the period from 1950 – 1951 in postdoctoral research at Cambridge University, he worked as an assistant at Istanbul University, where he married Suha Pamir, also a physics assistant, in 1952, and in 1953 he acquired the title of Associate Professor.

During 1957 – 1961 he worked at Brookhaven National Laboratory, Institute for Advanced Study at Princeton, New Jersey, and Columbia University. In 1960s, he worked on the Nonlinear Chiral Lagrangian, and produced results of relevance to Quantum Chromodynamics. Returning to Turkey in 1961, he accepted the title of Professor from Middle East Technical University (METU) and took part in the establishment of METU Department of Theoretical Physics. Continuing his work as a lecturer at METU until 1974, he formed a research group.

Being offered a position at Yale University in 1965, he started to work in both Yale University and METU, until 1974, when he decided to give up his position in METU and settle in the United States to continue with Yale. During these years, he took part in the formulation of E(6) grand unified theories.

Gursey died in 1992, in New Haven, Connecticut. He is survived by his son, Yusuf Gursey. The Feza Gursey Institute, founded by the joint effort of Booazici University and TUBYTAK in Turkey, is named in his honour.

FELIX EHRENHAFT

Felix Ehrenhaft (April 24, 1879 – March 4, 1952) was an Austrian physicist who contributed to atomic physics, to the measurement of electrical charges and to the optical properties of metal colloids. He was known for his maverick and controversial style. His fearless iconoclasm was greatly admired by philosopher Paul Feyerabend.

Biography

Ehrenhaft was born in Vienna to physician Leopold Ehrenhaft and Louise Eggar, the daughter of an Hungarian industrialist.

Ehrenhaft earned his doctorate from the University of Vienna in 1903, working on the optical properties of metallic colloids. He subsequently became assistant to Viktor von Lang.

Later Years

From the mid-1930s, Ehrenhaft's thinking started to diverge strikingly from the mainstream of physics. He observed many genuinely surprising and reproducible physical phenomena, usually of ultra-microscopic particles near the limits of perception. However, he was all too willing to adopt bizarre theories to explain experiments that were beset with interactions and multifactorial cause systems.

From the 1940s, Ehrenhaft's views became increasingly extreme and strident, eventually terminating his good friendship with Albert Einstein. He found it impossible to obtain either research funding or even a sympathetic hearing in the U.S.. In 1946, he returned to the University of Vienna where he held again his old position until his death. He became increasingly certain that he had observed magnetic monopoles; *magnetic currents*; and *magnetolysis*, the disassociation of liquids by magnets rather than electric current as in electrolysis.

A review of his life work can be found in the Austrian scientific journal "Acta physica Austriaca", and in the article by Rohatschek on photophoresis (see sources below).

FRIEDRICH ERNST DORN

Friedrich Ernst Dorn (27 July 1848 – 16 December 1916) was a German physicist who was the first to discover that a radioactive substance, later named radon, is emitted from radium.

Life and Work

Dorn was born in Guttstadt (Dobre Miasto), Province of Prussia, and died in Halle, Province of Saxony. He was educated at Konigsberg and went on to teach at the university level. In 1885, at Halle University, Dorn took over the position of personal *ordinarius* professor for theoretical physics from Anton Oberbeck.

Since Dorn was already an *ordinarius* professor, he was allowed to assume the title so as to not appear as having been demoted. In 1895, Dorn succeeded Hermann Knoblauch at Halle as the *ordinarius* professor for experimental physics and director of the physics institute. Dorn's previous duties were assumed by Karl Schmidt, who had been a Privatdozent and was called as an *extraordinarius* professor for theoretical physics.

In 1900, Dorn published a paper in which he described experiments that repeated and extended some earlier work on thorium by Ernest Rutherford. Dorn verified Rutherford's observation that a radioactive material was emitted by thorium, and discovered that a similar emission arose from the element radium. Additional work by Rutherford and Soddy showed that the same emission came from both thorium and radium, that it was a gas, and that it was actually a new element.

Dorn called the radioactive gaseous product from radium simply "emanation", but in 1904 Rutherford introduced the name "radium emanation" for the same material. Ramsay later suggested "niton", from the Latin word "nitens" meaning "shining". In 1923 the name was again changed, this time to radon by an international body of scientists.

Marshall and Marshall have examined the original papers leading to radon's discovery and their work should be consulted for a full treatment and extensive references. They conclude that it is actually Rutherford who should be awarded credit for radon's discovery since he was the first to detect the element being emitted from any radioisotope (thorium) and the first to demonstrate radon's gaseous nature. Rutherford also was the first to integrate his own work on radon with that of others on radon's atomic mass, its spectrum, and its position on the periodic table.

FRANCOIS ARAGO

Francois Jean Dominique Arago (February 26, 1786 – October 2, 1853) was a French mathematician, physicist, astronomer and politician.

Early Life and Work

Arago was born at Estagel, a small village near Perpignan, in the *departement* of Pyrenees-Orientales, Catalan France. He was the eldest of four brothers. Jean (1788-1836) emigrated to North America and became a general in the Mexican army. Jacques Etienne Victor (1799-1855) took part in Louis de Freycinet's exploring voyage in the *Uranie* from as 1817 to 1821, and on his return to France devoted himself to his journalism and the drama. The fourth brother, Etienne Vincent de (1802-1892), is said to have collaborated with Honore de Balzac in *The Heiress of Birague*, and from 1822 to 1847 wrote a great number of light dramatic pieces, mostly in collaboration.

Showing decided military tastes, Francois Arago was sent to the municipal college of Perpignan, where he began to study mathematics in preparation for the entrance examination of the polytechnic school. Within two years and a half he had mastered all the subjects prescribed for examination, and a great deal more, and, on going up for examination at Toulouse, he astounded his examiner by his knowledge of J. L. Lagrange.

Towards the close of 1803 Arago entered the Ecole Polytechnique, Paris, but apparently found the professors there incapable of imparting knowledge or maintaining discipline. The artillery service was his ambition, and in 1804, through the advice and recommendation of Simeon Poisson, he received the appointment of secretary to the Paris Observatory. He now became acquainted with Pierre-Simon Laplace, and through his influence was commissioned, with Jean-Baptiste Biot, to complete the meridianal measurements which had been begun by J. B. J. Delambre, and interrupted since the death of P. F. A. Mechain in 1804). Arago and Biot left Paris in 1806 and began operations along the mountains of Spain. Biot returned to Paris after they had determined the latitude of Formentera, the southernmost point to which they were to carry the survey. Arago continued the work until 1809, his purpose being to measure a meridian arc in order to determine the exact length of a metre.

After Biot's departure, the political ferment caused by the entrance of the French into Spain extended to the Balearic Islands, and the population suspected Arago's movements and his lighting of fires on the top of mola de l'Esclop as the activities of a spy for the invading army.

Their reaction was such that he was obliged to give himself up for imprisonment in the fortress of Bellver in June 1808. On July 28 he escaped from the island in a fishing-boat, and after an adventurous voyage he reached Algiers on August 3. From there he obtained a passage in a vessel bound for Marseille, but on August 16, just as the vessel was nearing Marseille, it fell into the hands of a Spanish corsair. With the rest the crew, Arago was taken to Roses, and imprisoned first in a windmill, and afterwards in a fortress, until the town fell into the hands of the French, when the prisoners were transferred to Palamos.

After three months' imprisonment, Arago and the others were released on the demand of the dey of Algiers, and again set sail for Marseille on the November 28, but then within sight of their port they were driven back by a northerly wind to Bougie on the coast of Africa.

Transport to Algiers by sea from this place would have occasioned a weary delay of three months; Arago, therefore, set out over land, guided by a Moslem priest, and reached it on Christmas Day. After six months in Algiers he once again, on the June 21, 1809, set sail for Marseille, where he had to undergo a monotonous and inhospitable quarantine in the lazaretto, before his difficulties were over. The first letter he received, while in the lazaretto, was from Alexander von Humboldt; and this was the origin of a connection which, in Arago's words, lasted over forty years without a single cloud ever having troubled it.

FREDERICK VINE

Frederick John Vine (born June 17, 1939) is a marine geologist and geophysicist and was a key contributor to the theory of plate tectonics.

Early Life

Vine was born in London, W4 and educated at Latymer Upper School and St. John's College, Cambridge where he studied Natural Sciences (BA, 1962) and marine geophysics (PhD, 1965).

Plate Tectonics

As a graduate student Fred Vine's Ph.D was 'magnetism in the seafloor', on which he worked along with his supervisor Drummond Matthews. Having met Harry Hess he was fully aware of his theories on sea floor spreading where the ocean bed effectively acts as a 'conveyor belt' moving away from the central ridge.. Vine's work, along with that of Drummond Matthews and Lawrence Morley of the Geological Survey of Canada, helped put the variations in the magnetic properties of the ocean crust into proper context. Specifically Vine and Matthews supported Dietz's (*Nature* 1961) idea that sea floor spreading was occurring at mid ocean ridges. Vine and Matthews showed that basalt created at a mid-ocean ridge records earth's current magnetic field polarity (and strength), thus turning Hess's theoretical 'conveyor belt' into a 'tape recorder'. Furthermore, they showed that magnetic reversals, suggested by Allan Cox (*Nature* 1963), can be seen as parallel strips as you travel perpendicularly away from the ridge crest.

Academic Career

Professor Vine had a distinguished career. He did important research with E.M. Moores on the Ophiolite within the Troodos mountains of southern Cyprus. He worked with R.A. Livermore and A.G.Smith on the history of Earth's magnetic field. He then did groundbreaking work on the electrical conductivity of rocks from the lower continental crust with R. G. Ross. In 1967 he became assistant professor of geology and geophysics at Princeton University. In 1970 he worked at the School of Environmental Sciences at the University of East Anglia, U.K., firstly as a Reader, then as Professor in 1974, and was Dean from 1977–1980, and again from 1993–1998. Since 1998, Vine has been a Professorial Fellow of the University of East Anglia. As of 2008 he remains at the university as Emeritus Professor.

FELIX ANDRIES VENING MEINESZ

Felix Andries Vening Meinesz (the Hague July 30, 1887-Amersfoort August 10, 1966) was a Dutch geophysicist and geodesist. He is known for his invention of a precise method for measuring gravity. Thanks to his invention, it became possible to measure gravity at sea, which led him to the discovery of gravity anomalies above the ocean floor. He later attributed these anomalies to continental drift.

Named after him are:

- a gravimeter, an apparatus to measure gravity
- a mathematical function used in geodesy
- a medal of the European Geophysical Society/European Geosciences Union
- a research school at Utrecht University
- Vening Meinesz crater on the Moon.

Biography

Vening Meinesz' father, Sjoerd Anne Meinesz, was mayor, first of Rotterdam, then of Amsterdam. He grew up in a protected environment. In 1910 he graduated in civil engineering in Delft. The same year he started working for the Dutch gravitational survey. In 1915 he wrote his dissertation on the defects of the gravimeters used at that time.

Vening Meinesz then designed a new gravimeter, which the KNMI (Royal Dutch Meteorological Institute) built. The apparatus has two pendula of the same size hanging in a frame but moving in opposite phases. With mirrors and lightbeams the difference in amplitude of the two pendula is captured on a film. Vening Meinesz had discovered that horizontal accelerations (as by waves on a boat) had no influence on the difference in amplitude between the two pendula. The recorded difference then is the amplitude of a theoretical, undisturbed pendulum. Now it became possible to measure gravity more accurately. Vening Meinesz started with measuring gravity all over the Netherlands, for which a network of 51 monitoring stations was created. This became a success, which encouraged him to do measurements at sea. A perfected gravimeter, hanging in a 'swing', was designed. The experiment was successful.

Now measuring gravity at sea had become possible. Between 1923 and 1929 the tall (over 2 metres) Vening Meinesz embarked in small submarines for some uncomfortable expeditions. His goal was to establish the exact shape of the geoid and the Earth. When one of his expeditions was made into a movie in 1935, Vening Meinesz became a hero of the Dutch cinema public. Besides, his research was in the international scientific spotlight. In 1927 he become a parttime professor in geodesy, cartography and geophysics at Utrecht University, and in 1937 he became professor at the Delft University of Technology as well.

In World War II, Vening Meinesz was involved in the Dutch resistance. After the war he could take up his tasks as a professor again. From 1945 to 1951 he was the director of the KNMI. He retired in 1957.

Research and Discoveries

The vast amounts of data that his expeditions yielded were analyzed and discussed together with other leading Dutch Earth scientists of the time J.H.F. Umbgrove, B.G. Escher and Ph.H. Kuenen, the results were published in 1948. An important result was the discovery of elongated belts of negative gravity anomalies along the oceanic trenches.

The mean gravity force appeared to be the same on land and at sea, which was in agreement with the principle of isostasy. Vening Meinesz was especially intrigued by the oceanic trenches. The coexisitence of active volcanism, large negative gravity anomalies and the sudden difference in terrain elevation could only be explained by assuming the Earth's crust was somehow pushed together at these places. As a geophysicist, he was prejudiced that the crust was too rigid to deform at that scale in such a way. His discoveries could be explained only with the development of the theory of plate tectonics in the '50s.

FLAXMAN CHARLES JOHN SPURRELL

Flaxman Charles John Spurrell (6 September 1842-25 February 1915), the archaeologist, geologist and photographer, was born in Mile End, Stepney, London, the eldest son of Dr. Flaxman Spurrell, M.D., F.R.C.S., and Ann Spurrell (who were also cousins). Shortly after his birth, his father moved to Bexley, Kent; later, Flaxman (junior) lived at The Priory, Picardy Road, Belvedere, now home to the Priory Conservative Club.

In the 1860s he began to examine flint implements in and around Crayford in Kent, and over the following decades published a large number of articles for the Kent Archaeological Society (of which his father was a founding member), the Essex Archaeological Society and Royal Archaeological Society, as well as other societies and groups. In 1895 he presented a number of pre-historic remains to the Natural History Museum, and later donated material to the Norwich Castle Museum.

He was a close friend of the egyptologist William Matthew Flinders Petrie, whom he helped to record discoveries made in, for example, Naqada and Tell el-Amarna in Egypt.

Flaxman Spurrell was also interested in photography, and some of his photographs are currently held by English Heritage.

Some years before his death, he retired to Bessingham Manor House in Norfolk, one of the seats of the Spurrell family, and was no longer active in the archaeological world. He died at The Den, Bessingham, in 1915, having married his cousin, Katherine Anne Spurrell, on 27 March 1912.

Flaxman Spurrell was educated at Epsom College and was a Fellow of Geological Society.

He was a nephew of Rev. Frederick Spurrell and an uncle of the biologist and author Herbert George Flaxman Spurrell.

FERDINAND VON RICHTHOFEN

Ferdinand Freiherr von Richthofen (May 5, 1833 – October 6, 1905) was a German traveller, geographer and scientist.

Biography

He was born in Carlsruhe, Prussian Silesia, and was educated in Breslau and Berlin. He travelled or studied in the Alps of Tyrol (the portion of what is now Bolzano-Bozen, Italy) and the Carpathians in Transylvania. In 1860 he joined the Eulenburg Expedition, a Prussian expedition which visited Ceylon, Japan, Taiwan, the Celebes, Java, the Philippines, Siam, Burma between 1860 and 1862. From 1862-868 he worked as a geologist in the United States discovering Goldfields in California. This was followed by several more trips of China, Japan, Burma and Java. He published his geographical, geological, economic, and ethnological findings in three volumes with an atlas. In China he located the dried-up lake bed of Lopnur.

He was also Professor of Geology at the University of Bonn beginning in 1875, Professor of Geography at the University of Leipzig in 1883, and Professor of Geography at the Friedrich Wilhelm University of Berlin in 1886. Among his most famous students was Sven Hedin, the Swedish explorer. He served as President of the German Geographical Society for many years, and founded the Berlin Hydrographical Institute.

He is noted for coining the terms "Seidenstraße" and "Seidenstraßen" = "Silk Road(s)" or "Silk Route(s)" in 1877.

He died in 1905 in Berlin.

When William Gill consulted him about a planned trip to China, he remarked:

'Hour after hour he gave up his valuable time to me, and opened volumes from his rich store of information. … Baron von Richtofen possesses in a remarkable manner the faculty of gathering up the details presented to his view; putting them together and generalising on them with rare judgement; forming out of what would be to a lesser genius, but scattered and unintelligible fragments, a uniform and comprehensive whole ... not one hint was given me that did not subsequently prove its value; his kind thoughts for my comfort and amusement were never ceasing, and his refined and cultivated intellect and genial manner rendered the recollections of my stay in the German capital some of the most pleasant of my life."

Ferdinand von Richthofen was an uncle of the World War I flying ace Manfred von Richthofen, best known as the "Red Baron".

The mountain range on the southern edge of the Gansu corridor in western China was named Richthofen Range after him, although the modern name is now Qilian Mountains.

FRIEDRICH MOHS

Friedrich Mohs (January 29, 1773-September 29, 1839) was a German geologist/mineralogist.

Career

Mohs, born in Gernrode, Germany, studied chemistry, mathematics and physics at the University of Halle and also studied at the Mining Academy in Freiberg, Saxony. After assuming the position of a foreman at a mine in 1801, Mohs moved in 1802 to Austria, where he was employed in trying to identify the minerals in a private collection of a Banker.

Mineral Properties

As part of this task, he started classifying minerals by their physical characteristics, in spite of their chemical composition, as had been done traditionally. This emphasis on physical characteristics was at odds with the prevailing chemical systematics. Minerals are now classified by chemical characteristics, but the physical properties are still useful in field examination.

Harness Scale

In 1812, Mohs became professor in Graz; in 1818, professor in Freiberg, Saxony; in 1826, professor in Vienna. In 1812, using relatively common minerals, he created a hardness scale that is still used today, called the Mohs' scale of mineral hardness. Mohs died during a trip to Italy, in Agordo near Belluno.

FREDERICK MCCOY

Sir Frederick McCoy, FRS (1817 – 16 May 1899) was a British palaeontologist and museum administrator, active in Australia.

Early Life

McCoy was the son of Dr. Simon McCoy, M.D. and was born in Dublin; some sources have his year of birth as 1823, but 1817 is the most likely. He was educated in that city and at Cambridge for the medical profession.

Palaeontology Career

McCoy's interests, however, became early centred in natural history, and especially in geology, and at the age of eighteen he published a *Catalogue of Organic Remains compiled from specimens exhibited in the Rotunda at Dublin* (1841). He assisted Sir RJ Griffith by studying the fossils of the carboniferous and silurian rocks of Ireland, and they prepared a joint *in 1844 appeared A Synopsis of the Character of Carboniferous Limestone Fossils of Ireland* (1844) and *Synopsis of the Silurian Fossils of Ireland* (1846).

In 1846 Sedgwick secured his services, and for at least four years he devoted himself to the determination and arrangement of the fossils in the Woodwardian Museum at Cambridge. Sedgwick wrote of him as "an excellent naturalist, an incomparable and most philosophical palaeontologist, and one of the steadiest and quickest workmen that ever undertook the arrangement of a museum" (*Life and Letters of Sedgwick*, ii. 194). Together they prepared the important and now classic work entitled *A Synopsis of the Classification of the British Palaeozoic Rocks, with a Systematic Description of the British Palaeozoic Fossils in the Geological Museum of the University of Cambridge* (1855). Meanwhile McCoy in 1850 had been appointed professor of geology in Queen's College, Belfast.

Late Life

To local societies he contributed many papers, and he continued his active scientific work for fifty-eight years—his last contribution, "Note on a new Australian Pterygotus," being printed in the *Geological Magazine* for May 1899. He was awarded the Murchison Medal of the Geological Society of London in 1879 and was elected F.R.S. in 1880, and was one of the first to receive the Hon. D.Sc. from the university of Cambridge. In 1886 he was made CMG, and in 1891 KCMG. He died in Melbourne on the 16 May 1899. Obituary (with bibliography) in Geol. Mag. 1899, p. 283.

FRED LONGSTAFFE

Dr. Fred J. Longstaffe is the Provost and VP Academic at the University of Western Ontario. He is a highly regarded leader in Earth Science research. His current focus is on applying knowledge of stable isotopes to various fields of study.

Longstaffe earned a BSc (Hon) from the University of Windsor and a PhD in Geology from McMaster University. In 1978, he attended the University of Alberta as a Killam Post-Doctoral Scholar. After that he joined that university's faculty in the Department of Geology. In 1987, Longstaffe moved to the University of Western as a full professor in Geology and opened the Laboratory for Stable Isotope Science. The labs principal research areas are environmental geochemistry and clastic diagenesis, with special emphasis on the application of stable isotopes and other biogeochemical methods to studies of the environment and climate change. The Departments of Geology and Geophysics were merged in 1993. He became the Chair of the newly formed Department of Earth Sciences. Dr. Longstaffe gave up that position in 1999 to take on the larger role of Dean of the Faculty of Science. In July 2005, Longstaffe became the university's Provost and VP Academic.

Dr. Longstaffe's research has attracted substantial funding from Natural Sciences and Engineering Research Council, Social Science and Humanities Research Council and Canada Foundation for

Innovation. His current research focuses on the use of stable isotopes to study earth and environmental science, ecosystems, oil sands, and anthropology.

Longstaffe has served as President of the Geological Association of Canada. He has frequently served on Natural Sciences and Engineering Research Council and Royal Society of Canada committees.

GERD BINNIG

Gerd Binnig (born July 20, 1947) is a German physicist, and a Nobel laureate.

He was born in Frankfurt am Main and played in the ruins of the city during his childhood. His family lived partly in Frankfurt and partly in Offenbach, and he attended school in both cities. At the age of 10, he decided to become a physicist, but he soon wondered whether he had made the right choice. He concentrated more on music, playing in a band. He also started playing the violin at 15 and played in his school orchestra.

In 1969, he married Lore Wagler, a psychologist, and they have a daughter born in Switzerland and a son born in California. His hobbies are reading, swimming and golf.

In 1978, he accepted an offer from IBM to join their Zurich research group. There, he met Heinrich Rohrer, with whom he shared the Nobel Prize in Physics in 1986 for their design of the scanning tunneling microscope (STM).

The team included Christoph Gerber and Edmund Weibel, and they were soon recognized with a number of prizes: the German Physics Prize, the Otto Klung Prize, the Hewlett Packard Prize, the King Faisal Prize, and ultimately, the Nobel Prize.

In 1994 Professor Gerd Binnig founded Definiens which turned in the year 2000 into a commercial enterprise. Today, companies and institutions around the world use Definiens' technology to maximize the value of images and thereby enabling better decisions. Definiens currently focuses on applications for Life Sciences and Earth Sciences.

In Life Sciences, Definiens' technology is used to accelerate the drug discovery, development, and diagnostics processes. In Earth Sciences, Definiens' technology enables satellite and aerial image classification and analysis with greater speed, accuracy and insight.

GIUSEPPE MERCALLI

Giuseppe Mercalli (May 21, 1850-March 19, 1914) was an Italian volcanologist.

Biography

Born in Milan, Mercalli was ordained a Roman Catholic priest and soon became a professor of the Natural Sciences at the seminary of Milan. He was removed from the professorship when he was suspected of liberalism for openly supporting a national monument to honour the great philosopher-priest Antonio Rosmini-Serbati.

Subsequently the Italian government appointed him a professor at Domodossola, followed by a post at Reggio di Calabria and finally a post at the Naples University. He was also director of the Vesuvius Observatory until the time of his death. Among his pupils was Giuseppe Moscati.

He is best remembered today for his Mercalli scale for measuring earthquakes which is still used today.

The Mercalli scale, unlike the more famous Richter scale, doesn't measure the actual energy released by an earthquake but how much effect an earthquake had on a given area, making it poorly suited for measuring earthquakes in sparsely populated areas, but ideal for comparing damage done by various tremors. The Mercalli scale gives a rating from I to XII, where I is felt only by a very few and XII has near total damage, few or no masonry structures remain standing, and objects are thrown into the air.

GEOFFREY HATTERSLEY-SMITH

Geoffrey Francis Hattersley-Smith (1923-) is an English born geologist and glaciologist. He attended Winchester College in Hampshire and graduated from New College, Oxford. From 1948-1950 he was the base leader for the Falkland Islands Dependencies Survey (now the British Antarctic Survey) on King George Island.

In 1951 he became a staff member with the Canadian Defence Research Board (DRB) (now part of the Department of National Defence. With the DRB he was part of several expeditions to places such as the Saint Elias Mountains in the Yukon and Cornwallis Island, Northwest Territories (now Nunavut). From 1953-1954 he led the joint Canada-United States expedition to Ellesmere Island In 1956 he received a Doctor of Philosophy from Oxford for his work on Ellesmeres glaciers.

In 1957 he began 16 years of research on Ellesmere Island. As part of the International Geophysical Year (1957-1958) he went to Lake Hazen and until 1973 worked either there or at Ward Hunt Island. In 1963 he set up a camp and conducted field research at Tanquary Fiord. The teams that he led named over 50 features on Ellesmere Island, such as Barbeau Peak and Turnabout River.

He was elected to the Royal Society of Canada in 1970 and in 1973 he retired as head of the DRB's Geotechnical Section and returned to England.

After returning to England he re-joined the British Antarctic Survey and was the secretary of the Antarctic Place-names Committee for the Foreign and Commonwealth Office in London. In 1984 the Advisory Committee on Antarctic Names named Cape Hattersley-Smith after him.

In 1990 Hattersley-Smith retired to Kent.

GEORGE MERCER DAWSON

George Mercer Dawson (August 1, 1849 – March 2, 1901) was a Canadian scientist and surveyor. He was born in Pictou, Nova Scotia, the son of Sir John William Dawson. By age 11, he was afflicted with tuberculosis of the spine (Pott's disease) that resulted in a deformed back and stunted his growth. However, his physical limitations did not deter Dawson from becoming one of Canada's greatest scientists. Tutors and his father provided his educational needs during his slow recovery from the illness. Dawson later attended the High School of Montreal and McGill University (part-time) before moving to London to study geology and palaeontology at the Royal School of Mines (now part of Imperial College London) beginning in 1869. Dawson graduated after three years with the highest marks in his class. Dawson received an LL.D. from Queen's University in 1890 and then from McGill University in 1891.

Dawson began his career in the 1870s as a professor of chemistry at Morrin College in Quebec City. He then performed extensive surveys of Western Canada in the 19th century beginning with the International Boundary Survey from 1872 to 1876. The result was a 387-page report called *Geology and Resources of the Region in the Vicinity of the 49th parallel from the Lake of the Woods to the Rocky Mountains, with Lists of Plants and Animals Collected, and Notes on the Fossils from the Killadeer Badlands currently part of Grasslands National Park.* This report established Dawson as a respected scientist.

During 1883 and 1884, Dawson travelled through the Canadian Rockies where he was tasked by the Canadian government to map out major mountains and mountain passes as well as significant rivers. Some of the many peaks he discovered were Mount Assiniboine 3,618 metres (11,870 ft) and Mount Temple 3,543 metres (11,620 ft). As a result of his field research, a map of his work was published in 1886 covering the Canadian Rockies from the US border to Red Deer Valley and Kicking Horse Pass.

In 1887, he led an expedition into the Yukon, developing some of the first maps of what later became the separate territory. His report was republished ten years later to satisfy the public's interest in the region as a result of the Klondike Gold Rush. Dawson City was named after him. Dawson Creek, British Columbia is also named in his honour.

Dawson became a staff member of the Geological Survey of Canada in 1875, progressed to assistant director in 1883 and finally to director in 1895.

Dawson died unexpectedly in Ottawa after a one day bout with acute bronchitis. He was interred in the family plot in the Mount Royal Cemetery in Montreal.

GEORGE V. CHILINGAR

George V. Chilingarian (he uses both Chilingar and Chilingarian as his last name) is a Professor of Civil and Petroleum Engineering at the University of Southern California (USC). He is one of the best-known petroleum geologists in the world and the founder of several prestigious journals in the oil and gas industry. Chilingar has published 61 books and hundreds of articles on geology, petroleum engineering and environmental engineering. He serves as president of the U.S. branch of the Russian Academy of Sciences and 17 of his books have been translated into Russian. In recognition of these contributions, the Russian Academy of Sciences has honoured him as a Knight of Arts and Sciences. He received his bachelor's and master's degrees in petroleum engineering and a Ph.D. in geology (with a minor in petroleum engineering), all at USC.

His greatest contribution to the petroleum industry may be a means of identifying oil-rich rock by analyzing the ratio of calcium to magnesium in core samples. This method was used in discovering one of Iran's largest oil fields, which was then named after Chilingar. He also played a key role in the development of Thailand's offshore oil reserves. Chilingar saw natural gas bubbles in the Gulf of Siam and redirected exploratory efforts, thus saving the nascent Thai oil industry.

In 2001, King Fahd of Saudi Arabia acknowledged Chilingar's significant contributions to the success of Saudi Aramco as well as the discovery and extraction of oil reserves around the world. The Saudi consul general in Los Angeles, Ambassador Mohammed A. Al-Salloum, presented the award, a globe signifying the worldwide reach and importance of the petroleum industry and Saudi Aramco.

He served as senior petroleum engineering adviser to the United Nations from 1967 to 1969, and then again from 1978 to 1987. He was also an energy policy adviser to California Governor Ronald Reagan in 1973.

GEORG AGRICOLA

Georgius Agricola (March 24, 1494 – November 21, 1555) was a German scholar and scientist. Known as "the father of mineralogy", he was born at Glauchau in Saxony. His real name was *Georg Bauer*; *Agricola* is the Latinised version of his name, *Bauer* meaning *peasant.* He is best known for his book De Re Metallica.

Life and Work

Gifted with a precocious intellect, Georg early threw himself into the pursuit of the "new learning," with such effect that at the age of twenty he was appointed Rector extraordinarius of Greek at the so-called Great School of Zwickau, and made his appearance as a writer on philology. After two years he gave up his appointment in order to pursue his studies at Leipzig, where, as rector, he received the support of the professor of classics, Peter Mosellanus (1493-1524), a celebrated humanist of the time, with whom he had already been in correspondence. Here he also devoted himself to the study of medicine, physics, and chemistry. After the death of Mosellanus he went to Italy from 1524 to 1526, where he took his doctor's degree.

He returned to Zwickau in 1527, and was chosen as town physician at Joachimsthal, a centre of mining and smelting works, his object being partly "to fill in the gaps in the art of healing," partly to test what had been written about mineralogy by careful observation of ores and the methods of their treatment. His thorough grounding in philology and philosophy had accustomed him to systematic thinking, and this enabled him to construct out of his studies and observations of minerals a logical system which he began to publish in 1528. Agricola's dialogue *Bermannus, sive de re metallica dialogus*, (1530) the first attempt to reduce to scientific order the knowledge won by practical work, brought Agricola into notice; it contained an approving letter from Erasmus at the beginning of the book.

In 1530 Prince Maurice of Saxony appointed him historiographer with an annual allowance, and he migrated to Chemnitz, the centre of the mining industry, in order to widen the range of his observations. The citizens showed their appreciation of his learning by appointing him town physician in 1533. In that year, he published a book about Greek and Roman weights and measures, *De Mensuis et Ponderibus.*

He was also elected burgomaster of Chemnitz. His popularity was, however, short-lived. Chemnitz was a violent centre of the Protestant movement, while Agricola never wavered in his allegiance to the old religion; and he was forced to resign his office. He now lived apart from the contentious movements of the time, devoting himself wholly to learning. His chief interest was still in mineralogy; but he occupied himself also with medical, mathematical, theological and historical subjects, his chief historical work being the *Dominatores Saxonici a prima origine ad hanc aetatem*, published at Freiberg. In 1544 he published the *De ortu et causis subterraneorum*, in which he laid the first foundations of a physical geology, and criticized the theories of the ancients. In 1545 followed the *De natura eorum quae effluunt e terra*; in 1546 the *De veteribus et novis metallis*, a comprehensive account of the discovery and occurrence of minerals and also more commonly known as De Natura Fossilium; in 1548 the *De animantibus subterraneis*; and in the two following years a number of smaller works on the metals.

GLAYDE WHITNEY

Glayde D. Whitney (1939–8 January 2002) was a behavioural geneticist and psychology professor at Florida State University. Beyond his work into the genetics of sensory system function in mice, in his later life he supported race and intelligence research and eugenics, and for these views was frequently accused of supporting scientific racism.

Biography

Whitney was born in Montana and grew up in Minnesota. He earned his bachelor's degree from University of Minnesota, as well as his doctorate from there in 1966. He then enlisted in the United States Air Force and served until 1969. He then worked as a postdoctoral fellow at the Institute for Behavioural Genetics with the University of Colorado, under Gerry McClearn and John DeFries. In 1970, Whitney was hired by the Florida State University to represent behavioural genetics in the psychobiology programme, where he would stay until his death. He considered himself to be "a Hubert Humphrey liberal."

Work in Behavioural Genetics

Whitney was the author of over 60 papers on the genetics of taste sensitivity in inbred mice. Support for some of this work came from a prestigious Claude Pepper Award for Research Excellence from the National Institute on Deafness and Other Communication Disorders (NIDCD) and in 1994, Glayde received the Manheimer Lectureship Award from the Monell Chemical Senses Centre, which recognizes career achievements of individuals in the chemosensory sciences. At the height of his genetics career he was the president of the Behaviour Genetics Association (BGA).

GEORGE DAVIS SNELL

George Davis Snell (December 19, 1903 – June 6, 1996) was an American mouse geneticist and basic transplant immunologist.

Work

George Snell shared the 1980 Nobel Prize in Physiology or Medicine with Baruj Benacerraf and Jean Dausset for their discoveries concerning "genetically determined structures on the cell surface that regulate immunological reactions". Snell specifically "discovered the genetic factors that determine the possibilities of transplanting tissue from one individual to another. It was Snell who introduced the concept of H antigens." Snell's work in mice led to the discovery of HLA, the major histocompatibility complex, in humans (and all vertebrates) that is analogous to the H-2 complex in mice. Recognition of these key genes was prerequisite to successful tissue and organ transplantation.

Life

George Snell was born in Bradford, Massachusetts, the youngest of three schildren. His father (who was born in Minnesota), worked as a secretary for the local YMCA; he invented a device for winding induction coils for motorboat engines. Snell was educated in the Brookline, Massachusetts schools and then enrolled at Dartmouth College in Hanover, New Hampshire where he continued his passion for mathematics and science, focusing on genetics. He received his Bachelor's degree from Dartmouth in 1926.

On the recommendation of John Gerould, his genetics professor at Dartmouth, Snell did graduate work at Harvard University with William E. Castle, the first American biologist to look for Mendelian inheritance in mammals. Snell earned his PhD from Harvard in 1930. His doctoral thesis was on genetic linkage in mice.

Snell then spent two years as a postdoctoral fellow at the University of Texas with H.J. Muller, who pioneered radiation genetics (and was also to win a Nobel Prize). Not surprisingly, Snell studied the genetic effects of x-rays on mice with Muller.

This experience "served to convince me that research was my real love," Snell wrote in his autobiography. " If it were to be research, mouse genetics was the clear choice and the Jackson Laboratory, founded in 1929 by Dr. Clarence Cook Little, one of Castle's earlier students, almost the inevitable selection as a place to work." The Jackson Laboratory was (and still is) the world's mecca for mouse genetics.

In 1935 Snell joined the staff of the Jackson Lab in Bar Harbor on beautiful Mt. Desert Island by the coast of Maine and he remained there for the entire balance of his long career. In Bar Harbor, he met and married Rhoda Carson. Together they had three sons, Thomas, Roy, and Peter. In his leisure time, Snell enjoyed skiing, a passion he developed during his years at Dartmouth, as well as tennis.

In 1988, he authored a substantial book, *Search for a Rational Ethic*, on the nature of ethics and the rules by which we live. It includes an evolution-based ethic founded on biological realities that he believed to be applicable to all human beings.

Snell died in Bar Harbor, Maine on June 6, 1996.

GOPALASAMUDRAM NARAYANA IYER RAMACHANDRAN

Gopalasamudram Narayana Iyer Ramachandran (8 October 1922-7 April 2001) is widely acknowledged as one of the most important Indian scientists of the 20th century, best known for his work that led to his creation of the Ramachandran plot for understanding peptide structure. He also made other major contributions in biology and physics.

Birth and Education

Ramachandran was born in the town of Ernakulam, Kerala, India. He joined Indian Institute of Science, Bangalore in 1942 in the Electrical Engineering Department. Quickly realizing his interest in physics, he switched to Department of Physics to complete his master's and doctoral thesis under the supervision of Nobel laureate Sir C. V. Raman. In 1942 he received a master's degree in physics from Madras University and received D.Sc. in 1947. Here he mostly studied crystal physics and crystal optics. During his studies he created an X-ray focusing mirror for the X-ray Microscope. The resulting field of crystal topography is used extensively in studies involving crystal growth and solid-state reactivity. Ramachandran then spent two years (1947–1949) at the Cavendish Laboratory in Cambridge, where he earned his Ph.D. for 'studies on X-ray diffuse scattering and its application to determination of elastic constants'.

Research

After completing his Ph.D, returned to Indian Institute of Science, Bangalore, India in 1949 as an assistant professor of physics. In 1952 he moved to Madras University as a professor and head, Department of Physics where he continued his work on crystal physics. But his interest shifted to the structure of biological macromolecules. Using X-ray diffraction Ramachandran along with Gopinath Kartha proposed and published the triple helical structure of collagen in 1954.

Wanting to tackle problems at a more fundamental level, Ramachandran decided to use this information to examine the various polypeptide conformations then known and also to develop a good 'yardstick' that could be used for examining and assessing any structure in general, but peptides in particular. The result which emerged from these calculations in 1962,-now commonly known as the Ramachandran plot-was published in the Journal of Molecular Biology in 1963 and has become an essential tool in the field of protein conformation. When it was first calculated, crystal structures had barely been obtained for any protein. From the mid 1960s onward Ramachandran studied many topics relating to the conformation of peptides including types of a-turns, conformation of prolyl residues, cis-peptide units, occurrence and need for non-planarity of the peptides, NMR coupling constants, peptides containing L and D residues and many others.

Ramachandran can be credited for bringing together into the one field of molecular biophysics the then disparate fields of X-ray crystallography, peptide synthesis, NMR and other optical studies, and physico-chemical experimentation.

In 1970 he founded the Molecular Biophysics Unit at the Indian Institute of Science which was later known as the Centre of Advanced Study in Biophysics and Crystallography.

Ramachandran and A.V. Lakshminarayana developed convolution-backprojection algorithms which greatly improved the quality and practicality of results obtainable by x-ray tomography. Compared to previously used methods, their algorithms considerably reduced computer processing time for image reconstruction, as well as providing more numerically accurate images. As a result, commercial manufacturers of x-ray tomographic scanners started building systems capable of reconstructing high resolution images that were almost photographically perfect. In 1971, they published their research in a paper ("Three dimensional reconstructions from radiographs and electron micrographs: Application of convolution instead of Fourier Transforms," Proc. Nat. Acad. Sci., vol. 68, pp. 2236-2240, 1971).

Notable awards that Ramachandran received include the Shanti Swarup Bhatnagar Award for Physics in India and the Fellowship of the Royal Society of London. In 1999 the International Union of Crystallography honoured him with the Ewald Prize for his 'outstanding contributions to crystallography'. In short, though Ramachandran did not receive the Nobel Prize, he will certainly be remembered for his contributions to science which were surely above a Nobel.

Later Years

During the last few years of his life he suffered a stroke and was affected by Parkinson's disease. Ramachandran died in 2001 at the age of 78.

GEORGE R. PRICE

George R. Price (1922–January 6, 1975) was an American population geneticist. Originally a physical chemist and later a science journalist, he moved to London in 1967, where he worked in theoretical biology at the Galton Laboratory, making three important contributions: first, rederiving W.D. Hamilton's work on kin selection with a new Price equation; second, introducing (with John Maynard Smith) the concept of the evolutionarily stable strategy (ESS), a central concept in game theory; and third, formalising Fisher's fundamental theorem of natural selection. A troubled man, Price converted to Christianity from atheism, and after giving all his possessions to the poor, committed suicide.

Early Life

Price was born in 1922, the younger brother of Edison. His father, an electrician, died when he was four. His mother was a former opera singer, and the family struggled through the Great Depression.

Having attended public school in New York, Price graduated with a degree in chemistry from University of Chicago in 1943 and received his doctorate in the subject from the same institution in 1946, having worked on the Manhattan Project.

In 1947 he married Julia Madigan, but their relationship was contentious because George was a militant atheist whilst his wife was a practicing Roman Catholic. They divorced in 1955, having had two daughters, Annamarie and Kathleen.

Early Career

Between 1946 and 1948, Price was an instructor in chemistry at Harvard University and consultant to Argonne National Laboratory. Later, he worked as a research associate in medicine at the University of Minnesota, working on, amongst other things, fluorescence microscopy and liver perfusion. In 1955 and 1956, he published two papers in the journal *Science* critisicing the apparently pseudoscientific claims of extra-sensory perception.

Continuing with science journalism, he tried to write a book entitled *No Easy Way* about the United States' Cold War with the Soviet Union and the People's Republic of China but complained that "the world kept changing faster than I could write about it", and so the book was never finished.

From 1961 to 1967, Price was employed by IBM as a consultant on graphic data processing. In 1966 he was treated for thyroid cancer, but the operation to remove the tumour left his shoulder partially paralysed and reliant on thyroxine medication. With the money from his medical insurance, he moved to the United Kingdom to start a new life in November 1967.

G. H. HARDY

Godfrey Harold Hardy (February 7, 1877 Cranleigh, Surrey, England – December 1, 1947 Cambridge, Cambridgeshire, England) was a prominent English mathematician, known for his achievements in number theory and mathematical analysis.

Non-mathematicians usually know him for *A Mathematician's Apology*, his essay from 1940 on the aesthetics of mathematics. The apology is often considered one of the best insights into the mind of a working mathematician written for the layman.

His relationship as mentor, from 1914 onwards, of the Indian mathematician Srinivasa Ramanujan has become celebrated. Hardy almost immediately recognized Ramanujan's extraordinary albeit untutored brilliance, and Hardy and Ramanujan became close collaborators. In an interview by Paul Erdos, when Hardy was asked what his greatest contribution to mathematics was, Hardy unhesitatingly replied that it was the discovery of Ramanujan. He called their collaboration "the one romantic incident in my life."

Life

G.H. Hardy was born 7 February 1877, in Cranleigh, Surrey, England, into a teaching family. His father was Bursar and Art Master at Cranleigh School; his mother had been a senior mistress at Lincoln Training College for teachers. Both parents were mathematically inclined.

Hardy's own natural affinity for mathematics was perceptible at a young age. When just two years old, he wrote numbers up to millions, and when taken to church he amused himself by factorizing the numbers of the hymns.

After schooling at Cranleigh, Hardy was awarded a scholarship to Winchester College for his mathematical work. In 1896 he entered Trinity College, Cambridge. After only two years of preparation he was fourth in the Mathematics Tripos examination. Years later, Hardy sought to abolish the Tripos system, as he felt that it was becoming more an end in itself than a means to an end. While at university, Hardy joined the Cambridge Apostles, an elite, intellectual secret society.

As the most important influence Hardy cites the self-study of *Cours d'analyse de l'Ecole Polytechnique* by the French mathematician Camille Jordan, through which he became acquainted with the more precise mathematics tradition in continental Europe. In 1900 he passed part II of the tripos and was awarded a fellowship. In 1903 he earned his M.A., which was the highest academic degree at English universities at that time. From 1906 onward he held the position of a lecturer, who had to teach six hours per week leaving him plenty of time for research. In 1919 he left Cambridge to take the Savilian Chair of Geometry at Oxford in the aftermath of the Bertrand Russell affair during World War I. He returned to Cambridge in 1931, where he was Sadleirian Professor until 1942.

The Indian Clerk (2007) is a novel by David Leavitt based on Hardy's life at Cambridge, including his discovery of and relationship with Srinivasa Ramanujan.

GABRIEL DOVER

Gabriel A. Dover (Gabby Dover) is a British geneticist. He is best known for coining the term molecular drive in 1982 to describe a putative third evolutionary force operating distinctly from natural selection and genetic drift. More generally, his research has been on the evolution of genes and genomes, particularly the complex processes that occur in multigene families such as ribosomal RNA genes. His recent work has focused on development in flies, in particular the co-evolution between the developmental regulatory elements involved in morphogenesis. His BSc is from the University of Leeds, and his PhD from the University of Cambridge. The majority of his career was spent at the Department of Genetics at the University of Cambridge. In 1992, Dover became a Professor of Genetics at the University of Leicester. He is currently a Research Fellow of the Leverhulme Trust.

Dover co-edited the textbook *Genome Evolution* (Academic Press, 1982) with Richard Flavell. He has also written a popular book on evolution, *Dear Mr Darwin: Letters on the Evolution of Life and Human Nature* (Weidenfeld & Nicolson, 2000), framed as an exchange of letters with Charles Darwin from beyond the grave. The book seeks to refute the selfish gene theory promulgated by Richard Dawkins.

GEORGE WELLS BEADLE

George Wells Beadle (October 22, 1903 – June 9, 1989) was an American scientist in the field of genetics, and Nobel Prize in Physiology or Medicine Nobel laureate who with Edward Lawrie Tatum discovered the role of genes in regulating biochemical events within cells. Beadle and Tatum's key experiments involved exposing the bread mold *Neurospora crassa* to x-rays, causing mutations. In a series of experiments, they showed that these mutations caused changes in specific enzymes involved in metabolic pathways. These experiments led them to propose a direct link between genes and enzymatic reactions, known as the "one gene, one enzyme" hypothesis.

Biography

Beadle was born in Wahoo, Nebraska. He received his Bachelor of Science degree in agronomy from the University of Nebraska's College of Agriculture in 1926 where he was a member of FarmHouse fraternity. At the recommendation of his advisor, Franklin D. Keim, he then entered graduate school in agronomy at Cornell University, intending to study ecology. He soon switched his focus to genetics and cytology, pursuing research on maize (corn) genetics under Rollins Adams Emerson—including some collaboration with Barbara McClintock. He received his Ph.D. from Cornell in 1931.

For post-doctoral work, Beadle joined Thomas Hunt Morgan's "fly lab" at the California Institute of Technology, where he worked with Alfred Sturtevant and others on *Drosophila* genetics. There, working with Boris Ephrussi, he helped develop a technique for transplanting foreign cells in fly larvae (creating a third eye in flies' abdomens); this technique was used to demonstrate that some mutations affecting eye colour involved genes that controlled specific metabolic steps in the production of eye pigment. In an effort to precisely characterize the reactions and substances involved, he recruited biochemist Edward Tatum to work on the pigment problem as well. They eventually isolated and identified the pigment precursor found in the "*vermilion*" mutant, but did so shortly after an independent German group. Over the course of his *Drosophila* work, Beadle was a professor at Harvard University, then Stanford University. With Tatum, Beadle switched his focus to a model organism more suited to biochemical genetics: *Neurospora.* By constructing mutant strains that required specific nutritional elements (amino acids or vitamins), they established that individual gene mutations were responsible for individual steps in the metabolism and synthesis of vital nutrients. This led, in 1941, to propose the "one gene-one enzyme hypothesis," the idea that a gene specifies a single enzyme, rather than a complex set of characteristics (as was generally assumed).

In 1946, with the support of Linus Pauling, Beadle was recruited to head the newly reorganized biology division of Caltech; the department was one of the prototypes of what would become known as *molecular biology.* During the early Cold War, Beadle was outspoken in his defense of colleagues under investigation for suspected Communist ties, and also worked on defining and publicizing the potential dangers of nuclear weapons-related radiation. In 1958, Beadle and Tatum were awarded the Nobel Prize in Physiology and Medicine for their work on biochemical genetics. Beadle went on to serve as president of the University of Chicago from 1961-1968, helping—through fund-raising and recruitment—to re-establish its reputation as a top research university. He published a book, *The Language of Life*, in 1966. Following his retirement as university president, Beadle returned to research, now on the evolutionary relationship between corn and teosinte. He continued research until the late 1970s, when Alzheimer's disease made continued intellectual work impossible. George Beadle died in 1989; his second wife Muriel Barnett Beadle died in 1994. He had one son, David (b. 1931), with his first wife Marion Hill Beadle.

GUIDO BARBUJANI

Guido Barbujani (born January 31, 1955) is an Italian population geneticist, evolutionist and literary author born in Adria, who has been working at the State University of New York at Stony Brook (NY), at the Padua and Bologna Universities, and is now a professor at the University of Ferrara since 1996.

Works

A population geneticist by training, has been working on several aspects of human genetic variation. In collaboration with Robert R. Sokal, he pioneered the statistical comparison of patterns of genetic and linguistic variation, showing that language differences may contribute to reproductive isolation, and hence promote genetic divergence between populations. His analyses of geographic patterns of genetic variation in Europe support Luca Cavalli-Sforza's Neolithic demic diffusion model, *i.e.* the idea that farming spread in the Neolithic mainly because farmers did, and not by cultural transmission. Two implications of this finding are that most Europeans' ancestors did not live in Europe, but in the Near East, up to Neolithic times, and that in their Westward expansion the early farmers carried with them their genes, their technologies, and possibly their languages too.

His studies of the amount of DNA differentiation among human populations, and of its spatial distribution, led to the conclusion that traditional human racial classification fails to account for most of the existing patterns of genetic variation. Rather, it seems that genetic variation is largely uncorrelated across genes, which, if confirmed, would explain why no consensus was ever reached on a catalog of human biological races. This activity has also resulted in publications for the general public. His recent DNA studies focus on genetic characterization of ancient human populations, such as Paleolithic anatomically-modern humans of Cro-Magnoid morphology, the Etruscans and the Neolithic (nuragic) Sardinians. Barbujani is the author of three novels.

GEOFFREY WILKINSON

Sir Geoffrey Wilkinson (14 July 1921 – 26 September 1996) was an English chemist.

Biography

Wilkinsonwas born in the village of Springside, near Todmorden in Yorkshire. His father, also a Geoffrey, was a master house painter and decorator; his mother worked in a local cotton mill. One of his uncles, an organist and choirmaster, had married into a family that owned a small chemical company making Epsom and Glauber's salts for the pharmaceutical industry. This is where he first developed an interest in chemistry. He was educated at the local council primary school and, after winning a County Scholarship in 1932, went to Todmorden Secondary School. There, he had the same physics teacher as Sir John Cockcroft, who received a Nobel Prize for "splitting the atom". Wilkinson's catalyst $RhCl(PPh_3)_3$

In 1939 he obtained a Royal Scholarship for study at Imperial College, London, from where he graduated in 1941. In 1942 Professor Friedrich Adolf Paneth was recruiting young chemists for the nuclear energy project. Wilkinson joined and was sent out to Canada, where he stayed in Montreal and later Chalk River Laboratories until he could leave in 1946. For the next four years he worked with Professor Glenn T. Seaborg at Berkeley, California, mostly on nuclear taxonomy. He then became a Research Associate at the Massachusetts Institute of Technology and began to return to his first interest as a student-transition metal complexes of ligands such as carbon monoxide and olefins. He was then at the Harvard University from September 1951 until he returned to England in December 1955, with a sabbatical break of nine months in Copenhagen. At Harvard, he still did some nuclear work on excitation functions for protons in cobalt, but had already begun to work on olefin complexes.

In June 1955 he was appointed to the chair of Inorganic Chemistry at Imperial College in the University of London, and from then on worked almost entirely on the complexes of transition metals. He was married, with two daughters.

GUNTER WIRTHS

Gunter Wirths was a German chemist who was an authority on uranium production, especially reactor-grade. He worked at *Auergesellschaft* in the production of uranium for the *Heereswaffenamt* and its *Uranverein* project. In 1945, he was sent the Soviet Union to work on the Russian atomic bomb project. When he was released from the Soviet Union, he settled in West Germany, and worked at the Degussa company.

Career

Wirths was a colleague of Nikolaus Riehl, who was the director of the scientific headquarters of *Auergesellschaft*. *Auergesellschaft* had a substantial amount of "waste" uranium from which it had extracted radium. After reading a paper in 1939 by Siegfried Flugge, on the technical use of nuclear energy from uranium, Riehl recognized a business opportunity for the company, and, in July of that year, went to the *Heereswaffenamt* (HWA, Army Ordnance Office) to discuss the production of uranium. The HWA was interested and Riehl committed corporate resources to the task. The HWA eventually provided an order for the production of uranium oxide, which took place in the Auergesellschaft plant in Oranienburg, north of Berlin. It was this that got Wirths involved with the production of uranium metal, which *Auergesellschaft* did for the *Uranverein* project of the *Heereswaffenamt*.

GEORGE M. WHITESIDES

George M. Whitesides (b. August 3, 1939, Louisville, Kentucky) is an American chemist and professor of chemistry at Harvard University. He is best known for his work in the areas of NMR spectroscopy, organometallic chemistry, molecular self-assembly, soft lithography, microfabrication, microfluidics, and nanotechnology. Whitesides is also known for his "outline system" for writing scientific papers. As of March 2008, he has the highest Hirsch index rating of all living chemists.

Education and Academic Career

Whitesides attended secondary school at Phillips Andover and graduated in 1957. He received his A.B. degree from Harvard College in 1960 and earned a Ph.D. in chemistry from the California Institute of Technology in 1964. Under the tutelage of John D. Roberts, Whitesides' graduate work focused on the use of NMR spectroscopy in organic chemistry. Among other research endeavors, he studied spin-spin coupling in a variety of organic compounds and the structure of Grignard reagents in solution.

Research at MIT

Whitesides began his independent career as an assistant professor at the Massachusetts Institute of Technology in 1963 and remained there until 1982. While at MIT, he played a pivotal role in the development of the Corey-House-Posner-Whitesides reaction, which now bears his name.

Research at Harvard

In 1982, Whitesides moved his laboratory to the Department of Chemistry at Harvard University, his alma mater. He has served tenures as chairman of the Chemistry Department (1986-89) and associate Dean of the Faculty of Arts and Sciences (1989-92).

Current Research

Whitesides is currently the Woodford L. and Ann A. Flowers University Professor at Harvard, one of only 21 University Professorships at the institution. He maintains an active research group of over 35 graduate and postdoctoral students with a four-person office support staff and lab space covering more than 6, 000 square feet. According to the biography on his Web site, Whitesides' current research interests include "physical and organic chemistry, materials science, biophysics, complexity, surface science, microfluidics, self-assembly, micro-and nanotechnology, science for developing economies, origin of life, and cell-surface biochemistry." The single primary objective of his lab is "to fundamentally change the paradigms of science."

GLENN T. SEABORG

Glenn Theodore Seaborg (Swedish: *Glenn Teodor Sjoberg*) (April 19, 1912 – February 25, 1999) won the 1951 Nobel Prize in Chemistry for "discoveries in the chemistry of the transuranium elements, " contributed to the discovery and isolation of ten elements, developed the actinide concept and was the first to propose the actinide series which led to the current arrangement of the Periodic Table of the Elements.

He spent most of his career as an educator and research scientist at the University of California, Berkeley where he became the second Chancellor in its history and served as a University Professor. Seaborg advised ten presidents from Truman to Clinton on nuclear policy and was the chairman of the United States Atomic Energy Commission from 1961 to 1971 where he pushed for commercial nuclear energy and peaceful applications of nuclear science.

Throughout his career, Seaborg worked for arms control. He was signator to the Franck Report and contributed to the achievement of the Limited Test Ban Treaty, the Nuclear Non-Proliferation Treaty, and the Comprehensive Test Ban Treaty. Seaborg was a well-known advocate for science education and federal funding for pure research. He was a key contributor to the report "A Nation at Risk" as a member of President Reagan's National Commission on Excellence in Education and was the principal author of the Seaborg Report on academic science issued in the closing days of the Eisenhower administration.

Seaborg was the principal or co-discoverer of ten elements: plutonium, americium, curium, berkelium, californium, einsteinium, fermium, mendelevium, nobelium and element 106, which was named seaborgium in his honour while he was still living. He also developed more than 100 atomic isotopes, and is credited with important contributions to the separation of the isotope of uranium used in the atomic bomb at Hiroshima.

Early in his career, Seaborg was a pioneer in nuclear medicine and developed numerous isotopes of elements with important applications in the diagnosis and treatment of diseases, most notably iodine-131, which is used in the treatment of thyroid disease. In addition to his theoretical work in the development of the *actinide concept* which placed the actinide series beneath the lanthanide series on the periodic table, Seaborg proposed the placement of super-heavy elements in the transactinide and superactinide series. After sharing the 1951 Nobel Prize in Chemistry with Edwin McMillan, he received approximately 50 honorary doctorates and numerous other awards and honors.

The list of things named after Seaborg ranges from his atomic element to an asteroid. Seaborg was a prolific author, penning more than 50 books and 500 journal articles, often in collaboration with others. He received so many awards and honors that he was once listed in the Guinness Book of World Records as the person with the longest entry in *Who's Who in America.*

Biography

Of Swedish ancestry, Seaborg was born in Ishpeming, Michigan, the son of Herman Theodore (Ted) and Selma Olivia Erickson Seaborg. He had one sister, Jeanette. When Glenn Seaborg was a boy, the family moved to the Seaborg Home in a subdivision called Home Gardens, that was later annexed to the City of South Gate, California, a suburb of Los Angeles.

He kept a daily journal from 1927 until he suffered a stroke in 1998. As a youth, Seaborg was both a devoted sports fan and an avid movie buff. His mother encouraged him to become a book-keeper as she felt his literary interests were impractical. He did not take an interest in science until his junior year when he was inspired by Dwight Logan Reid, a chemistry and physics teacher at David Starr Jordan High School in Watts.

He graduated from Jordan in 1929 at the top of his class and received a bachelor's degree in chemistry at the University of California, Los Angeles in 1934. While at UCLA, he was invited by his German professor to meet Albert Einstein, an experience that had a profound impact on Seaborg and served as a model of graciousness for his encounters with aspiring students in later years. Seaborg worked his way through school as a stevedore (longshoreman), fruit packer and laboratory assistant.

GEORGE ANDREW OLAH

George Andrew Olah (born May 22, 1927 in Budapest, as *Olah Gyorgy*) is a Hungarian-born American chemist. He was significant in stabilizing and in studying carbocations via superacids. He won a Nobel Prize in Chemistry in 1994. Soon after, he was awarded the Priestley Medal, the highest honour granted by the American Chemical Society.

Life

Olah studied, then taught, at what is now Budapest University of Technology and Economics. As a result of the 1956 Hungarian Revolution, he and his family moved briefly to England and then to Canada where he joined Dow Chemical in Sarnia, Ontario, with another Hungarian chemist, Stephen J. Kuhn. Olah's pioneering work on carbocations started during his eight years with Dow. In 1965 he returned to academia at Case Western Reserve University and then to University of Southern California in 1977. In 1971, Olah became a naturalized citizen of the United States.

Olah is currently a distinguished professor at the University of Southern California and the director of the Loker Hydrocarbon Research Institute. In 2005, Olah wrote an essay promoting the methanol economy.

GIULIO NATTA

Giulio Natta (February 26, 1903, Imperia-Bergamo, 2 May 1979) was an Italian chemist, who won a Nobel Prize in Chemistry in 1963 with Karl Ziegler for work on high polymers. He was born in Imperia, Italy, on February 26, 1903. He graduated in Chemical Engineering at the Politecnico di Milano in 1924. In 1927 he passed the exams for becoming a professor there. In 1933 he became a full professor and the director of the Institute of General Chemistry of Pavia University, where he stayed until 1935. In that year he was appointed full professor in physical chemistry at the University of Rome. From 1936 to 1938 he moved as a full professor and director of the Institute of Industrial Chemistry at the Politecnico di Torino.

In 1938 he took the head of the Department of chemical engineering at Politecnico di Milano university, in a somehow criticized manner, when his predecessor Mario Giacomo Levi was forced to step down as a consequence of racial laws against Jews being introduced in fascist Italy.

His work at the Politecnico led to the improvement of earlier work by Ziegler and to the development of the Ziegler-Natta catalyst. He won a Nobel Prize in Chemistry in 1963 with Karl Ziegler for work on high polymers.

He was diagnosed with Parkinson's disease in 1956. His condition became severe enough in 1963, that his son had to help him in Stockholm during the Noble Prize Award Ceremony and a colleague had to give the lecture. Prof. Natta died on May 2, 1979.

Natta is buried in the cemetery of Bergamo.

GILBERT N. LEWIS

Gilbert Newton Lewis (October 23, 1875-March 23, 1946) was a famous American physical chemist known for his Lewis dot structures, his 1916 paper "The Atom and the Molecule", which is the foundation of modern valence bond theory, developed in coordination with Irving Langmuir, and his 1923 textbook *Thermodynamics and the Free Energy of Chemical Substances*, written in coordination with Merle Randall, one of the founding books in chemical thermodynamics. In 1926, Lewis coined the term "photon" for the smallest unit of radiant energy. He was a brother of Alpha Chi Sigma, the professional chemistry fraternity.

Career

After earning his Ph.D., he stayed as an instructor for a year before taking a travelling fellowship, studying under the physical chemist Wilhelm Ostwald at Leipzig and Walther Nernst at Gottingen. He then returned to Harvard as an instructor for three more years, and in 1904 left to become superintendent of weights and measures for the Bureau of Science of the Philippine Islands in Manila. The next year he returned to Cambridge when the Massachusetts Institute of Technology (MIT) appointed him to a faculty position, in which he had a chance to join a group of outstanding physical chemists under the direction of Arthur Amos Noyes. He quickly rose in rank, becoming assistant professor in 1907, associate professor on 1908, and full professor in 1911. He left MIT to become professor of physical chemistry and dean of the College of Chemistry at the University of California, Berkeley in 1912. Lewis Hall at Berkeley, built in 1948, is named in his honour.

GERMAIN HENRI HESS

Germain Henri Hess (August 7, 1802–November 30, 1850) was a Swiss-born Russian chemist and doctor who formulated Hess's Law, an early principle of thermochemistry.

Early Days

Born in Geneva, Switzerland, his father was an artist and in 1805 moved the family to Russia to find work. Beginning in 1822, Hess studied medicine at the University of Tartu. He qualified as a physician in 1825.

Hess turned to chemistry after a meeting with Jons Jakob Berzelius, the famous Swedish chemist, and went to Stockholm University to study under him. On his return to Russia, Hess joined an expedition to study the geology of the Urals before setting up a medical practice in Irkutsk.

Contributions to Chemistry

In 1830, Hess took up chemistry full time, researching and teaching, and later became a professor at the Saint Petersburg Technological Institute. His most famous paper, outlining his law on thermochemistry, was published there in 1840. His principle came to be called Hess's Law, which holds that in a series of chemical reactions, the total energy gained or lost depends only on the initial and final states, regardless of the number of steps. This is also known as the law of constant heat summation.

Further Studies and Final Days

Hess's other work concerned the investigation of minerals, including analysis of silver telluride (Ag_2Te), which was named Hessite in his honour. He also discovered that the oxidation of sugars yielded saccharic acid.

Hess was the author of a textbook on chemistry that was the standard Russian work for several decades. He died in St. Petersburg.

GILBERT WHITE

Gilbert White (18 July 1720 – 26 June 1793) was a pioneering naturalist and ornithologist.

White was born in his grandfather's vicarage at Selborne in Hampshire. He was educated by a private tutor in Basingstoke before going to Oriel College, Oxford. He obtained his deacon's orders in 1746, being fully ordained in 1749, and subsequently held several curacies in Hampshire and Wiltshire, including Selborne's neighbouring parishes of Newton Valence and Farringdon, as well as Selborne itself on four separate occasions. In 1752/53 White held the office of Junior Proctor at Oxford and was Dean of Oriel. In 1757 he became non-resident perpetual curate of Moreton Pinkney in Northamptonshire. After the death of his father in 1758, White moved back into the family home at *The Wakes* in Selborne, which he eventually inherited in 1763. In 1784 he became curate of Selborne for the fourth time, remaining so until his death. Having studied at Oriel at the behest of his uncle, he was ineligible to be considered for the permanent living of Selborne, which was in the gift of Magdalen College.

White is best known for his *The Natural History and Antiquities of Selborne* (1789). This was a compilation of his letters to Thomas Pennant, the leading British zoologist of the day, and the Hon. Daines Barrington, an English barrister and another Fellow of the Royal Society. These letters contained White's discoveries about local birds, animals and plants. He believed in distinguishing birds by observation rather than by collecting specimens, and was thus one of the first people to separate the similar-looking Chiffchaff, Willow Warbler and Wood Warbler by means of their song.

White is regarded by many as England's first ecologist and one of the founders of modern respect for nature. He said of the earthworm (1770):

> Earthworms, though in appearance a small and despicable link in the chain of nature, yet, if lost, would make a lamentable chasm [...] worms seem to be the great promoters of vegetation, which would proceed but lamely without them...

White and William Markwick collected records of the dates of emergence of more than 400 plant and animal species, White recording in Hampshire and Markwick in Sussex between 1768 and 1793. These data, summarised in *The Natural History and Antiquities of Selborne* as the earliest and latest dates for each event over the 25-year period, are among the earliest examples of modern phenology. His 1783/4 diary corroborates the dramatic climatic impacts of the volcanic 'Laki haze' that spread from Iceland with lethal consequences across Europe.

White's frequent accounts of a tortoise inherited from his aunt in *The Natural History and Antiquities of Selborne* form the basis for Verlyn Klinkenborg's book, *Timothy; or, Notes of an Abject Reptile* (2006), as well as for Sylvia Townsend Warner's *The Portrait of a Tortoise* (1946).

His house in Selborne, *The Wakes*, now contains the Gilbert White Museum, as well as the Oates Memorial Museum, commemorating Frank and Lawrence Oates. A biography of White, by Richard Mabey was published by Century Hutchinson in 1986, and won the Whitbread Biography of the Year award.

A documentary about White, presented by historian Michael Wood, was broadcast by BBC Four in 2006. Gilbert White's famous work has been continuously in print since its first publication and is one of the most frequently published books in the English language. The paperback edition of *The Illustrated Natural History of Selborne* was last reprinted by Thames & Hudson in 2007.

HEINZ POSE

Rudolf Heinz Pose (10 April 1905 in Konigsberg – 13 November 1975 in Dresden) was a German nuclear physicist.

He did pioneering work which contributed to the understanding nuclear energy levels. He worked on the German nuclear energy project *Uranverein*. After World War II, the Soviet Union sent him to establish and head Laboratory V in Obninsk. From 1957, he was at the *Joint Institute for Nuclear Research* in Dubna, Russia. He settled in East Germany in 1959, and he held teaching posts and directed nuclear physics institutes at the *Technische Hochschule* Dresden.

Education

Pose studied physics, mathematics, and chemistry at the University of Konigsberg, the Ludwig Maximilian University of Munich, the Georg-August University of Gottingen, and the Martin Luther University of Halle-Wittenberg. He received his doctorate at Halle, in 1928, under the Nobel laureate in Physics Gustav Hertz.

Career

From 1928 Pose was an unsalaried assistant and from 1930 a regular assistant to the physicist Gerhard Hoffmann, who was doing research in nuclear reaction measurements. In 1929, Pose studied the nuclear reactions of aluminum nuclei bombarded with alpha particles. His experiments showed the existence of discrete energy levels in the nucleus. His pioneering work described for the first time the effect of resonance transformation in a nuclear process. On the basis of these works and his Habilitation, Pose was awarded a teaching contract for atomic physics in 1934. He continued to study these nuclear reactions in other light (low atomic number) nuclei through the 1930s. In 1939, he was awarded an unscheduled/adjunct (*auberplanmabige*) professorship at Halle.

During World War II, Pose was delegated to various organizations to carry on nuclear research and development activities. From 1940, he worked for the *Kaiser-Wilhelm Gesellschaft's Institut fur Physik* (KWIP, Kaiser Wilhelm Institute for Physics) on the German nuclear energy project *Uranverein.* He worked with Werner Maurer on proof of spontaneous neutron emission of uranium and thorium. From 1942, he was at the Physikalisch-Technische Reichsanstalt, where Abraham Esau was President, and also held the title of Plenipotentiary (*Bevollmachtiger*) for Nuclear Physics-as such, he controlled German nuclear research.

Some of the research was carried out at the *Versuchsstelle* (testing station) of the *Heereswaffenamt* (HWA, Army Ordnance Office) in Gottow; Kurt Diebner, was director of the facility. The testing station is where Pose and Ernst Rexer compared the effectiveness of neutron production in a paraffin-moderated reactor using uranium plates, rods, and cubes. Internal reports (See section below: Internal Reports.) on their activities were classified Top Secret and had limited distribution. The G-1 experiment performed at the HWA testing station had lattices of 6,800 uranium oxide cubes (about 25 tons) in the neutron moderator paraffin. Their work verified Karl Heinz Hocker's calculations that cubes were better than rods, and rods were better than plates. In June 1944, he went to the Physics Institute of the University of Leipzig to work on cyclotron development.

HANS CHRISTIAN ORSTED

Hans Christian Orsted (August 14, 1777 – March 9, 1851) was a Danish physicist and chemist. He shaped post-Kantian philosophy and advances in science throughout the late nineteenth century. He is best known for discovering the relationship between electricity and magnetism known as electromagnetism. He was also the first modern thinker to explicitly describe and name the thought experiment.

Early Life and Studies

Orsted developed his interest in science while working as a young boy for his father, Soren Christian Orsted, who owned a pharmacy. He and his brother, Anders Sandoe Orsted, received most of their early education through self-study at home, leaving home for Copenhagen in 1793 to take entrance exams for the University of Copenhagen. The brothers passed and distinguished themselves academically at the University. By 1796, Orsted received honours for his papers in both aesthetics and physics.

In 1801, Hans received a travel scholarship and public grant that enabled him to spend three years travelling in Europe. In Germany, he met Johann Wilhelm Ritter, a physicist who believed there was a connection between electricity and magnetism. The connection made sense to Orsted since he believed in the unity of nature, and, therefore, that a relationship must exist between most natural phenomena. Their conversations drew Orsted into the study of physics. He became a professor at the University of Copenhagen in 1806 and continued his research with electric currents and acoustics. Under his guidance, the University developed a comprehensive physics and chemistry programme and established new laboratories.

Death and Legacy

Orsted died in 1851, and was buried in the Assistens Cemetery in Copenhagen. The 100 danske kroner note issued from 1950 to 1970 features an engraving of Orsted. Today, the buildings which are home to the Department of Chemistry and the Institute for Mathematical Sciences at the University of Copenhagen, are named *The H.C. Orsted Institute* in his honour. Also, the first Danish satellite, launched 1999, was named Orsted in his honour.

HENRY MOSELEY

Henry Gwyn Jeffreys Moseley (November 23, 1887 – August 10, 1915) was an English physicist. His main contributions to science were the quantitative justification of the previously empirical concept of atomic number, and Moseley's law. This law advanced chemistry by immediately sorting the elements of the periodic table in a more logical order. It also advanced basic physics by providing independent support for the Bohr model of the Rutherford/Antonius Van den Broek nuclear atom containing positive nuclear charge equal to atomic number.

Biography

Henry Moseley was born in Weymouth, Dorset, on the south west coast of England in 1887. His father Henry Nottidge Moseley was a naturalist, a Professor of Anatomy and physiology at Oxford and a member of the Challenger Expedition. His mother was Amabel, daughter of the conchologist John Gwyn Jeffreys. He attended Eton College on a King's scholarship. In 1906, he entered Trinity College of the University of Oxford, and on graduation from that institution in 1910 went to Manchester University to work with Ernest Rutherford. During his first year at Manchester, he had a full teaching load, but after a year he was relieved of his teaching duties and began full-time research.

In 1913, by using x-ray spectra obtained by diffraction in crystals, he found a systematic relation between wavelength and atomic number, Moseley's law. Previous to this, atomic numbers or elemental numbers had been thought of as a semi-arbitrary sequential ordering-number, based on sequence of atomic masses, but altered when necessary (for example, by Dimitri Mendeleev) to put an element in the appropriate place in the periodic table. For example, cobalt and nickel had been assigned atomic numbers of 27 and 28, respectively, based on their chemical properties, since they have nearly identical atomic mass (in fact, cobalt's atomic mass is larger than nickel's, which would have reversed them had they been placed in the periodic table strictly according to this criterion). Moseley's experiments were able to show directly that cobalt and nickel have clearly differing atomic numbers of 27 and 28, and are correctly placed in the periodic table by an objective measure. Moseley's discovery thus showed that atomic numbers were not arbitrary, but have an experimentally measurable basis.

In addition, Moseley showed that there were gaps in the atomic number sequence at numbers 43, 61, 72, and 75. These spaces are now known, respectively, to be the places of the radioactive very rare elements technetium and promethium, and the last two discovered naturally-occurring stable elements hafnium (discovered 1923) and rhenium (discovered 1925). None were known in Moseley's time.

Mendeleev had previously predicted technetium, and Bohuslav Brauner had previously predicted promethium; Moseley confirmed their predictions, predicted the two additional undiscovered elements, and argued that there were no other gaps in the periodic table between aluminum and gold. This last matter had been an issue, particularly with the rare earths. Moseley was able to demonstrate that the lanthanoid series of rare-earth elements, *i.e.* lanthanum through lutetium inclusive, must have 15 members—no more and no less.

The number of lanthanoids was an issue very far from being settled by the chemistry of that time, which could not yet provide pure samples of all the rare earth salts, and in some cases was chemically unable to tell mixtures of two very similar elements from pure materials. Moseley's instrument was able to sort out these problems, some of which had occupied chemists for years, almost immediately. He predicted the existence of element 61, a lanthanoid whose existence was previously unsuspected.(Many years later element 61 *i.e.* promethium was created artificially.)

In 1914, Moseley resigned at Manchester to return to Oxford to pursue his research, but when World War I broke out, he turned down a job offer and enlisted in the Royal Engineers. He fought at Gallipoli, where he was killed in action by a sniper in 1915, shot through the head while in the act of telephoning an order.

Many speculated that he should have won the Nobel Prize, but was unable to because it is only awarded to the living. It is speculated that because of Moseley's death in the War that the British and other world governments began a policy of no longer allowing their scientists to enlist for combat.

Only twenty-seven years old at death, Moseley could in many scientists' opinions have contributed much to the knowledge of atomic structure had he lived. As Niels Bohr once said in 1962, *"You see actually the Rutherford work [the nuclear atom] was not taken seriously. We cannot understand today, but it was not taken seriously at all. There was no mention of it any place. The great change came from Moseley."*

HARRIE MASSEY

Sir Harrie Stewart Wilson Massey (16 May 1908-27 November 1983) was an influential Australian mathematical physicist. He worked primarily in the fields of atomic and atmospheric physics.

Life and Career

Harrie Massey was born in St. Kilda, Melbourne, Australia, but grew up in the rural community of Hoddles Creek. Massey enrolled in the local state school in 1913. At the age of 16 he won a Senior Government Scholarship to the University of Melbourne. There he studied physics and chemistry and graduated with a first class honours BSc in 1927. He stayed on to study mathematics and was awarded another first class degree, a BA, in 1929. At that time, the university did not offer a PhD programme but, clearly gifted, he took on an MSc with both experimental and theoretical components. The former dealt with soft X-ray deflection from metal surfaces and the latter with wave mechanics. His external examiner was Ralph Fowler from the University of Cambridge who was Paul Dirac's PhD supervisor.

In 1929, with the benefit of another scholarship, Massey went to Trinity College, Cambridge to perform research at the Cavendish Laboratory led by Ernest Rutherford. Fowler was appointed as Massey's supervisor although it was clear that he did not need any supervision *per se*. Massey obtained his PhD on the *The Collision of Material Particles* in 1932. He co-authored a book on atomic collision processes with Nevill Mott shortly afterwards. He then became a lecturer at the Queen's University of Belfast in 1933 and left to take up a chair in Mathematics at University College London five years later. This was to create a strong academic link between QUB and UCL which persists to this day.

During the Second World War he worked for the Admiralty Mining Establishment. He had a great influence on the future careers of nearly every scientist that worked there including David Bates, who was invited to join the staff at UCL, and Robert Boyd, who was offered a research assistant post. Francis Crick was introduced to Maurice Wilkins by Massey.

Massey was made head of the UCL Physics department in 1950 and remained its head after the department was merged with Astronomy in 1973. He retired in 1975.

He was the first chairman of the British National Committee for Space Research and helped found the European Space Research Organization as well as the Mullard Space Science Laboratory at UCL.

HENDRIK LORENTZ

Hendrik Antoon Lorentz (July 18, 1853 – February 4, 1928) was a Dutch physicist who shared the 1902 Nobel Prize in Physics with Pieter Zeeman for the discovery and theoretical explanation of the Zeeman effect. He also derived the transformation equations subsequently used by Albert Einstein to describe space and time.

Biography

Hendrik Lorentz was born in Arnhem, Gelderland, the son of Gerrit Frederik Lorentz (1822 – 1893), a shopkeeper, and Geertruida van Ginkel (1826 – 1861). In 1862, after his mother's death, his father married Luberta Hupkes. From 1866-1869 he attended the newly established high school in Arnhem, and in 1870 he passed the exams in classical languages which were then required for admission to University. Lorentz studied physics and mathematics at the University of Leiden, where he was strongly influenced by the teaching of astronomy professor Frederik Kaiser; it was his influence that led him to become a physicist. After earning a bachelor's degree, he returned to Arnhem in 1872 to teach high school classes in mathematics, but he continued his studies in Leiden next to his teaching position. In 1875 Lorentz earned a doctoral degree under Pieter Rijke on a thesis entitled *"Over de theorie der terugkaatsing en breking van het licht"* (On the theory of reflection and refraction of light), in which he refined the electromagnetic theory of James Clerk Maxwell.

In 1881 Hendrik married Aletta Catharina Kaiser, niece of Frederik Kaiser. She was the daughter of Johann Wilhelm Kaiser, director of the Amsterdam's Engraving School and professor of Fine Arts, and designer of the first Dutch postage stamps (1852). Later Kaiser was the Director of the National Gallery of Amsterdam. Hendrik and Aletta's eldest daughter Geertruida Luberta Lorentz was to become a physicist as well.

Professor in Leiden

In 1878, only 24 years of age, Lorentz was appointed to the newly established chair in theoretical physics at the University of Leiden. On January 25 1878, he delivered his inaugural lecture on *"De moleculaire theorien in de natuurkunde"* (The molecular theories in physics). During the first twenty years in Leiden, Lorentz was primarily interested in the theory of electromagnetism to explain the relationship of electricity, magnetism, and light. After that, he extended his research to a much wider area while still focusing on theoretical physics. From his publications, it appears that Lorentz made contributions to mechanics, thermodynamics, hydrodynamics, kinetic theories, solid state theory, light, and propagation. His most important contributions were in the area of electromagnetism, the electron theory, and relativity.

Lorentz theorized that the atoms might consist of charged particles and suggested that the oscillations of these charged particles were the source of light. When colleague and former student of Lorentz Pieter Zeeman discovered the Zeeman effect in 1896, Lorentz supplied its theoretical interpretation. The experimental and theoretical work was honoured with the Nobel prize in physics in 1902. Lorentz' name is now associated with the Lorentz-Lorenz formula, the Lorentz force, the Lorentzian distribution, and the Lorentz transformation.

HENDRIK ANTHONY KRAMERS

Hendrik Anthony Kramers (Rotterdam, February 2, 1894 – Oegstgeest, April 24, 1952) was a Dutch physicist, who was generally known by the first name *Hans*. Hans was the son of Hendrik Kramers, a physician, and Jeanne Susanne Breukelman. On October

25, 1920 he was married to Anna Petersen. They had three daughters and one son.

In 1912 Hans finished secondary education (in Dutch: HBS) in Rotterdam, and studied mathematics and physics at the University of Leiden, where he obtained a master's degree in 1916. Kramers wanted to obtain foreign experience, but his first choice, Max Born in Gottingen, was not reachable because of the first world war. Because Denmark was neutral in this war, as was The Netherlands, he travelled (by ship, overland was impossible) to Copenhagen, where he visited unannounced the then still relatively unknown Niels Bohr. Bohr took him on as a PhD student and Hans prepared his dissertation under Bohr's direction. Although Kramers did most of his doctoral research (on intensities of atomic transitions) in Copenhagen, he obtained his formal Ph.D. in Leiden (on May 8, 1919).

After working for almost ten years in Bohr's group and becoming an associate professor at the university of Copenhagen, Kramers left Denmark in 1926 and returned to his native land. He became a full professor in theoretical physics at the university of Utrecht. In 1934 he left Utrecht and succeeded Ehrenfest in Leiden. From 1931 until his death he held also a cross appointment at the Delft University of Technology.

Kramers was one of the founders of the Mathematisch Centrum in Amsterdam. He won the Lorentz Medal in 1947 and Hughes Medal in 1951.

Kramers lends his name to the Kramers crater on the Moon, the Kramers-Heisenberg formula, the Wentzel–Kramers–Brillouin approximation, the Kramers–Kronig relation, Kramers-Wannier duality, the Kramers model for polymer chains, Kramers-Anderson superexchange, and Kramers' degeneracy theorem.

HAGEN KLEINERT

Hagen Kleinert is Professor of Theoretical Physics at the Free University of Berlin, Germany (since 1968), Honourary Professor at the Kyrgyz-Russian Slavic University, and Honourary Member of the Russian Academy of Creative Endeavours. For his contributions to particle and solid state physics he was awarded the Max Born prize 2008 with Medal.

Kleinert has written more than 370 papers on mathematical physics and the physics of elementary particles, nuclei, solid state, liquid crystals, biomembranes, microemulsions, polymers, and theory of financial markets. He has written several books on theoretical physics. His most notable book *Path Integrals in Quantum Mechanics, Statistics, Polymer Physics, and Financial Market* has been published in four editions since 1990 with the latest two editions including chapters on the application of path integrals in financial markets. This book has received enthusiastic reviews.

After his first years as a student at Universitat Hannover and Georgia Institute of Technology, he learned as a graduate student General Relativity from George Gamov, one of the fathers of the Big Bang theory. As a young professor in 1972, Kleinert visited Caltech and was impressed by noted US physicist Richard Feynman. He discovered how to use Feynman's path integrals to solve the path integral of the hydrogen atom. This work greatly extended the applicable range of Feynman's techniques. Later, Kleinert was to collaborate with Feynman in some of the latter's last work. This has led to a mathematical method for converting divergent weak-coupling power series into convergent strong-coupling ones. This so-called Variational Perturbation Theory yields at present the most accurate theory of critical exponents observable close to second-order phase transitions, as confirmed for superfluid helium in satellite experiments.

Within the quantum field theories of quarks he found the origin of the algebra of Regge residues conjectured by N. Cabibbo, L. Horwitz, and Y. Ne'eman (see p.232 in Ref.).

Together with K. Maki he clarified the structure of the icosahedral phase of quasicrystals.

For superconductors he predicted in 1982 a tricritical point in the phase diagram between type-I and type-II superconductors where the order of the transition changes from second to first. The predictions were confirmed in 2002 by Monte Carlo computer simulations.

The theory is based on a new disorder field theory, which Kleinert developed in the books on *Gauge Fields in Condensed Matter.* In this theory, the statistical properties of fluctuating vortex or defect lines are described as elementary excitations with the help pf fields, whose Feynman diagrams are the pictures of the lines. The disorder field theory is a dual version of the order field theory of L.D. Landau for phase transitions.

At the 1978 summer school in Erice he proposed the existence of broken supersymmetry in atomic nuclei, which has meanwhile been observed experimentally.

His theory of collective quantum fields and the Hadronization of Quark Theories are prototypes for numerous developments in the theory of condensed matter, nuclear and elementary particle physics.

In 1986 he introduced stiffness into the theory of strings, which normally possess only tension. In this way he greatly improved the physical properties of strings. Since the Russian physicist A. Polyakov proposed simultaneously a similar extension, the result is called the Polyakov-Kleinert string.

Together with A. Chervyakov developed an extension of the theory of distributions from linear spaces to semigroups by defining also their products uniquely (in the mathematical theory, only linear combinations are defined). The extension became possible by the physical requirement that the path integrals must be invariant under coordinate transformations. This property is necessary for the equivalence of the path integral formulation to Schrodinger theory.

As an alternative to string theory, Kleinert used the complete analogy between non-Euclidean geometry and the geometry of crystals with defects to construct a model of the universe called World Crystal or Planck-Kleinert crystal which has, at distances of the Planck length, quite a different physics than string theory.

In this model, matter creates defects in spacetime which generate curvature and all the effects of general relativity. This theory inspired Italian artist Laura Pesce to create glass sculptures entitled "world crystal".

Kleinert is a senior member of the faculty for the International Relativistic Astrophysics Ph.D. (IRAP) Project, which forms part of the internationalo network for astrophysics. He was also involved in the European Science Foundation's project Cosmology in the Laboratory.

HEIKE KAMERLINGH ONNES

Heike Kamerlingh Onnes (September 21, 1853 – February 21, 1926) was a Dutch physicist. His scientific career was spent exploring extremely cold refrigeration techniques and the associated phenomena.

Biography

Kamerlingh Onnes was born in Groningen, Netherlands. His father, Harm Kamerlingh Onnes, was a brickworks owner. His mother was Anna Gerdina Coers of Arnhem.

In 1870, Kamerlingh Onnes attended the University of Groningen. He studied under Robert Bunsen and Gustav Kirchhoff at the University of Heidelberg from 1871 to 1873. Again at Groningen, he obtained his masters in 1878 and a doctorate in 1879. His thesis was "Nieuwe bewijzen voor de aswenteling der aarde" (*tr.* New proofs of the rotation of the earth). From 1878 to 1882 he was assistant to Johannes Bosscha, the director of the Polytechnic in Delft, for whom he substituted as lecturer in 1881 and 1882.

From 1882 to 1923 Kamerlingh Onnes served as professor of experimental physics at the University of Leiden. In 1904 he founded a very large cryogenics laboratory and invited other researchers to the location, which made him highly regarded in the scientific community. In 1908, he was the first physicist to liquify helium, using cryostats. Using the Joule-Thomson effect, he lowered the temperature to less than one degree above absolute zero, reaching

0.9 K. At the time this was the coldest temperature achieved on earth. The original equipment is at the Boerhaave Museum in Leiden.

He was married to Maria Adriana Wilhelmina Elisabeth Bijleveld (m. 1887) and had a child named Albert.

Superconductivity

Kamerlingh Onnes conducted (in 1911) electrical analysis of pure metals (mercury, tin and lead) at very low temperatures. Some, such as William Thomson (Lord Kelvin), believed that electrons flowing through a conductor would come to a complete halt or, in other words, metal resisitivity will become infinity at absolute zero. Others, including Kamerlingh Onnes, felt that a conductor's electrical resistance would steadily decrease and drop to nil. Augustus Matthiessen pointed out when the temperature decreases, the metal conductivity usually improves or in other words, the electrical resisitivy usually decreases with temperature. At 4.2 kelvin the resistance was zero according to the observation of Kamerlingh Onnes and his co-workers. The drop to zero was experimentally observed to be abrupt. Kamerlingh Onnes stated that the "*Mercury has passed into a new state, which on account of its extraordinary electrical properties may be called the superconductive state*". He published more articles about the phenomenon, initially referring to it as "*supraconductivity*" and, only later adopting the term "superconductivity".

Kamerlingh Onnes received widespread recognition for his work, including the 1913 Nobel Prize in Physics for (in the words of the committee) "*his investigations on the properties of matter at low temperatures which led, inter alia, to the production of liquid helium*".

Death and Afterwards

Kamerlingh Onnes died in Leiden. Some of the instruments he devised for his experiments can still be seen at the Boerhaave Museum in Leiden. The apparatus he used to first liquefy helium is on display in the lobby of the physics department at Leiden University, where the low temperature lab is also named in his honour. His student and successor as director of the lab Willem

Hendrik Keesom was the first person who was able to solidify helium, in 1926.

The Onnes-effect referring to the creeping of superfluid Helium is named in his honour.

The Kamerlingh Onnes crater on the Moon was named after him by the IAU.

HELMUT HONL

Helmut Honl (1903 in Mannheim, Germany – 1981) was a German theoretical physicist who made contributions to quantum mechanics and the understanding of atomic and molecular structure.

From 1921 to circa 1923, Honl studied at the University of Heidelberg and the University of Gottingen, followed by the University of Munich, where he studied under Arnold Sommerfeld. He was granted his doctor of philosophy in 1926. In 1929, he became assistant to Paul Peter Ewald at the Stuttgart Technische Hochschule until 1933, after which he was a Privatdozent.

Even before acquiring his doctorate at Munich, Honl had done seminal work which contributed to the advancement of quantum mechanics and the understanding of atomic and molecular structure and spectra. Some of his work was done in collaboration with Fritz London. As is the case in any fast developing field with a high level of interest, others independently make similar findings. This was the case with his work on the intensity of Zeeman effect spectral lines. Both Honl and Samuel Goudsmit and Ralph de Laer Kronig published results in 1925.

Their work was promptly put into use. In the first paper of the trilogy which launched the matrix mechanics formulation of quantum theory in 1925, Werner Heisenberg, a former student of Sommerfeld, working with Max Born at the University of Gottingen, used the work of Honl, Kronig, and Goudsmit, referring to it as the "*Goudsmit-Kronig-Honl* formula."

At this time, there were three centres of development for quantum mechanics and the interpretation of atomic and molecular structure, based on atomic and molecular spectroscopy, especially the Sommerfeld-Bohr model: the Theoretical Physics Institute at the University of Munich, under Arnold Sommerfeld, the Institute of Theoretical Physics at the University of Gottingen, under Max Born, and the Institute of Theoretical Physics, under Niels Bohr. These three institutes effectively formed a consortium for the exchange of assistants and researchers. Furthermore, with Sommerfeld educating such capable physicists, when they were called to other facilities, they effectively became extensions of Sommerfeld's Institute of Theoretical Physics.

This was the case with Honl when he went to the Stuttgart Technische Hochschule to work with Paul Peter Ewald, who received his Ph.D. under Sommerfeld and became ordinarius professor of theoretical physics at Stuttgart Technische Hochschule in 1921. At Stuttgart, Ewald and Honl worked on the quantum theory atomic and molecular structure and solid-state physics. They developed a theoretical model of electron densities and the atomic scattering factor in solids. Their work has been referenced in the literature as the Ewald-Honl-Brill model (after the German physicist Rudolf Brill).

HEINRICH HERTZ

Heinrich Rudolf Hertz (February 22, 1857 – January 1, 1894) was a German physicist who clarified and expanded the electromagnetic theory of light that had been put forth by Maxwell. He was the first to satisfactorily demonstrate the existence of electromagnetic waves by building an apparatus to produce and detect VHF or UHF radio waves.

Biography

Hertz was born in Hamburg, Germany, into a prosperous and cultured Hanseatic family. His father, Gustav Ferdinand Hertz, was a barrister and later a senator. His mother was the former Anna Elisabeth Pfefferkorn. He had three younger brothers and one younger sister.

While studying at the gymnasium of Hamburg, he showed an aptitude for sciences as well as languages, learning Arabic and Sanskrit. He studied sciences and engineering in the German cities of Dresden, Munich and Berlin, where he studied under Gustav R. Kirchhoff and Hermann von Helmholtz.

In 1880, Hertz obtained his PhD from the University of Berlin; and remained for post-doctoral study under Helmholtz. In 1883, Hertz took a post as a lecturer in theoretical physics at the University of Kiel. In 1885, Hertz became a full professor at the University of Karlsruhe where he discovered electromagnetic waves.

Death at age 36

In 1892, an infection was diagnosed (after a bout of severe migraines) and Hertz underwent some operations to correct the illness. He died of Wegener's granulomatosis at the age of 36 in Bonn, Germany in 1894. His wife, Elizabeth Hertz (maiden name: Elizabeth Doll) did not marry again. Heinrich Hertz left two daughters, Joanna and Mathilde. Subsequently, all three women left Germany in the 1930s to England, after the rise of Adolf Hitler. Charles Susskind interviewed Mathilde Hertz in the 1960s and he later published a book on Heinrich Hertz. Heinrich Hertz's daughters never married and so he does not have any descendants, according to the book by Susskind.

HERMANN VON HELMHOLTZ

Hermann Ludwig Ferdinand von Helmholtz (August 31, 1821 – September 8, 1894) was a German physician and physicist who made significant contributions to several widely varied areas of modern science. In physiology and physiological psychology, he is known for his mathematics of the eye, theories of vision, ideas on the visual perception of space, colour vision research, and on the sensation of tone, perception of sound, and empiricism. In physics, he is known for his theories on the conservation of energy, work in electrodynamics, chemical thermodynamics, and on a mechanical foundation of thermodynamics. As a philosopher, he is known for his philosophy of science, ideas on the relation between the laws of perception and the laws of nature, the science of aesthetics, and ideas on the civilizing power of science. A large German association of research institutions, the Helmholtz Association, is named after him.

Early Life

Helmholtz was the son of the Potsdam Gymnasium headmaster, Ferdinand Helmholtz, who had studied classical philology and philosophy, and who was a close friend of the publisher and philosopher Immanuel Hermann Fichte. Helmholtz's work is influenced by the philosophy of Fichte and Kant. He tried to trace their theories in empirical matters like physiology.

As a young man, Helmholtz was interested in natural science, but his father wanted him to study medicine at the Charite because there was financial support for medical students. Helmholtz wrote about many topics ranging from the age of the Earth to the origin of the solar system.

Sensory Physiology

The sensory physiology of Helmholtz was the basis of the work of Wilhelm Wundt, a student of Helmholtz, who is considered one of the founders of experimental psychology. He, more explicitly than Helmholtz, described his research as a form of empirical philosophy and as a study of the mind as something separate. Helmholtz had in his early refutal of the speculative early nineteenth century tradition of *Naturphilosophie* stressed the importance of materialism, and was focusing more on the unity of "mind" and body.

HOWARD GEORGI

Howard Mason Georgi III, born in 1947 in San Bernardino, California, is Harvard College Professor and Mallinckrodt Professor of Physics at Harvard University. He has, for many years, taught an advanced freshman physics course, "Physics 16" in the fall semester.

He is also Director of Undergraduate Studies in Physics and Master of Leverett House, where he asks all students to endearingly call him "*Chief*," while his wife Ann Georgi commands the name "Coach." He graduated from Harvard in 1967 and obtained his Ph.D. from Yale University in 1971. He was Junior Fellow in the Harvard Society of Fellows from 1973-1976 and a Senior Fellow from 1982-1998.

In 1995 he was elected to the National Academy of Sciences and received the Sakurai Prize; in 2000 he shared the Dirac Medal with Jogesh Pati and Helen Quinn. He has advised a number of notable students, including Andrew G. Cohen, Adam Falk, Benjamin Grinstein, John Hagelin, Lawrence J. Hall, David B. Kaplan, Michael Luke, Aneesh Manohar, Ann Nelson and Lisa Randall.

He is best known for early work in Grand Unification and gauge coupling unification within SU(5) and SO(10) groups (see Georgi-Glashow model). He later proposed the supersymmetric Standard Model with Savas Dimopoulos in 1981. After the measurements of the three Standard Model gauge couplings at LEP I in 1991, it was shown that particle content of the MSSM, in contrast to the Standard Model alone, led to precision gauge coupling unification.

He has since worked on several different areas of physics including composite Higgs models, heavy quark effective theory, dimensional deconstruction, little Higgs, and unparticle theories.

Georgi has been a strong advocate for women in science.

Georgi in 2006 together with Vadim Alexeevich Kuzmin received the Pomeranchuk Prize of the Alikhanov Institute for Theoretical and Experimental Physics (ITEP).

Georgi has published several books the best known of which is *Lie Algebras in Particle Physics* published by World Scientific. He has also published *The Physics of Waves* and *Weak Interactions and Modern Particle Theory.*

Unparticle physics is a theory that there exists matter that cannot be explained in terms of particles, because its components are scale invariant. Howard Georgi proposed this theory in the spring of 2007 in the papers "Unparticle Physics" and "Another Odd Thing About Unparticle Physics".

HENDRIK CASIMIR

Hendrik Brugt Gerhard Casimir (July 15, 1909 in 's-Gravenhage, Netherlands– May 4, 2000 in Heeze) was a Dutch physicist best known for his research on the two-fluid model of superconductors (together with C. J. Gorter) in 1934 and the Casimir effect (together with D. Polder) in 1948.

Biography

He studied theoretical physics at the University of Leiden under Paul Ehrenfest, where he received his Ph.D. in 1931. His PhD thesis dealt with the quantum mechanics of a rigid spinning body and the group theory of the rotations of molecules. During that time he also spent some time in Copenhagen with Niels Bohr. After receiving his Ph.D. he worked as an assistant to Wolfgang Pauli at Zurich. In 1938, he became a physics professor at Leiden University. At that time, he was actively studying both heat conduction and electrical conduction, and contributed to the attainment of millikelvin temperatures.

In 1942, during World War II, Casimir moved to the Philips Research Laboratories in Eindhoven, the Netherlands. He remained an active scientist and in 1945 wrote a well-known paper on Lars Onsager's principle of microscopic reversibility. He became a co-director of Philips Research Laboratories in 1946 and a member of the board of directors of the company in 1956. He retired from Philips in 1972.

Although he spent much of his professional life in industry, Hendrik Casimir was one of the great Dutch theoretical physicists. Casimir made many contributions to science during his years in research from 1931 to 1950. These contributions include: pure mathematics, Lie groups (1931); hyperfine structure, calculation of nuclear quadrupole moments, (1935); low temperature physics, magnetism, thermodynamics of superconductors, paramagnetic relaxation (1935-1942); applications of Onsager's theory of irreversible phenomena (1942-1950). He helped found the European Physical Society and became its president from 1972 till 1975. In 1979 he was one of the key speakers at CERN's 25th anniversary celebrations.

While at Philips Research Labs, in 1948 Casimir, collaborating with Dirk Polder, predicted the quantum mechanical attraction between conducting plates now known as the Casimir effect, which has important consequences in Micro Electro-Mechanical Systems (MEMS), among others.

He was awarded six honorary doctor degrees by universities outside the Netherlands. He received numerous awards and prizes. He was a Foreign Associate of the National Academy of Engineering.

HANS BETHE

Hans Albrecht Bethe (July 2, 1906 – March 6, 2005) was a German-American physicist, and Nobel laureate in physics for his work on the theory of stellar nucleosynthesis. Bethe also made important contributions to quantum electrodynamics, nuclear physics and particle astrophysics. During World War II, he was head of the Theoretical Division at the secret Los Alamos laboratory developing the first atomic bombs. There he played a key role in calculating the critical mass of the weapons, and did theoretical work on the implosion method used in both the Trinity test and the "Fat Man" weapon dropped on Nagasaki, Japan.

During the early 1950s, Bethe also played an important role in the development of the larger hydrogen bomb, though he had originally joined the project with the hope of proving it could not be made. Bethe later campaigned together with Albert Einstein in the Emergency Committee of Atomic Scientists against nuclear testing and the nuclear arms race. He influenced the White House to sign the ban of atmospheric nuclear tests in 1963 and the 1972 Anti-Ballistic Missile Treaty, SALT I. His scientific research never ceased even into the later years of his life. He is one of the few scientists who can claim a major paper in his field every decade of his career, which spanned nearly sixty years. Freeman Dyson called Bethe the "supreme problem solver of the 20th century."

Early Years

Bethe was born in Strassburg, Germany, which since 1919 has been in France. Although his mother was Jewish, he was raised in the religion of his father, Christianity. Bethe studied physics at JWG University, Frankfurt, and went on to earn his doctorate from the University of Munich with supervisor Arnold Sommerfeld, after which he did postdoctoral stints in Cambridge and at Enrico Fermi's laboratory in Rome. He was influenced by Fermi's simplicity and Sommerfeld's rigor in approaching problems, and these qualities influenced his own later research.

Bethe left Germany in 1933 when the Nazis came to power and he lost his job at the University of Tubingen, moving first to England where he held a provisory position of Lecturer for the year 1933-1934 and in the fall of 1934, a fellowship at the University of Bristol. In England, Bethe worked with the theoretician Rudolf Peierls on a comprehensive theory of the deuteron. In 1929, Bethe made an important contribution to solid state physics and chemistry, with his formulation of the basic concepts of crystal field theory. His paper is regarded as the starting point for all serious later discussions of the topic. In 1930, he devised a formula for the energy loss of swift charged particles in matter called the Bethe formula, which is now as important as it was then.

In 1935 Bethe moved to the United States, and joined the faculty at Cornell University, a position which he occupied for the rest his career. During 1948-1949 he was a Visiting Professor at Columbia University. At Cornell, Bethe became known as one of the leading theoretical physicists of his generation, and along with upcoming physicists such as cyclotron pioneer Milton Stanley Livingston, and later, after the war, experimentalist Robert R. Wilson and theoretician Robert Bacher, put Cornell on the world physics map. Together with Robert Bacher and Livingston, Bethe published a series of three articles which summarized most of what was known on the subject of nuclear physics until that time, an account that became informally known as "Bethe's Bible", and remained the standard work on the subject for many years. In this account, he also continued where others left off, filling in gaps from the older literature. From 1935-1938, he studied nuclear reactions and reaction cross sections, carbon-oxygen-nitrogen cycle, leading to his important contribution to stellar nucleosynthesis. This research was later useful to Bethe in more quantitatively developing Niels Bohr's theory of the compound nucleus.

Bethe became a naturalized citizen of the United States in 1941. He was an honorary member of the International Academy of Science.

HOMI J. BHABHA

Homi Jehangir Bhabha, (October 30, 1909 – January 24, 1966) was an Indian nuclear physicist who had a major role in the development of the Indian atomic energy programme and is considered to be the father of India's nuclear programme. Bhabha was born into a prominent family, through which he was related to Dinshaw Maneckji Petit, Muhammad Ali Jinnah, Homi K Bhabha and Dorab Tata. After receiving his early education at Bombay schools and at the Royal Institute of Science, he attended Caius College of Cambridge University to pursue studies in mechanical engineering. After taking the mechanical engineering Tripos, he pursued studies under Paul Dirac to complete the Mathematics Tripos. Meanwhile, he worked at the Cavendish Laboratory while working towards his doctorate in theoretical physics under R. H. Fowler. During this time, he embarked on groundbreaking research into the absorption of cosmic rays and electron shower production. Afterwards, he published a string of widely-accepted papers on his theories regarding cosmic ray showers.

World War II broke out in September 1939 while Bhabha was vacationing in India. He chose to remain in India until the war ended. In the meantime, he accepted a position at the Indian Institute of Science in Bangalore, headed by Nobel laureate C. V. Raman. He established the Cosmic Ray Research Unit at the institute, and began to work on the theory of the movement of point particles. In 1945, he established the Tata Institute of Fundamental Research in Bombay, and the Atomic Energy Commission of India three years later. In the 1950s, Bhabha represented India in International Atomic Energy Forums, and served as President of the United Nations Conference on the Peaceful Uses of Atomic Energy in Geneva, Switzerland in 1955. He later served as the member of the Indian Cabinet's Scientific Advisory Committee and set up the Indian National Committee for Space Research with Vikram Sarabhai. In January 1966, Bhabha died in a plane crash near Mont Blanc, while heading to Vienna, Austria to attend a meeting of the International Atomic Energy Agency's Scientific Advisory Committee.

Early Life

Bhabha was born in Bombay to Jehangir Hormaji Bhabha, an Oxford-educated barrister, and Meherbai Framji Panday, a wealthy Parsi family living in Bombay, India Bhabha, at his birth, was directly linked to India's most prominent mercantile families. Through his mother, Bhabha was the great-grandson of Sir Dinshaw Maneckji Petit, a textiles entrepreneur noted for his philanthropic efforts, and therefore distantly related by marriage to Muhammad Ali Jinnah through his second wife, Rattanbai Petit, who was the elder Petit's granddaughter. Through his father, Bhabha was the grandson of Hormusji Bhabha, CIE, the Inspector-General of Education in Mysore, and the nephew of Meherbai Hormusji, who was married to Dorab Tata, the eldest son of Jamsetji Tata. He is also a distant relative of similarly named post-colonial theorist Homi K Bhabha.

Bhabha received his early education at Bombay's Cathedral Grammar School, which became the Cathedral and John Connon School in 1922 after merging with the John Connon School, run by the city's Scottish Education Society. He entered Elphinstone College at age 15 after passing his Senior Cambridge Examination with Honours. He then attended the Royal Institute of Science until 1927 before joining Caius College of Cambridge University, the alma mater of his uncle Dorab Tata. His father and uncle Dorab planned for Bhabha to obtain an engineering degree from Cambridge and then return to India, where would join the Tata Iron and Steel Company in Jamshedpur. However, during his studies, Bhabha felt more of an interest in the field of mathematics, instead of engineering. In 1928, Bhabha wrote to his father, informing him of his mixed feelings about his intended specialty: "I seriously say to you that business or job as an engineer is not the thing for me. It is totally foreign to my nature and radically opposed to my temperament and opinions. Physics is my line. I know I shall do great things here. For, each man can do best and excel in only that thing of which he is passionately fond, in which he believes, as I do, that he has the ability to do it, that he is in fact born and destined to do it. My success will not depend on what A or B thinks of me. My success will be what I make of my work. Besides, India is not a land where science cannot be carried on"

I am burning with a desire to do physics. I will and must do it sometime. It is my only ambition. I have no desire to be a 'successful' man or the head of a big firm. There are intelligent people who like that and let them do it. I hear you saying 'But you are not Socrates or Einstein'. No—and that is what Berlioz's father said to Berlioz. He called him a useless musician when he was young—Hector Berlioz who now accepted as one of the world's greatest geniuses and France's greatest musician. How can anybody else know at what time what one will do, if there is nothing to show.... It is no use saying to Beethoven 'You must be a scientist for it is great thing' when he did not care two hoots for science; or to Socrates 'Be an engineer; it is work of intelligent man'. It is not in the nature of things. I therefore earnestly implore you to let me do physics."

HANNES ALFVEN

Hannes Olof Gosta Alfven (May 30, 1908; Norrkoping, Sweden – April 2, 1995; Djursholm, Sweden) was a Swedish plasma physicist and Nobel laureate for his work on the theory of magnetohydrodynamics. He was originally trained as an electrical power engineer and later moved to research and teaching in the fields of plasma physics. Alfven made many contributions to plasma physics, including theories describing the behaviour of aurorae, the Van Allen radiation belts, the effect of magnetic storms on the Earth's magnetic field, the terrestrial magnetosphere, and the dynamics of plasmas in the Milky Way galaxy.

Biography

In 1937, Alfven argued that if plasma pervaded the universe, it could then carry electric currents capable of generating a galactic magnetic field. After winning the Nobel Prize for his works in magnetohydrodynamics, he emphasized that:

> *In order to understand the phenomena in a certain plasma region, it is necessary to map not only the magnetic but also the electric field and the electric currents. Space is filled with a network of currents which transfer energy and momentum over large or very large distances. The currents often pinch to filamentary or surface currents. The latter are likely to give space, as also interstellar and intergalactic space, a cellular structure.*

His theoretical work on field-aligned electric currents in the aurora (based on earlier work by Kristian Birkeland) was confirmed by satellite observations, in 1974, resulting in the discovery of Birkeland currents.

Education

Alfven received his PhD from the University of Uppsala in 1934. His thesis was titled "Investigations of the Ultra-short Electromagnetic Waves."

Early Years

In 1934, Alfven taught physics at both the University of Uppsala and the Nobel Institute for Physics in Stockholm, Sweden. In 1940, he became professor of electromagnetic theory and electrical measurements at the Royal Institute of Technology in Stockholm. In 1945, he acquired the nonappointive position of Chair of Electronics. His title was changed to Chair of Plasma Physics in 1963. In 1954-1955, Alfven was a Fulbright Scholar at the University of Maryland, College Park. In 1967, after leaving Sweden and spending time in the Soviet Union, he moved to the United States. Alfven worked in the departments of electrical engineering at both the University of California, San Diego and the University of Southern California.

Alfven considered himself an electrical engineer foremost. During his scientific career, prior to winning the Nobel Prize, Alfven was not generally recognized as a leading innovator in the scientific community (though they were using his work). He enjoyed the assertion that he was guilty of a fault or offence by the entry into areas not previously explored in astrophysics levelled by other cosmologists and theoreticians.

HAROLD WILLIAMS

Dr. Harold Williams, (born March 14, 1934) is one of the premier field geologists in the history of geology and the foremost expert on the Appalachian Mountains of North America. An expert on the evolution and tectonic development of mountain belts, Williams advanced the theory of colliding super-continents in the 1960's and 1970's by helping to transform the notion of Continental Drift into the Theory of Plate Tectonics.

Williams was born in St. John's, Newfoundland and attended Memorial University of Newfoundland earning a diploma in Engineering and a B.Sc degree (1956) and a M.Sc degree (1958) on a Dominion Command scholarship. He earned a Ph.D from the University of Toronto in 1961. He thereafter joined the Geological Survey of Canada (GSC), where he the gained the reputation of being an expert field geologist and outstanding scientist

He left the GSC in 1968 and joined the faculty at Memorial University of Newfoundland, where he was the first to receive the prestigious title of University Research Professor (1984) and the first to be appointed Alexander Murray Professor (1990). He was the first to win both the Past President's Medal and the Logan Medal of the Geological Association of Canada.

He was elected Fellow of the Royal Society of Canada at age 38, a very rare accolade, and 15 years later was awarded the Miller Medal by its Academy of Science. First winner of the R.J.W. Douglas Medal of the Canadian Society of Petroleum Geologists, he was also the first geoscientist to be awarded an Isaac Walton Killam Memorial Fellowship and the first scientist of any kind to hold this award for four full years. He has over 250 publications to his credit and for several years in the past three decades has been the most cited Canadian geoscientist in the world.

Williams was among the first to describe the evidence for the existence of the Iapetus Ocean, the predecessor of the modern Atlantic Ocean. A sampling of these rocks is preserved and protected in Gros Morne National Park of western Newfoundland, which has qualified for UNESCO World Heritage Site recognition under his advocacy. Williams is perhaps best known for producing the world's first tectonic lithofacies map and the first geological map of the entire Appalachian Mountains in the U.S. and Canada in 1978.

HOWEL WILLIAMS

Howel Williams (1898-1980) was a noted American geologist and volcanologist. He was born of Welsh parents in Liverpool, England, on October 12, 1898. He received a BA in geography in 1923 and an MA in archaeology in 1924 from Liverpool University. He studied geology at the Imperial College of Science and Technology in London; his twin brother David Williams also became a geologist. Howel Williams moved to the University of California at Berkeley in 1926. In 1928 he was awarded the degree of D.Sc. from the University of Liverpool and published his first papers on the geology of various California volcanic regions. Williams was a member of the National Academy of Sciences.

He published many studies on the volcanoes of California, but is most noted for his "The Geology of Crater Lake National Park" in which he recognized the nature of the collapse of the crater and extended the work to develop the principles of volcanic caldera formation. He did extensive early work on the geology of Central America (often sketch-mapping from the windows of second-class buses), and of the Galapagos Islands. In Latin America, Williams put to good use his early background in archeology. For instance, he used petrographic techniques to trace the origin of stone used in the giant Olmec sculptures of La Venta, Tabasco Mexico.

Williams was a master of the art of field sketching, formerly practiced by many naturalists. Many of his papers were illustrated with his meticulously done pen and ink drawings. His drawings of the microscopic features of rocks of all types were used exclusively in the very successful textbook, *Petrography*, by Williams, Turner, and Gilbert.

ISAAC NEWTON

Sir Isaac Newton, (4 January 1643 – 31 March 1727 [OS: 25 December 1642 – 20 March 1726]) was an English physicist, mathematician, astronomer, natural philosopher, alchemist and theologian. His *Philosophiæ Naturalis Principia Mathematica*, published in 1687, is considered to be the most influential book in the history of science. In this work, Newton described universal gravitation and the three laws of motion, laying the groundwork for classical mechanics, which dominated the scientific view of the physical universe for the next three centuries and is the basis for modern engineering. Newton showed that the motions of objects on Earth and of celestial bodies are governed by the same set of natural laws by demonstrating the consistency between Kepler's laws of planetary motion and his theory of gravitation, thus removing the last doubts about heliocentrism and advancing the scientific revolution.

In mechanics, Newton enunciated the principles of conservation of momentum and angular momentum. In optics, he invented the reflecting telescope and developed a theory of colour based on the observation that a prism decomposes white light into a visible spectrum. He also formulated an empirical law of cooling and studied the speed of sound.

In mathematics, Newton shares the credit with Gottfried Leibniz for the development of calculus. He also demonstrated the generalized binomial theorem, developed the so-called "Newton's method" for approximating the zeroes of a function, and contributed to the study of power series.

In a 2005 poll of the Royal Society asking who had the greater effect on the history of science, Newton was deemed much more influential than Albert Einstein.

Biography

Isaac Newton was born on 4 January 1643 [OS: 25 December 1642] at Woolsthorpe Manor in Woolsthorpe-by-Colsterworth, a hamlet in the county of Lincolnshire. At the time of Newton's birth, England had not adopted the latest papal calendar and therefore his date of birth was recorded as Christmas Day, 25 December 1642.

Newton was born three months after the death of his father. Born prematurely, he was a small child; his mother Hannah Ayscough reportedly said that he could have fit inside a quart mug. When Newton was three, his mother remarried and went to live with her new husband, the Reverend Barnabus Smith, leaving her son in the care of his maternal grandmother, Margery Ayscough. The young Isaac disliked his stepfather and held some enmity towards his mother for marrying him, as revealed by this entry in a list of sins committed up to the age of 19: *Threatening my father and mother Smith to burn them and the house over them.*

According to E.T. Bell and H. Eves:

Newton began his schooling in the village schools and was later sent to The King's School, Grantham, where he became the top student in the school. At King's, he lodged with the local apothecary, William Clarke and eventually became engaged to the apothecary's stepdaughter, Anne Storer, before he went off to the University of

Cambridge at the age of 19. As Newton became engrossed in his studies, the romance cooled and Miss Storer married someone else. It is said he kept a warm memory of this love, but Newton had no other recorded "sweet-hearts" and never married.

There are rumours that he remained a virgin. However, Bell and Eves' sources for this claim, William Stukeley and Mrs. Vincent (the former Miss Storer — actually named Katherine, not Anne), merely say that Newton entertained "a passion" for Storer while he lodged at the Clarke house.

From the age of about twelve until he was seventeen, Newton was educated at The King's School, Grantham (where his signature can still be seen upon a library window sill).

He was removed from school, and by October 1659, he was to be found at Woolsthorpe-by-Colsterworth, where his mother, widowed by now for a second time, attempted to make a farmer of him. He was, by later reports of his contemporaries, thoroughly unhappy with the work. It appears to have been Henry Stokes, master at the King's School, who persuaded his mother to send him back to school so that he might complete his education. This he did at the age of eighteen, achieving an admirable final report.

In June 1661, he was admitted to Trinity College, Cambridge. According to John Stillwell, he entered Trinity as a sizar. At that time, the college's teachings were based on those of Aristotle, but Newton preferred to read the more advanced ideas of modern philosophers such as Descartes and astronomers such as Copernicus, Galileo, and Kepler.

In 1665, he discovered the generalized binomial theorem and began to develop a mathematical theory that would later become calculus. Soon after Newton had obtained his degree in August of 1665, the University closed down as a precaution against the Great Plague. Although he had been undistinguished as a Cambridge student, Newton's private studies at his home in Woolsthorpe over the subsequent two years saw the development of his theories on calculus, optics and the law of gravitation.

Later Life

In the 1690s Newton wrote a number of religious tracts dealing with the literal interpretation of the Bible. Henry More's belief in the universe and rejection of Cartesian dualism may have influenced Newton's religious ideas. A manuscript he sent to John Locke in which he disputed the existence of the Trinity was never published. Later works — *The Chronology of Ancient Kingdoms Amended* (1728) and *Observations Upon the Prophecies of Daniel and the Apocalypse of St. John* (1733) — were published after his death. He also devoted a great deal of time to alchemy (see above).

Newton was also a member of the Parliament of England from 1689 to 1690 and in 1701, but his only recorded comments were to complain about a cold draft in the chamber and request that the window be closed.

Newton moved to London to take up the post of warden of the Royal Mint in 1696, a position that he had obtained through the patronage of Charles Montagu, 1st Earl of Halifax, then Chancellor of the Exchequer. He took charge of England's great recoining, somewhat treading on the toes of Master Lucas (and securing the job of deputy comptroller of the temporary Chester branch for Edmond Halley).

Newton became perhaps the best-known Master of the Mint upon Lucas' death in 1699, a position Newton held until his death. These appointments were intended as sinecures, but Newton took them seriously, retiring from his Cambridge duties in 1701, and exercising his power to reform the currency and punish clippers and counterfeiters.

As Master of the Mint in 1717 Newton unofficially moved the Pound Sterling from the silver standard to the gold standard by creating a relationship between gold coins and the silver penny in the "Law of Queen Anne"; these were all great reforms at the time, adding considerably to the wealth and stability of England. It was his work at the Mint, rather than his earlier contributions to science, that earned him a knighthood from Queen Anne in 1705.

Newton was made President of the Royal Society in 1703 and an associate of the French Academie des Sciences. In his position at the Royal Society, Newton made an enemy of John Flamsteed, the Astronomer Royal, by prematurely publishing Flamsteed's star catalogue, which Newton had used in his studies.

Newton died in London on 31 March 1727 [OS: 20 March 1726], and was buried in Westminster Abbey. His half-niece, Catherine Barton Conduitt, served as his hostess in social affairs at his house on Jermyn Street in London; he was her "very loving Uncle," according to his letter to her when she was recovering from smallpox. Although Newton, who had no children, had divested much of his estate onto relatives in his last years, he actually died intestate.

After his death, Newton's body was discovered to have have had massive amounts of mercury in it, probably resulting from his alchemical pursuits. Mercury poisoning could explain Newton's eccentricity in late life.

IGOR KURCHATOV

Igor Vasilyevich Kurchatov (January 12, 1903 – February 7, 1960) was a Soviet/Russian physicist. He was the leader of the Soviet atomic bomb project. Kurchatov was born in Simsky Zavod, Ufa Governorate (now the town of Sim, Chelyabinsk Oblast). After completing Simferopol gymnasium [1]1, he studied physics at Crimea State University and ship building at the Polytechnical Institute in Petrograd. In 1924-1925, Kurchatov was a research assistant at the faculty of Physics of the Polytechnic Institute in Baku, the present-day Azerbaijan State Oil Academy. In 1925 he moved to the Physico-Technical Institute, where he worked (under Abram Fedorovich Ioffe) on various problems connected with radioactivity. In 1932, he received funding for his own nuclear science research team, which built the Soviet Union's first cyclotron (September 21, 1939).

Igor Kurchatov and his apprentice Georgy Flyorov discovered the basic ideas of the uranium chain reaction and the nuclear reactor concept in the 1930s. In 1942 Kurchatov declared: "At breaking up of kernels in a kilogram of uranium, the energy released must be equal to the explosion of 20,000 tons of trotyl." This announcement was practically verified during the atomic bombing of Hiroshima.

When war broke out between Germany and the USSR in 1941, Kurchatov switched his research first to protecting shipping from magnetic mines, and later to tank armour. In 1943 the NKVD obtained a copy of a secret British report by the MAUD Committee concerning the feasibility of atomic weapons, which led Stalin to order the commencement of a Soviet nuclear programme (albeit with very limited resources). Ioffe recommended Kurchatov to Molotov, and Kurchatov was appointed director of the nascent programme later that year. The Soviet atomic bomb project remained a relatively low priority until information from spy Klaus Fuchs and later the destruction of Hiroshima and Nagasaki goaded Stalin into action. Stalin ordered Kurchatov to produce a bomb by 1948, and put the ruthless Lavrenty Beria in direct command of the project. The project took over the town of Sarov in the Gorki Oblast (now Nizhny Novgorod Oblast) on the Volga, and renamed it *Arzamas-16*.

The team (which included other prominent Soviet nuclear scientists such as Julii Borisovich Khariton and Yakov Borisovich Zel'dovich) was assisted both by public disclosures made by the U.S. government and by further information supplied by Fuchs, but Kurchatov and Beria (fearing the intelligence was misinformation) insisted his scientists retest everything themselves. Beria in particular would use the intelligence as a third-party check on the conclusions of the teams of scientists.

On August 29, 1949 the team detonated First Lightning, its initial test device (a plutonium implosion bomb) at the Semipalatinsk Test Site. Kurchatov later remarked that his main feeling at the time was one of relief, as he was confident that had the weapon failed, Stalin would have had him shot.

Kurchatov subsequently worked on the Soviet hydrogen bomb programme (1953), but later worked for the peaceful use of nuclear technology, and advocated against nuclear bomb tests. Among the projects held under Kurchatov were the first cyclotron in Moscow (1949), the first Atomic Reactor in Europe (1946), the first industrial Nuclear power plant in the world (1954), the first Nuclear reactor for Submarines in the world (1959), Nuclear Icebreakers (*Lenin*, both the world's first nuclear powered surface ship and the first nuclear powered civilian vessel, 1959).

During the A-bomb programme, Kurchatov swore he wouldn't cut his beard until the programme succeeded, and he continued to wear a large beard (often cut into eccentric styles) for the remainder of his life, earning him the nickname "The Beard". Kurchatov died in Moscow in 1960 of a blood clot in his brain, and his ashes were buried in the Kremlin Wall Necropolis on Red Square.

Two towns bear his name: Kurchatov Township, the headquarters of the STS, and Kurchatov near Kursk (the site of a nuclear power station). The Kurchatov crater on the Moon and the asteroid 2352 Kurchatov are also named after him.

IVAN YEFREMOV

Ivan Antonovich (real patronymic *Antipovich*) *Yefremov*, sometimes spelled *Ivan Antonovich Efremov* was a Soviet paleontologist and science fiction author. He originated taphonomy, the study of fossilization patterns.

Biography

Born in the village of Vyritsa in St. Petersburg's province on the 22nd (old style 9th) of April, 1908. Yefremov includes the year 1907 in his biography in order to begin his labour activity earlier. His parents divorced during the Russian Revolution. His mother married a Red Army commander and left the children in Herson to be cared for by an aunt who soon died of typhus. He then joined a Red Army company as a "son of the regiment" and reached Perekop with it. In 1921 he was demobilized and went to Petrograd (today's Saint Petersburg) to study. There, he managed to complete his education. He later commented that "the Revolution was also my own liberation from philistinism". During his young years he had to combine his studies with different kinds of labour. In 1924 under the influence of academician Sushkin he became interested with palaeontology. Yefremov was admitted into the Leningrad State University but did not graduate. From the middle of 1930 he took part in several paleontological expeditions on Volga region, Ural, Central Asia. He became a Laboratory Head in the Institute of Palaeontology. 1935 he passed an external exam in Leningrad Mining Institute. In the same year he became a Candidate of biological science, and in 1941—a Doctor of biological science.

In the 1940s Yefremov developed a new field of science called taphonomy: the monograph "Taphonomy" was published in 1950 and many regulations of it were successfully employed during his expedition on Gobi desert in Mongolia. In these years he became a famous scientist and won the State Prize.

The first belles-lettres story of Ivan Yefremov was first published in 1944. In 1949 the historical novel *The Land of Foam* (*Great Arc*, 1946) was published. But he became most famous with his novel *Andromeda Nebula* (*Andromeda: A Space-Age Tale*, 1957). This book is the hymn to a whole-hearted world of communist future of mankind that reached the stars and changed the Earth into blooming garden. There is no more inequality between people, the social structure of the society allows each person to reach elevations of self-development. The all-Universe communication system called Great Circle includes mankind in the interstellar family of rational creatures. This book became a moral guiding line for many soviet people.

IGNACY DOMEYKO

Ignacy Domeyko (July 31, 1802 – January 23, 1889, Santiago de Chile) was a famous 19th-century Lithuanian-Polish geologist and mineralogist (born in Imperial Russia, present-day Belarus, former Polish-Lithuanian Commonwealth). After the youth spent in partitioned Poland, he participated in the Polish national uprising-the November Uprising, and after its failure he was forced to leave the Polish lands. He spent part of his life in France and eventually settled in Chile, of which he gained a citizenship and where he lived for about 50 years. He made major contributions to the study of Chilean geography, geology and mineralogy. He is seen as having close ties with several countries, and thus in 2002, when UNESCO organized a series of events in his memory, he was referred to as a "citizen of the world".

Life

Domeyko was born in Russian partition of the former Polish-Lithuanian Commonwealth, at Niedywiadka Manor (Bear Cub Manor), near Nieoewie (Nyasvizh), Nowogrodek (Navahradak) district, Minsk Governorate, Imperial Russia (now Karelichy district, Belarus). In his time, he was subject of the Russian Tsar. Domeyko had, however, been brought up in the culture of the Polish-Lithuanian Commonwealth, a multicultural entity that had been destroyed shortly before his birth, in the partitions of Poland (the last of which occurred in 1795). For this reason, and because he subsequently spent most of his life in Chile, he is considered a person of national importance to four countries: Belarus, Chile, Lithuania and Poland.

Domeyko studied at Imperial University of Vilna under Jedrzej Œniadecki. Involved in Vilna in the Philomathes, a secret student organization dedicated to studying Polish culture and restoring Polish independence, he was a close friend of Adam Mickiewicz, the greatest Polish Romantic poet and Alexander Pushkin's rival as the greatest poet of East-central and Eastern Europe.

After participating in the November 1830 Uprising, an insurrection that sought to revive the Poland-Lithuania Commonwealth, in 1831 Domeyko was forced to emigrate to France, as remaining in Poland would force him to than face Russian reprisals. After a trip through Germany, he arrived in France, where he would obtain the title of an engineer in Paris at the *Ecole des Mines.*

In 1838 he left for Chile. After becoming a citizen of Chile in 1849, Domeyko stated *"I may never change my citizenship now, however god gives a hope for me, that anywhere-even it will be Cordillera, or Paneriai-i will die as Lithuanian"*. Domeyko lived in Chile until May 22, 1884, when he returned for an extended visit to Europe. He stayed four years in (still partitioned) Poland, receiving an honorary doctorate from the Jagiellonian University in Krakow (in the Austrian partition) and touring Europe, then returned to Chile.

ISABEL CLIFTON COOKSON

Isabel Clifton Cookson (December 25, 1893-July 1, 1973) was an Australian botanist who specialised in palaeobotany and palynology.

Cookson was born at Hawthorn, Victoria, she attended the Methodist Ladies' College at Kew and gained honours in anatomy, physiology and botany in the senior public examination. She went on to study for her BSc at the University of Melbourne and graduated in 1916 with majors in botany and zoology. When she completed her studies she became a demonstrator at the university, and between 1916 and 1917 received a government research scholarship and the MacBain research scholarship in biology, amongst other awards to study the flora of the Northern Territory. She contributed illustrations for the 1917 book *The Flora of the Northern Territory* by Alfred J. Ewart and O. B. Davies.

She continued working at the University of Melbourne, until she visited the Imperial College of Science and Technology between 1925 and 1926, and, on a return visit in the University of Manchester between 1926 and 1927. At Manchester she began a long and productive academic relationship with W. H. Lang, Lang named the genus *Cooksonia* in her honour. Form 1929 her research focussed on palaeobotany, she wrote several papers on fossil plants including early vascular plants from the Silurian and Early Devonian which helped to shape theories of early land-plant evolution. She also studied more resent coal forming deposits. Her work on the early terrestrial fossil plants of Victoria and field work showing associated graptolites and plants led to her research thesis and to a D.Sc. from the University of Melbourne in 1932.

In 1930 she was appointed lecturer in botany at the University of Melbourne. From the 1940s she worked on fossil spores, pollen and phytoplankton and their relationship with palaeogeography and championed the usefulness of plant microfossils for oil exploration. The Council for Scientific and Industrial Research established in 1949 a pollen research unit under her leadership. In 1952 she was appointed a research fellow in botany, and retired in 1959. She was active in her retirement, 30 of her 86 scientific papers were published after 1959.

Since 1976 the Botanical Society of America has awarded the Isabel Cookson Award to the best paper on palaeobotany presented at their annual meeting at the bequest of Cookson. Cookson Place in the Canberra suburb of Banks is also named in her honour.

The standard author abbreviation *Cookson* is used to indicate this individual as the author when citing a botanical name.

IAN WILMUT

Prof. Sir Ian Wilmut (born July 7, 1944) is an English embryologist and is currently one of the leaders of the Queen's Medical Research Institute at the University of Edinburgh. He is best known as the man who played a supervisory, but not a scientific, role in the team that in 1996 first cloned a mammal, a Finn Dorset lamb named Dolly. He was granted an OBE in 1999 for services to embryo development. In December 2007 it was announced that he would be knighted in the 2008 New Year Honours.

Biography

Wilmut was born in Hampton Lucy, Warwickshire), England, and became interested in biology while working as a farmhand.

His father, Leonard Wilmut, was a maths teacher who had a severe case of diabetes that caused blindness.

Wilmut met Christopher Polge, who had discovered cryopreservation in 1949, and became fascinated with the research. He earlier desired to embark on a naval career, but was unable to do so because of his colour blindness. He was a student of the former Boy's High School, in Scarborough, where his father taught.

After attending the University of Nottingham for his undergraduate degree, Wilmut was awarded a Ph.D. from Cambridge in 1971; his subsequent research led to the birth of the first calf from a frozen embryo — "Frosty" — in 1973.

Steen Willadsen, at Cambridge, England, was the first to clone a mammal from differentiated cells, from sheep embryos, in 1984.

In 1995, Keith Campbell and Bill Ritchie succeeded in producing a pair of lambs, Megan and Morag from embryonic cells. Dolly the sheep, a Finn Dorset sheep, named after the singer, Dolly Parton, was born in 1996. Dolly was the first clone derived from adult cells. She died early, in 2003, at 6 years old. In 1998 another sheep Polly was created. She was made from genetically altered skin cells to contain a human gene.

He was knighted in the 2008 New Year Honours for "services to science".

It has been reported that Wilmut is abandoning cloning in light of Shinya Yamanaka's work on induced pluripotent stem cells.

It has been reported that the Queen has been petitioned to deny Wilmut's honour.

IRWIN ROSE

Irwin A. Rose (born 16 July 1926) is an American biologist. Along with Aaron Ciechanover and Avram Hershko, he was awarded the 2004 Nobel Prize in Chemistry for the discovery of ubiquitin-mediated protein degradation.

Rose attended Washington State University for one year prior to serving in the Navy during WWII. Upon returning from the war he received his B.S. in 1948 and his Ph.D. in biochemistry in 1952, both from the University of Chicago. He is currently a distinguished professor-in-residence at the Department of Physiology and Biophysics of the College of Medicine at the University of California, Irvine.

Irwin (Ernie) trained several postdoctoral fellows while at the Fox Chase Cancer Centre in Philadelphia, where the groundbreaking Ub work was done. These included Art Haas, the first to see Ubiquitin chains, Keith Wilkinson, the one to first identify APF-1 as Ubiquitin, and Cecile Pickart, a world class enzymologist in many parts of the Ub system.

Ernie would frequently tour the lab, with a harmonica, when Avram and Aaron were there working in the summer with Keith and Art.

IVAN VLADIMIROVICH MICHURIN

Ivan Vladimirovich Michurin (October 27 [O.S. October 15] 1855–June 7, 1935), a Russian practitioner selectionist, Honourable Member of the Soviet Academy of Sciences (1935), academician of the Lenin All-Union Academy of Agriculture (1935).

In 1875, Michurin leased a strip of land of about 500 square metres not far from Tambov, began collecting plants, and started his research in pomology and selection. In 1899, he acquired a much bigger strip of land of about 130,000 square metres and moved all of his plants there.

In 1920, right after the end of the Russian Civil War, Vladimir Lenin ordered People's Commissar of Agriculture Semion Sereda to organize an analytic research on Michurin's works and practical achievements. On September 11, 1922, Mikhail Kalinin visited Michurin at Lenin's personal request. On November 20, 1923, the Council of People's Commissars recognized Michurin's "fruit garden" as an institution of state importance. In 1928, the Soviets established a selectionist genetic station on the basis of Michurin's garden, which would be re-organized into the Michurin Central Genetic Laboratory in 1934.

Michurin made a major contribution in the development of genetics, especially in the field of pomology. In his cytogenetic laboratory, he researched cell structure and experimented with artificial polyploidy. Michurin studied the aspects of heredity in connection with the natural course of ontogenesis and external influence, creating a whole new concept of predominance. He proved that predominance depends on heredity, ontogenesis, and phylogenesis of the initial cell structure and also on individual features of hybrids and conditions of cultivation. In his works, Michurin assumed a possibility of changing genotype under external influence.

Michurin was one of the founding fathers of scientific agricultural selection. He worked on hybridization of plants of similar and different origins, cultivating methods in connection with the natural course of ontogenesis, directing the process of predominance, evaluation and selection of seedlings, acceleration of process of selection with the help of physical and chemical factors.

Michurin's method of crossing of geographically distant plants would be widely used by other selectionists. He worked out theoretical basis and some practical means for hybridization of geographically distant plants. Michurin also proposed means for overcoming the genetic barrier of incompatibility during the process of hybridization, such as pollination of the young hybrids during their first florescence, preliminary vegetative crossing, use of a "mediator", pollination with the mix of different kinds of pollen etc.

The Soviets began to cultivate Michurin's hybrids of apple, pear, cherry, rowan and others. Michurin was the one to start cultivation of his hybrids of grape, apricot, sweet cherry and other southern plants in the northern climates.

During the Lysenkoism campaign, Michurin (without his intentions as after his death) was promoted as a Soviet leader in theory of evolution, the Soviet propaganda contrasting the "productive" "Soviet Michurinist Biology"with the "fruitless" "capitalist" *Weismanist-Morganist-Mendelist* genetics. In fact, Michurin's theory of influence of the environment on the heredity was a variant of Lamarckism. He maintained the position that the task of a selectioner is to assist and enhance the natural selection. The following Michurin's phrase was widely popularized in the Soviet Union: (*"We cannot wait for favors from Nature. To take them from it—that is our task."*)

For this reason, in the Soviet Union he was portrayed as the only true follower of Darwinism.

Throughout all his life Michurin worked to create new sorts of fruit plants. He introduced over 300 new species. He was awarded the Order of Lenin and Order of the Red Banner of Labour for his achievements.

ISRAEL SHAHAK

Israel Shahak (April 28, 1933 – July 2, 2001) was a Polish-born Israeli Professor of Chemistry at Hebrew University in Jerusalem, the former president of the Israeli League for Human and Civil Rights, and an outspoken critic of the Israeli government. Shahak's writings on Judaism have been the source of considerable controversy.

Biography

Born in Warsaw, Poland, Shahak was the youngest child of a cultured Polish Jewish family. After Germany occupied Poland, his family was forced into the Warsaw Ghetto. His brother escaped and joined the Royal Air Force and his father disappeared. His mother paid a poor Catholic family to hide him, but when her money ran out he was returned, and in 1943 they were both sent to Bergen-Belsen concentration camp. Israel Shahak was liberated in 1945, and shortly thereafter emigrated to the British Mandate of Palestine, where he volunteered for a kibbutz, but was turned down as "too weedy".

After graduating from high school, Shahak served in the Israel Defense Forces (IDF) in an elite regiment. After completing service with the IDF, he attended Hebrew University where he received his doctorate in chemistry. In 1961, he left Israel for the United States to study as a postdoctoral student at Stanford University. He returned two years later to become a teacher and researcher in chemistry at Hebrew University, where he remained until his retirement in 1990.

After the 1967 Six-Day War Shahak became critical of Israel's treatment of Palestinians, and a supporter of a Palestinian state, and wrote many articles and several books outlining his views of Israeli society and Judaism.

Shahak died in Israel at the age of 68 due to complications from diabetes. In an obituary, writing of Shahak's work for human rights, Christopher Hitchens wrote:-

'His home on Bartenura Street in Jerusalem was a library of information about the human rights of the oppressed. The families of prisoners, the staff of closed and censored publications, the victims of eviction and confiscation—none were ever turned away. I have met influential "civil society" Palestinians alive today who were protected as students when Israel was a professor of chemistry at the Hebrew University; from him they learned never to generalize about Jews. And they respected him not just for his consistent stand against discrimination but also because—he never condescended to them. He detested nationalism and religion and made no secret of his contempt for the grasping Arafat entourage. But, as he once put it to me, "I will now only meet with Palestinian spokesmen when we are out of the country. I have some severe criticisms to present to them. But I cannot do this while they are living under occupation and I can 'visit' them as a privileged citizen." This apparently small point of ethical etiquette contains almost the whole dimension of what is missing from our present discourse: the element of elementary dignity and genuine mutual recognition.'

ILYA PRIGOGINE

Ilya, Viscount Prigogine (January 25, 1917 – May 28, 2003) was a Russian-born naturalized Belgian physicist and Nobel Laureate chemist noted for his work on dissipative structures, complex systems, and irreversibility.

Biography

Prigogine was born in Moscow a few months before the Russian Revolution of 1917. His father, Roman Prigogine, was a chemical engineer at the Moscow Institute of Technology. Because the family was critical toward the new Soviet system, they left Russia in 1921.

They first went to Germany and in 1929 to Belgium, where Prigogine received Belgian nationality in 1949.

Prigogine studied chemistry at the Free University of Brussels, now split into the Universite Libre de Bruxelles and the Vrije Universiteit Brussel, where in 1950 he became professor. In 1959, he was appointed director of the International Solvay Institute in Brussels, Belgium.

In that year he also started teaching at the University of Texas at Austin in the United States, where he later was appointed Regental Professor and Ashbel Smith Professor of Physics and Chemical Engineering. In 1967 he co-founded there what is now called The Centre for Complex Quantum Systems. In that year he also returned to Belgium where he became director of the *Centre for Statistical Mechanics and Thermodynamics.*

He was a member of numerous scientific organizations, and received numerous awards, prizes and 53 honorary degrees. In 1955 Ilya Prigogine was awarded the Francqui Prize for Exact Sciences. For this study in irreversible thermodynamics he received the Rumford Medal in 1976 and in 1977 the Nobel Prize in Chemistry. In 1989 he was awarded the title of Viscount by the King of Belgium. Until his death he was president of the International Academy of Science and was in 1997 one of the founders of the International Commission on Distance Education (CODE), a worldwide accreditation agency.

IGNACY LUKASIEWICZ

Jan Jozef Ignacy Lukasiewicz (1822-1882) was a Polish pharmacist of Armenian descent who devised the first method of distilling kerosene from seep oil. He was the founder of the Polish oil industry and one of the pioneers of oil industry in the world. Among his achievements were the construction of modern kerosene lamp (1853), founding of the first oil well (1854) in Poland and the building of the first oil refinery in Poland (1856).

Lukasiewicz became a wealthy man and one of the most prominent philanthropists in Galicia. Because of his support for the economical development of the region, a popular saying was coined attributing all paved roads to his guldens.

Biography

Ignacy Lukasiewicz was born March 8, 1822 in Zaduszniki near Mielec, in the Austrian empire (after the partition of Poland). His parents were Apolonia nee Cewietlik and Jozef Lukasiewicz, a member of local intelligentsia and a veteran of Koeciuszko's Uprising. His parents rented a small manor in Zaduszniki, but soon after Ignacy's birth had to move to Rzeszow due to economical difficulties. There Ignacy started his studies at the local gymnasium, but had to abandon it in 1836. To help his parents, Ignacy Lukasiewicz moved to Lancut where he started to work as a pharmacist's assistant. At the same time he became involved in various political organizations supporting the idea of restoration of Polish sovereignty. In 1840 he returned to Rzeszow, where he continued to practice at the pharmacy of Edward Hubl.

In 1845 he met Edward Dembowski, who admitted Lukasiewicz to the illegal *Centralization of the Polish Democratic Society*. The aim of that organization was to prepare an all-national uprising against the partitioning powers. Because of that, on February 19, 1846 Lukasiewicz was arrested by the Austrian authorities and imprisoned in Lwow. On December 27, 1847 he was released from prison due to lack of evidence, but for the rest of his life he was regarded as *politically insecure*. He was also ordered to remain in Lwow.

There Lukasiewicz started working for the *Pod Zot Gwiazd* pharmacy owned by Piotr Mikolasch. On his insistence Lukasiewicz was allowed to leave Lwow and join the Krakow University. After several years of studies, financed mostly by Mikolasch, he managed to pass all his university examinations except pharmacognosy, what prevented him from graduation. Finally, on July 30, 1852 Lukasiewicz graduated from the faculty of pharmacy of the University of Vienna. He then returned to Lwow. Lukasiewicz had long been interested in the potential of seep oil as a cheap alternative to the more expensive whale oil. In 1853 Jan Zeh, together with his associate

Lukasiewicz, was the first in the world to distill clear kerosene from seep oil, Canada's Abraham Gesner having first refined kerosene from coal in 1846. On July 31, 1853, Lukasiewicz made one of his kerosene lamps available to a local hospital to illuminate an emergency surgical operation. The date is considered the starting point of modern oil industry.

In early 1854 Lukasiewicz moved to Gorlice, where he continued his work. He set up many companies together with entrepreneurs and landowners. That same year, he opened the world's first oil "mine" at Bobrka, near Krosno (still operational as of 2006). At the same time Lukasiewicz continued his work on kerosene lamps. Later that year he set up the first kerosene street lamp in Gorlice's borough of Zawodzie.

In the following years he opened several other oil wells, each of them as a joint-venture with various local merchants and businessmen. In 1856 in Ulaszowice near Jaso he opened an "oil distillery", that is the first industrial oil refinery in the world. As the demand for kerosene was still low, the plant initially produced mostly artificial asphalt, machine oil and lubricants. The refinery was destroyed in a fire in 1859, but was rebuilt in Polanka near Krosno the following year.

In 1863 Lukasiewicz, who moved to Jaso in 1858, was already a wealthy man. He openly supported the January Uprising and financed help for the refugees. In 1865 he bought a large manor and the village of Chorkowka. There he established yet another oil refinery. Having gained one of the largest fortunes in Galicia, Lukasiewicz promoted the development of oil industry in the area of Dukla and Gorlice. He gave his name to several oil-mining enterprises in the area, including the oil wells of Ropianka, Wilsznia, Smereczne, Ropa and Wojtowa.

He also became the benefactor of the region and founded a spa resort in Bobrka, a chapel in Chorkowka and a large church in Zrecin. As one of the best-known businessmen of his times, he was elected to the Galician Sejm. In 1877 Lukasiewicz also organized the first Oil Industry Congress and founded the National Oil Society. Ignacy Lukasiewicz died January 7, 1882, of pneumonia. He was buried at the small cemetery of Zrecin, next to the Gothic Revival church he had financed.

IRVING LANGMUIR

Irving Langmuir (January 31, 1881 in Brooklyn, New York – August 16, 1957 in Woods Hole, Massachusetts) was an American chemist and physicist. His most noted publication was the famous 1919 article "The Arrangement of Electrons in Atoms and Molecules" in which, building on Gilbert N. Lewis's cubical atom theory and Walther Kossel's chemical bonding theory, he outlined his "concentric theory of atomic structure". While at G.E., from 1909-1950, Langmuir advanced several basic fields of physics and chemistry, invented the gas-filled incandescent lamp, the hydrogen welding technique, and was awarded the 1932 Nobel Prize for Chemistry for his work in surface chemistry. He was the first industrial chemist to become a Nobel laureate. The Langmuir Laboratory for Atmospheric Research near Socorro, New Mexico was named in his honour as was the American Chemical Society journal for Surface Science, called Langmuir. A residential building is named after him on the Stony Brook University campus.

Life

Irving Langmuir was born in Brooklyn, New York on January 31, 1881. He was the third child of four of Charles Langmuir and Sadie, nee Comings. During his childhood, Langmuir's parents encouraged him to carefully observe nature and to keep a detailed record of his various observations. When Irving was eleven, it was discovered that he had poor eyesight. When this problem was corrected, details that had previously eluded him were revealed. Because of this, his interest in nature and the various complications of nature was heightened.

During his childhood, Langmuir was greatly influenced by his older brother, Arthur Langmuir. Arthur was a research chemist who encouraged Irving to be curious about nature and how things work. Arthur helped Irving set up his first chemistry lab in the corner of his bedroom, and he was content to answer the myriad of questions that Irving would pose. Langmuir's hobbies included mountaineering, skiing, piloting his own plane, and classical music. In addition to his professional interest in the politics of atomic energy, he was deeply concerned about wilderness conservation.

Education

Langmuir attended his early education at various schools and institutes in America and Paris (1892-1895). He graduated with a B.S. in metallurgical engineering from the Columbia University School of Mines (the first mining and metallurgy school in the U.S., established, 1864 and presently known as Fu Foundation School of Engineering and Applied Science) in 1903. He earned his Ph.D. degree in 1906 under Nobel laureate Walther Nernst in Gottingen, for research done using the "Nernst glower", an electric lamp invented by Nernst. His doctoral thesis was entitled "On the Partial Recombination of Dissolved Gases During Cooling." He later did postgraduate work in chemistry. Langmuir then taught at Stevens Institute of Technology in Hoboken, New Jersey, until 1909, when he began working at the General Electric research laboratory (Schenectady, New York). In 1912, he married Marion Mersereau.

Bibliography

Ahmed, Akbar S.: *Jinnah, Pakistan, and Islamic Identity: The Search for Saladin,* 1997.

Allen, G. : *New Education: American Opinion,* May issue, 1971.

Alva, Joachim: *Leaders of India,* Bombay, Thacker & Co., Ltd., 1943

Arabinda Poddar : *Tagore : The Political Personality,* Kolkata, Indiana, 2004.

Beaumont, Roger : *Sword of the Raj: the British Army in India, 1747-1947,* Indianapolis, Bobbs-Merrill, 1977.

Branch, Katherine. *Guide to Scientific Biography.* San Diego: University Library, San Diego State University, 1981.

Christopher J. : *An Indian Rural Economy: The Tamiland Countryside,* Oxford, Clarendon Press, 1984.

DeLong, G. F.: *The Dutch in America, 1609-1974,* Boston, Twayne Publishers, 1975.

Desai, A.R. : *Social Background of Indian Nationalism,* Bombay, Popular Prakashan, 1966.

Duignan, P.A. : *The Ideal and the Ethics of Authenticity in Leadership,* Orlando, Florida, 1997.

Ebon, Martin: *Maharishi, The Guru,* New American Library, 1968.

Evers, C. & Lakomski, G. : *Knowing Educational Administration,* Oxford, Pergamon, 1991.

Fisher, Michael : *A Clash of Cultures: Awadh the British, and the Mughals,* New Delhi, Manohar, 1987.

Furth, H.G. : *The World of Grown-ups: Children's Conceptions of Society,* New York, Elsevier North Holland, 1980.

Gardner, H. : *Multiple Intelligences: The Theory in Practice,* New Yrok, Basic Books, 1993.

Ghoshal, U. N.: A *History of Indian Political Ideas.* London, 1966.

Grace, G. : *School Leadership: Beyond Educational Management*, London, Falmer, 1995.

Harris, H. S.: *Hegel's Development: Towards the Sunlight 1770-1801*, Oxford, Clarendon Press, 1972

Hilbert, D.R. : *Color and Color Perception: A Study in Anthropocentric Realism*, Stanford, CSLI, 1987.

Jacobsen, Hans-Adolf: *Karl Haushofer: Leben und Werk*, Harald Boldt Verlag, Boppard 1979.

Jeong-kyu : *Historic Factors Influencing Korean Higher Education*, Seoul, Jimoondang, 2000.

John L.: *The Islamic Threat : Myth or Reality?* 1999.

Koning, K. de and Martin, M. : *Participatory Research in Health: Issues and Experiences*, London, Zed Books, 1996.

Lee, Jeong-kyu : *Historic Factors Influencing Korean Higher Education*, Seoul, Jimoondang, 2000.

Lovett, T. : *Radical Approaches to Adult Education: A Reader*, London, Croom Helm, 1988.

McGinn, C. : *The Subjective View: Secondary Qualities and Indexical Thoughts*, Oxford, Oxford University Press, 1983.

Muldoon, S. and H. Carrington : *The Projection of the Astral Body*, New York, Samuel Weiser and Company, 1970.

Nuna, S.C. : *Education and Development*, NIEPA, New Delhi, 1987.

Okech, J.G.; Asiachi, A.J. : *Curriculum Development for Schools*, Nairobi, Educational Research Publications, 1992.

Poster, C. and Kruger, A. : *Community Education in the Western World*, London, Routledge, 1990.

Ramesh Chandra, *Government and Politics of India*, New York, St. Martin's Press, 1995.

Roberts, K., White, G.E. and Parker, H.J. : *The Character-Training Industry, Adventure Training Schemes in Britain*, Newton Abbot, David and Charles, 1974.

Roderick, R. : *Habermas and the Foundations of Critical Theory*, Basingstoke, Macmillan, 1986.

Ruse, M.: *The Philosophy of Biology*, London, Hutchinson, 1973.

Scott, C. : *Social Education*, Boston, Ginn and Co., 1908.

Seyla Benhabib: *The Reluctant Modernism of Hannah Arendt*, Rowan and Littlefield Publishers, 2003.

Simkins, T. : *Non-formal Education and Development*, Manchester, Manchester University, 1977.

Smith, M.K. : *Local Education, Community, Conversation, Action*, Buckingham, Open University Press, 1994.

Stenhouse, L. : *Authority, Education and Emancipation*, London, Heinemann, 1983.

Storing, Herbert; Murray Dry: *The Anti-Federalist*, Chicago: University of Chicago Press, 2006.

Thakur, Ramesh Chandra, *Government and Politics of India*, New York, St. Martin's Press, 1995.

Thomas, Edward J. : *The Life of Buddha as Legend and History*, London, Routledge and Kegan Paul, 1927.

Tinker, Hugh: *Experiment with Freedom, India and Pakistan 1947*, London, Oxford UP, 1967.

Tsurumi, E. Patricia : *Colonial Education in Korea and Taiwan*, Princeton, Princeton University Press, 1984.

Tully, Mark : *India: Forty Years of Independence*, New York, Braziller, 1988.

Van der Veer, Peter : *Religious Nationalism: Hindus and Muslims in India*, Berkeley, University of California Press, 1994.

Vincent, Rose : *The French in India: From Diamond Traders to Sanskrit Scholars*, Bombay, Popular Prakashan, 1990.

Waldron, Jeremy: *God, Locke and Equality*, Cambridge Uni, Press, 2002.

Williams, J.E., & Morland, J.K. : *Race, Color, and the Young Child*, Chapel Hill, University of North Carolina Press, 1976.

Yasin, Mohammad : *Indian Politics : Processes, Issues and Trends,* New Delhi, Kanishka, 2004.

Yong, Tan Tai and Kudaisya, Gyanesh: *The Aftermath of Partition in South Asia*, London, Routledge, 2000.

Zubrowski, Bernie: *Raceways*, Boston, MA, A Boston Children's Museum Activity Book, 1985.

Index

D

E

F

G

H

I

J

L

M

N

O

P

R

S

T

Y

❑❑❑